Teachers for the South

History of Schools and Schooling

Alan R. Sadovnik and Susan F. Semel
General Editors

Vol. 6

PETER LANG
New York • Washington, D.C./Baltimore • Boston
Bern • Frankfurt am Main • Berlin • Vienna • Paris

Clinton B. Allison

Teachers for the South

Pedagogy and Educationists in the University of Tennessee, 1844–1995

PETER LANG
New York • Washington, D.C./Baltimore • Boston
Bern • Frankfurt am Main • Berlin • Vienna • Paris

Library of Congress Cataloging-in-Publication Data

Allison, Clinton B.
Teachers for the South: pedagogy and educationists
in the University of Tennessee, 1844–1995 / Clinton B. Allison.
p. cm.—(History of schools and schooling; v. 6)
Includes bibliographical references and index.
1. Teachers—Training of—Tennessee—Knoxville—History.
2. University of Tennessee, Knoxville College of Education—History. 3. Teacher
educators—Tennessee—Knoxville—History. I. Title. II. Series.
LB2193.K56A45   370'.711—dc21   97-17931
ISBN 0-8204-3841-3
ISSN 1089-0678

Die Deutsche Bibliothek-CIP-Einheitsaufnahme

Allison, Clinton B.:
Teachers for the south: pedagogy and educationists in the University
of Tennessee 1844–1995/Clinton B. Allison.
–New York; Washington, D.C./Baltimore; Boston; Bern;
Frankfurt am Main; Berlin; Vienna; Paris: Lang.
(History of schools and schooling; Vol. 6)
ISBN 0-8204-3841-3

Cover design by Nona Reuter.

The paper in this book meets the guidelines for permanence and durability
of the Committee on Production Guidelines for Book Longevity
of the Council of Library Resources.

© 1998 Peter Lang Publishing, Inc., New York

Printed in the United States of America.

To Lloyd P. Williams, my professor, and William L. Butefish, my colleague.

Table of Contents

Preface

Rather than any thought of writing a book, it was simply curiosity that motivated me to first begin looking in the University of Tennessee archives for information on the College of Education. People have different ways of trying to feel at home in the places where they spend their time. Historians' usual way of understanding an institution, an idea, or a place is by learning how it developed and changed over time, and they are often uncomfortable without such knowledge. In 1969, I came to UT with a new Ph.D. in history of education. It was boom times for the College of Education. I was one of 157 faculty members, and the college could not hire new faculty fast enough to keep pace with enrollment growth—fifteen to twenty new assistant professors were hired each year. The dean and associate deans arrived at the same time that I did, and even most of the older professors had been at UT only since the 1950s. (There were only nineteen faculty members in the college in 1946.) Except for the recent past, no one seemed to know much about the college's history. True, some mentioned the famous Summer School of the South for teachers that was held at UT at the turn of the century, which led me to the limited secondary material on the summer school, the Summer School of the South papers, and the 110 boxes of papers of its superintendent, Philander P. Claxton. I spent so much time in Special Collections in the Hoskins Library that the helpful staff assigned me a study (directly behind a replica of Estes Kefauver's senate office), making it easy to keep poking through more and more archival boxes. When I had collected three file-cabinet drawers of documents on the college, I had no choice but to write its history.

This history is a case study in southern teacher education. It is not the type of in-house institutional history that retiring teary-eyed deans or professors write to make alumni, students, and faculty feel good about the service that their colleges have given to local schools and communities. With a broader audience in mind, I critically examine a number of topics related to teacher education and schooling in this southern institution, including attitudes toward and treatment of teacher education in the university, educationists' efforts to earn acceptance by arts and science professors and university administrators, scholarship or the lack thereof by faculty and students, service to the "field," educationists' continuing social reform missions, and gender and racial issues.

As a long-time professor in the UT College of Education, I am not a neutral or objective observer; but I try to keep my bias in check, particularly in my accounts of the last thirty years when I was often an active participant in the events I describe. As a subjective statement, I reveal that I opposed the proposals for competence-based teacher education in the mid-1970s, chaired the College of Education Goals Committee in 1982–1983, was a member of the steering committee for New College in 1991–1992, and supported the appointment of Richard Wisniewski as dean and consider him a friend. In the last chapter, whenever possible, I avoid using the names of individual professors.

The latest cycle of critiques of teacher education and "reforms" in schools of education has created an interest in gaining historical leverage on teacher education. Recent histories have been limited to northern and western institutions: Geraldine Joncich Clifford and James W. Guthrie, *Ed School: A Brief for Professional Education*, 1988 (California); Jurgen Herbst, *And Sadly Teach*, 1989 (Massachusetts and the Midwest); and Robert A. Levin, *Educating Elementary Teachers*, 1994 (Pennsylvania and New Hampshire). This is the first book-length study of the history of teacher education in the South.

The major theme of the first chapter is the ambivalence of the university faculty toward educating schoolteachers, even as the university evolved from a military school with a classical curriculum to a land-grant institution. Beginning with the establishment of a Teachers' Course in 1844, the university periodically created and abandoned teacher education programs. I describe the substance and spirit of summer normal institutes, so important in the training of southern teachers, in some detail. I continue the theme of ambivalence in the second chapter as, with great fanfare, the university created a new Teachers' Department in 1890 and then allowed it to die, unmourned, in 1896. Questionable scholarship was the major issue in the short,

unhappy life of the department. The trustees established the department with the understanding that it would be "in no sense a normal
department" but an intellectual preparation of teachers; they, and the
university president, were never satisfied with the academic quality of
the department. A positive topic is the admission of "lady teachers" in
the department. As in other southern states, teacher education was
the back door through which women entered the state university.

The central place of the University of Tennessee in the turn-of-the-
century southern education campaigns is the topic for the fourth and
fifth chapters. The contributions and power of northern philanthropy
in the life of UT's teacher education programs began with grants by
the General Education Board (GEB) and the Southern Education Board
(SEB) to establish a department of education patterned after Teachers
College, Columbia University. The GEB also underwrote the famous
Summer School of the South that brought many of America's best-
known scholars to Knoxville to educate teachers and train them as
agents in the southern school campaigns; 20,000 teachers attended
in the first ten years of the summer school. The SEB established its
Bureau of Information and Investigation in Knoxville. The Bureau,
administered by educationist P. P. Claxton, provided propaganda for
public schooling and industrial education throughout the South. In addition, the GEB funded a professor of secondary education in each
southern state to act as an agent for the campaigns. In chapter 4, I analyze the activities of the Tennessee professors of secondary education.

Struggles of educationists to find a place for themselves in an often
antagonistic university environment is the theme of the fifth and sixth
chapters. An antieducationist university administrator was a special
nemesis. In the fundamentalist religious climate of Tennessee in the
1920s, he discharged an education professor, ostensibly for teaching
evolution; and in the subsequent "great professor trial," he fired five
other professors from across the university who supported the educationist, bringing a censure from the American Association of University Professors. Throughout their history at UT, education professors
found more support outside the university than within it. Latching
onto the national country-life movement in the 1920s and 1930s,
they developed an extensive project to uplift rural life and improve
rural schools. Tennessee educationists shared the progressive education faith in the power of schooling to transform society and in the
survey as the major instrument to effect change. They also shared
progressives' willingness to impose "superior, modern" values on the

less privileged. In the depression years, teacher education did surprisingly well, expanding its programs during a time of financial retrenchment. In order to survive, educationists had gained experience in lobbying and had become adept at promoting themselves to constituencies outside the university.

Despite the drop in enrollment during the Second World War and continuing complaints about mistreatment by the university, the 1940s was another period of expansion for the college. Although the South was often behind other sections of the country in pedagogical progressivism, the educationists at UT portrayed themselves as leading a region-wide progressive reform movement. The president of the university responded with highly publicized attacks on progressive pedagogy. I examine a continuing theme of this study in chapter 7: when educationists are under attack, they reorganize. The college responded to criticisms with a major revision of the teacher education curriculum in the 1950s. It developed a competency-based program two decades before competency-based education became a national phenomenon.

The final chapter paints the history of the last generation in broad strokes. Baby boomers in school created a severe teacher shortage, and the college grew spectacularly. With growth in the size of the faculty, the college began to lose its distinctive southern character. During the criticisms of public schools and teacher education of the 1980s, another generation of university administrators expressed dissatisfaction with the quality of the college, and campus administrators took an active role in recruiting a dean who they thought could help create a college of education of which the university could be proud. With much opposition from some faculty, the new dean furnished leadership for major reforms: significantly higher academic requirements for teaching candidates, a full-year internship, and a postbaccalaureate teacher education program. Finally, with the support of corporate grants, a New College of Education was created.

Of those who help in the making of a book there is no end.

A summer faculty development grant from the UT Graduate School helped with time to begin the project, and an academic leave supported by the cultural studies in education unit for Spring semester 1996 was invaluable time for writing. The cultural studies faculty and the unit secretary, Jo Allen, have protected my time, tolerated my preoccupation with educationists' past, and cheered me on as I finished the book. Richard Wisniewski encouraged this project throughout his tenure as dean. I appreciate colleagues William Butefish, Lynn Cagle, and Joan Paul who read portions of the manuscript. They helped me look around my blinders and prodded me into reconsidering arguable conclusions. I particularly appreciate my fellow historian Joan Paul for her numerous courtesies and unfailing support. I am grateful to graduate students who helped with archival research over many years, including Joe L. Kincheloe, David Williams, Mike Story, Norma Tedder, Donald E. Miller, and W. Todd Groce. Charlotte Duncan read and proofread the manuscript with a sharp eye for comma faults and lapses in reasoning; those that remain in the work are not her fault. Librarians as a species are special people, and this work could not have been constructed without the unfailing help of the UT special collections staff, particularly Nick Wyman, John Dobson, Special Collections Librarian Emeritus, and his successor, James B. Lloyd. As always, I deeply appreciate the support of my family, particularly my beloved wife, Claudia.

I thank the New York University Press for permission to reprint parts of "Early Professors of Education: Three Case Studies" which appeared as chapter 3 in *The Professors of Teaching: An Inquiry* (1989), edited by Richard Wisniewski and Edward R. Ducharme. And I thank the *Journal of Thought* for its permission to reprint in slightly different form "Training Dixie's Teachers: The University of Tennessee's Summer Normal Institutes," which was published in volume 18 (Fall 1983).

Chapter 1

The Nineteenth Century Phoenix of Teacher Education

A major theme of this book is the ambivalence of the University of Tennessee toward teacher education that resulted in the death and resurrection of one program after another in pedagogy. The university was in and out of teacher training for much of the nineteenth century. Many colleges and universities of the time publicized the education of teachers for the lower schools as a major service of the institution, a way of justifying its existence to those who looked on a college as a playground for rich men's sons. In the antebellum South, when college presidents in their annual reports wrote of the responsibility of their colleges and universities to provide teachers for the common schools, they did not mean that there were curricula specifically organized to train teachers to teach but that there were invariably young men who had undergone the rigors of the classical curriculum and whose prospects were so poor that they had to teach for a few years in order to keep body and soul together.

In 1828 small, struggling East Tennessee College (predecessor of the University of Tennessee) moved from downtown Knoxville to its first building on "the Hill" a mile west of town. In 1840, in the long unrealized hope of creating a medical school, the college was renamed East Tennessee University. The university had five professors, including the president, and ninety-five students, forty-seven of whom were in the preparatory department. A major occupation of the faculty was attempting to maintain student discipline and their own safety from their charges. Assaulting the president or professors or breaking their windows were grounds for expulsion. Students were also forbidden, among other things, to go armed, fight, use turbulent words, wear "women's apparel," lie, or attend a "dancing party or any public festive entertainment" in Knoxville.[1]

The 1834 Tennessee Constitutional Convention charged the college with promoting establishment of public schools. Teacher preparation was a way for the trustees to fulfill their mandate; besides, they needed the students. After university president Joseph Estabrook declared in 1838 that he did "not consider a classical education indispensable, or even necessary to the teachers of our common schools," the faculty developed a program for teachers that included, in addition to regular academic subjects, a course entitled the "art of school teaching." Teacher training was part of the newly created English Department (later named English and Scientific), the modern or nonclassical curriculum. The "art of school teaching" appeared in the 1844 catalogue of the university. This was very early for a public institution to undertake training in pedagogy—the first public normal school in the United States was not established until 1839—and East Tennessee University may have been the first state college or university to offer such a course. The university catalog in 1844 announced that two young men from each county in East Tennessee would be allowed to enroll without tuition to qualify themselves for the "business of teaching" if they were 16 years old, able to read and write, could produce testimonials of good moral character, had "good natural talents," and would agree, after completion of the two-year course of study, to devote the succeeding three years to teaching in East Tennessee. The university did not award degrees to or consider those who completed the course graduates. With some exaggeration, university historian Stanley Folmsbee wrote that the "English and Scientific Department was in effect a forerunner of a college of education."[2]

Unfortunately, as was to be typical of attempts to train teachers for generations, the teachers' course was stillborn. The art of school teaching course disappeared from the catalog, without explanation, the next year, and the university dropped any semblance of a special program for training teachers in 1849. Although the university continued to give free tuition to men who said they were preparing to teach in public schools, the university did not establish another teacher- education program until after the Civil War.[3]

State-mandated systems of public schools in the post-Civil War South began to operate in earnest only after the stain of Reconstruction was removed from them. This cleansing action required the repeal of radical Republican-inspired public school legislation and, after a decent interval, the creation of less ambitious systems of schools by conservative Democratic legislators. Throughout the South, for a half century, public school systems existed mainly on paper. Among their problems were the pitifully ill-prepared teachers. Without the state-mandated common schools that existed elsewhere, the South lacked normal schools and other teacher-training institutions. The Peabody Educational Fund, established in 1867, attempted to stimulate a modicum of training opportunities by providing grants for short-term institutes, such as those conducted by the university that I discuss later in this chapter.[4]

Tennessee exemplifies the South's experience. The Radical Republican legislature established a state system of public schools in 1867, but the Democrats repealed it when they returned to power in 1869; in 1873, however, the Democratic General Assembly passed a weaker school law that is the foundation of Tennessee's present public school system. At that time, East Tennessee University was a small, all-male military school with uniforms and discipline patterned after West Point. The classical curriculum was still dominant. In 1869, after a difficult and sometimes bitter struggle, the legislature designated the school as Tennessee's land-grant university under the Morrill Act. The endowment, however, remained in danger for several years. East Tennessee University received it largely because of the Union sentiments of trustees and faculty, and, when conservative Democrats returned to power in October 1869, the endowment was immediately in peril. The Democrats insisted that Knoxville was too remote to serve most of the children of the state and that some healthy and eligible (and more Democratic) place in West Tennessee should be found. In 1871 the legislature's failure to override Governor Senter's veto by five votes averted efforts to deprive the university of the federal land grant.[5]

Ambivalence about the establishment of teacher education was part of a much larger struggle over the basic purposes of the institution as a land-grant university. For decades there was a great debate within the university over the meaning of the land-grant designation. Most of the faculty and the president (the Reverend Thomas Humes, Episcopalian rector and Unionist) looked upon agricultural and mechanical arts as merely a branch of the university. On the other hand, Judge Oliver P. Temple, long-time and energetic board of trustee member, constantly pushed and shoved for a transformation of the university from a classical school to a predominantly agricultural and mechanical institution. He opposed not only the elitists on the faculty but also farmers' sons with an unfortunate tendency to wish to study Latin and Greek.[6]

The faculty was uneasy about any departure from the rigors of the classical curriculum. Under the "Purpose of the College of Agriculture and the Mechanical Arts" in the 1873 catalogue, students were warned that:

A most important purpose of this, as of other forms of education, is mental discipline. To attain this end, the scientific and philosophical branches of study will be taught with the greatest possible thoroughness. The indolent student will find in this department no refuge from the strict and thorough drill of the classical course.[7]

Casting envious eyes on the appropriations for lower schools under the education act of 1873 and wishing to be of greater service to the state, President Humes suggested to his faculty of eight professors "the propriety of adding a Normal Course" to the offerings of the university. A three-professor committee was to consider the proposal and report its recommendations at the next regularly scheduled meeting of the faculty. A week later, at the appointed time, the requested report was delayed "till tomorrow." The committee did not make the report the next day or, as is typical of faculty committees, for weeks to come. Rather, the faculty returned to the type of pressing problems that occupied much of their attention in the period. At the next regular meeting, the faculty reduced the rank of two cadets "for playing the ball near the college building." At the May 19 meeting, Cadet Ring was summoned and "charged with unbecoming conduct in the Dining Hall, in throwing a dish of meat out of the window" and suspended for the rest of the term. Three days later, Professor John Payne lamented that the cadet "was still on the College grounds and conducting himself improperly." The faculty voted to have him removed immediately. Finally, on May 30, the subject of normal instruction resurfaced, and the committee, augmented by President Humes, was ordered "to report on Monday next." The minutes of the faculty for Monday were terse and unrevealing: "The Committee on the Normal Course reported certain recommendations which with certain amendments were adopted and ordered printed in the catalogue."[8]

The Normal Department was to encourage and promote public schools in Tennessee and "to supply the urgent demand for competent teachers." Those who wished to pursue the three-year, nondegree-granting course had to be eighteen years old, to affirm their intention to teach in the public schools of Tennessee for at least two years, and to be "suited by his character, capacity, and acquirements to be instructed in East Tennessee University for that purpose." They were required to present a certificate from their county superintendent of public schools attesting that they had met these conditions before they could be admitted. Since the university was a military school, the faculty advised—or warned—prospective teachers that they would "be under the same College regulations and discipline as other students."[9]

In 1875 Humes reported that he was pleased with the university's progress. The student body was growing—a total of 318 students enrolled in June 1874—although most were still in college preparatory courses. The hope for the future, as he saw it, was with the public schools. As they developed in quality as well as in numbers, qualified students would increase and the "evil" of preparing students for the freshman class at the university would "no doubt be gradually remedied."[10]

Humes was eager to develop, at least in the minds of public officials and citizens, a close relationship between the university and the public schools, in part because a recognition of the university as the capstone of the public school system could be used to justify state appropriations and, in part, because he recognized a "mutual interdependence" between public schools and the university. Not only would improved public schools send better scholars, but the university in turn would send forth "well-educated and competent teachers for the public schools." He particularly liked the state superintendent's suggestion that legislators appoint prospective teachers, selected on the basis of competitive examinations in their district, who would be designated "state students." Many former students of the university were already teaching in public schools, but the proposed plan would greatly increase their numbers, and, Humes insisted, "except as regards the past graduates of the College who have become instructors, would improve the average quality." Any idea that an auspicious beginning in teacher education had commenced was soon dashed. The Normal Department immediately disappeared from catalogs, not to reappear until 1879. Since the faculty or trustees did not publicly acknowledge its demise, it seems to have died a natural death from lack of interest by both prospective students and university authorities.[11]

Despite the aborting of the Normal Department, the university continued to recognize both the need for trained teachers and the possibility of gaining support from the legislature by offering normal instruction. From 1876 to 1878, professors visited and often taught in the omnipresent teachers' institutes. English Professor Richard

Kirkpatrick, who served as president of the Tennessee Teachers Association during this period, was particularly active in conducting teacher institutes. Because he was also charged with recruiting students for the university during his travels across the state, the trustees were enthusiastic about his work. In Spring 1878, the faculty requested the trustees to dispatch more professors, at university expense, to the numerous institutes conducted during the summer vacation. They approved sending one professor, and, in overly legalistic language, agreed "to pay the actual necessary expense of said agent or Representative during the time he shall be engaged as contemplated in the proposition submitted to the Committee."[12]

At the same meeting a special committee of the trustees considered a faculty proposition to create a summer normal school to which they would admit teachers without charge. Sizable funds were involved, and the trustees attempted a compromise. They confessed that the university didn't have the money to support an institute, but they didn't "wish to be understood as discouraging so laudable an enterprise." They offered the university buildings to professors who were willing to teach in the summer institutes without pay.[13]

Summer Normal Institutes

With free use of a campus building, faculty donation of time, and a grant of $500 from the Peabody Fund, the university held its first summer normal institute in 1880. The state superintendent designated the university's program one of three State Institutes, as differentiated from the more numerous and less prestigious county institutes. The summer normal institutes held under the auspices of the university between 1880 and 1898 became a welcome fixture of summertime in Knoxville. Townspeople of all ages as well as teachers attended the formal sessions, enjoyed the evening entertainment scheduled by the institute directors, and went on out-of-town excursions. And the local newspapers gave extensive coverage to the activities of the institutes.[14]

For the isolated, rural Tennessee teacher, the summer trip to Knoxville was made as attractive and enjoyable as possible. Railroads granted special railroad rates for teachers who were attending the institute, and members of the faculty met "ladies who come unattended" at the train. Textbooks were either furnished free or at wholesale prices. Teachers were told not to worry if they were unable to buy their books, even at the reduced price, just to bring such as they had. They were assured that boarding houses were available at reasonable rates and that horse-drawn omnibuses would "run to and from the hill every day" during the institute's session. Even their unavoidable minor discomforts and inconveniences would be easy to bear because of the valuable experiences that awaited them. The *Knoxville Daily Chronicle* reported that they arrived ready to "doff their sparkling cloaks and fall to work with peasant hearts and arms." Their enthusiasm did not abate; the newspaper announced a few days later that even though the weather was "tolerable hot" and "the hill hard to climb," the teachers were so "absorbed that they with eyes all aglow with interest, imitate the lecturer in all he does."[15]

In commenting on institutes generally, Edgar Wallace Knight, a southern historian of education, once complained that their "work at best was doubtless fragmentary and haphazard and the effort to make the lectures entertaining was sometimes ridiculous." Certainly too much work in the classroom was stupefying and, as exciting as the curriculum of the institute was, organizers planned other activities. Once or twice a week at the Opera House, nationally known speakers, including John Eaton, United States Commissioner of Education, and J. L. M. Curry, General Agent of the Peabody Fund, addressed the teachers. Some highly praised talks seem of doubtful interest: "Yesterday the optional hour was occupied by Rev. J. H. Martin, D. D., of Atlanta, who furnished much pleasure to all by reading from poems about Florida written by himself during his recent visit to that State." A hit of the 1882 institute at the Opera House was Mrs. L. C. French, the elocution instructor, who demonstrated what quality elocution was all about. *"The* Piece" in her repertoire was "The Sioux Chief's Daughter." "It alone," according to a local newspaper, "would prove Mrs. French's success as an elocutionist."[16]

There were interesting and valuable things for the teachers to do in their leisure time without leaving the hill. Stereopticon exhibits were always a popular feature with up to 200 teachers meeting in the evenings to see famous views of rugged mountain peaks and placid lakes. And Col. Samuel Lockett, the institute principal, gave a number of the more fortunate teachers "a peep at the Moon" through the university's excellent telescope.[17]

Out-of-town excursions (teachers had not yet discovered the wisdom of calling them field trips) were eagerly anticipated. And some teachers were bitterly disappointed when a Saturday holiday to Coal Creek to study the geology of the mines had to be abandoned when not enough of their colleagues were willing or were able to pay the seventy-five cents excursion railway rate. The *Knoxville Daily Chronicle* was squarely on the side of the teachers: "The railway showed the independent spirit all the way through and in the minds of many, charged an exorbitant price."[18]

Two years later the teachers, on special coaches, were able to go not only to the Coal Creek mines but also to the zinc works and on to Jellico, on the Kentucky border. The railroad rates were obviously attractive because 125 other citizens, including "quite a number of Knoxville's young ladies," joined about forty teachers. The train left the station before 8:00 in the morning "with many expectant hearts aboard, whose fondest wishes were realized ere the setting of the sun." The wishes must not have been too exalted as the chief excitement reported by a newspaper correspondent who accompanied the institute members was, in addition to some "breathtaking scenes," the killing of a cow by the train shortly before it arrived back in Knoxville. Teachers as well as cows were sometimes accident prone. A decade later the institute took an all-day excursion to the Holbrook Normal School in Fountain City, just north of Knoxville. The obviously bored reporter for the *Knoxville Tribune* ventured that "about the most interesting feature of the day's doings was when some of the party fell in Mr. French's new lake. They were, however, "pulled out before drowning." An agent for the American Book Company seemed to make it all right by buying a soda for everyone. The state superintendent reported in 1896 that the institutes were becoming more dedicated to teacher training and less to "popular entertainment." It is probably a coincidence that they disappeared shortly thereafter.[19]

The presence of persons on the excursion who were not teachers was in keeping with the tradition of the institutes. Often a majority of those attending institute functions, including regular class presentations, were lay persons. From the first year, the institute directors made clear that they did not intend the activities on the hill to be exclusively for teachers; they also invited the general public: "We trust friends of education in our city will encourage the normal school with their presence." Not only should parents attend in the interest of their children, but the "sunshine of the public presence" would elevate the quality of educational discussions. Particularly, young men and women who didn't know how to use their spare time wisely were urged to attend. The state superintendent acknowledged that the inviting of influential lay persons to speak and others to attend sessions was "potent in molding public sentiment" on behalf of public schools.[20]

Systematic or methodical instruction was difficult because of the coming and going not only of visitors but of the teachers as well, who seemed to drift in and out much as they pleased. They were allowed to enroll even in the last week of the institute, and many who enrolled at the beginning stayed only for a week or two, although a teacher had to attend at least half of the sessions to receive a certificate. However, the faculty assured teachers that even if they could attend only part of the sessions, it would be "of great advantage to them."[21]

The curriculum of the institutes was a mixture of academic courses (the content often little changed from that offered in the regular collegiate year) and lessons in pedagogy. In the first institute, as an example, the faculty gave daily instruction in geography, history, mathematics, botany, and geology; and they devoted one hour each week to agriculture and another to music and calisthenics. Knox County School Superintendent Frank Smith taught pedagogy from 10:15 to 11:00 Monday through Thursday, alternating between courses in "Primary Teaching" and "School Economy."[22]

In teacher education, students stridently, wistfully, and continually demand relevancy. In the summer normal institutes, that demand was for more on how to teach rather than on the disciplines. During the second institute, the teachers and the public were assured that its purpose was "not to teach subject matter" but to help teachers gain knowledge, "which has been learned by the observations of the most skilled instructors in the world, on how to teach." However, a year later, the fifteen faculty members of the institute, including eight professors from the University of Tennessee, were still offering a curriculum weighted in favor of traditional liberal arts courses, although the first grade, consisting of those who had not attended the previous summer, studied "Elementary Method of Instruction" and the second grade, the "Theory and Practice of Teaching." The trustees indicated, however, that the study of pedagogy permeated the curriculum: "The instruction in all subjects had distinctly in view 'how to teach,' rather than the teaching of the subject." Despite those protests, the university professors who dominated the institutes taught their specialties. Professor Joynes presented learned, detailed lectures on the structure of the English language to the often semiliterate teachers. By the end of the first week of the 1883 institute, history professor Smith had lectured on the events leading to the discovery of America, explorers and their claims, establishment of permanent settlements, causes of the French and Indian Wars, and the Revolutionary War. And Colonel Lockettt had lectured on experimental physics and explained, "in a very lucid manner, some really knotty and intricate points in mathematics." Lockett's versatility was further demonstrated by the "admirable" work in his class in sketching.[23]

The coming and going of the students was sometimes matched by the footloose faculty. The *Daily Chronicle* for July 3, 1883, reported that the institute's history teacher, Miss Conway of Memphis, had telephoned that she was leaving for Saratoga the next day and a replacement would have to be found. Mr. Frank M. Smith of Little Rock agreed to take her place. A week later, however, the paper reported that Smith had left that morning for the West on business and that "Professor W. L. McSpadden of Rogersville, who is remembered here as a successful teacher, would take his place."[24]

Over the life of the institute, its two most popular faculty members were probably Thomas C. Karns of Union City, the mainstay of teacher education in the university, and Mrs. L. C. French, the only "lady member" of the faculty in its early years, who packed teachers and townspeople into her lectures on elocution. Karns appears to have done the best job of balancing subject content and teaching methodology. His "talks" on algebra, geography, and history "were practical and to the point," and his lessons on teaching children to read "by the word and script method" were extremely popular with the teachers, especially when he used a real "class of little ones" to demonstrate his methods.[25]

The stated purposes of the institute in improving teaching methods, as reported by the *Daily Chronicle,* had an equal level of credence and the same amount of puffery as the patent medicine advertisements in the same newspaper:

> New and more complete methods for the instruction of young people are being discovered continually, rendering the old system obsolete. It will be the object of the Institute to make known these new discoveries in teaching, and lay down specific and unquestioned rules for adoption in all schools in the state.

The institute could have offered much less and still carried many of the teachers far from where they were, for they were often unfamiliar with the barest rudiments of teaching methods. As an example, Professor Louis Soldan, a visiting faculty member in the 1880s, found it necessary to suggest to the teachers that they prepare lessons before class because it would enable them to put the material "in a new light and ask better questions." By the 1890s, more restraint was evident in claims for the institute. The state superintendent cautioned that a short institute could do no more than provide "the hint—the valuable hint—upon which the ingenuity and natural intelligence of the teacher will lead him to improve."[26]

Over two or three summers, the institute curriculum included instruction on an impressive array of topics, including principles of pedagogy (with emphasis on the need for popular, tax-supported schooling and the separation of church and state), organization and graduation of schools, school discipline, map drawing, object lessons, and methods of teaching the basic subjects. Concern with teaching reading was paramount; and since methods of teaching reading is one of the political issues of our day and an indication of one's place on the political spectrum (phonetics on the right, whole language on the left), it might be instructive to know that whole word or "look and say" rather than phonetics did not originate as an insidious plot by the pink-progressive Teachers College faculty in the radical 1930s but was forcefully pushed more than a century ago in that hotbed of subversion—the University of Tennessee Summer Normal Institute. Professor Karns was particularly successful in propagandizing for the word method by taking a small class of children who had never been to school and demonstrating "what could be done in a few minutes by using this method."[27]

Superintendent Frank Smith used Spencerian charts with their flourishes and curlicues in his penmanship lessons, but such teaching aids were rare. The lecture was the chief means of instruction; having recently replaced recitations, it did not suffer from the condemnation that has been visited on it since in teacher-training institutions. "Instruction will be largely oral," the *Knoxville Sunday Chronicle* reported at the beginning of the 1883 session, but added that "the valuable collections in the university Cabinet and Museum will be used for illustrating sciences taught." And by the 1890s some presentations anticipated the show-and-tell projects so often associated with elementary school methods of teaching. For example, Miss Doak of Nashville prepared a thirty-square-foot sand map of Tennessee:

All the principal ranges of mountains and valleys were neatly molded out as they exist; little scraps of iron and pieces of coal were placed where such bodies of minerals are known to exist. Kernels of wheat, corn and oats, where they were grown and the rivers and railroads were indicated by different colored strings of yarn and the whole was a very clever design and made up a splendid and impressive object lesson.[28]

The institute instructors were not hesitant to engage in character education. If the development of children's characters was more important than the furnishing of their minds in the lower schools, surely the same should be true of the training of teachers. Above all, most boards of education of the time wanted teachers to personify ideal values and habits that children were to emulate, and Protestant religious values and observances were, of course, included. Each day of the institute began with at least fifteen minutes of devotional exercises. Independence Day 1883 was typical: Professor Dinwiddie was in charge of opening exercises that included singing, reading Scripture, and prayer. Later in the week a lecture was presented on the necessity of keeping church and state separate, though the need for the church to be responsible for religious education, "without which education may be a powerful engine for doing evil," was recognized.[29]

In the summer of 1898, the Southern Biblical Assembly held its convention in Knoxville during the term of the normal institute, and the teachers were promised that the evening speakers and stereopticon views of Bible lands, scenes, and characters would alone "be worth the time and expense of attending the summer school." In addition, the faculty devoted several of the afternoon sessions of the assembly to "Bible Study in the Secular and Public Schools." "Every Christian teacher will be interested in this subject," the Knoxville Journal editorialized. Nineteenth-century educators seldom perceived a conflict between their advocacy of universal tax-supported, public schooling, including separation of church and state, and their whole-hearted support of the teaching of general Protestant values and the use of religious rituals in the classroom. Institute faculty contemptuously denounced theories of the evolution of humans from lower forms. State Superintendent W. S. Doak spoke of the "disastrous tendencies" of the time when "a certain class of scientists" made a lot of noise and spoke a good deal of nonsense about "man's" place on the earth. He went on to assure the teachers that God had made them moral agents. Recitation of "memory gems" by the institute instructors and participants often followed devotional exercises. These were short, often mawkish maxims frequently in verse:

So nigh is grandeur to our dust,
So near is God to man;
When Duty whispers low, "Thou must"
The Youth replies, "I can."[30]

The Protestant ethic received full, unbridled support from the institute instructors, particularly stress on cleanliness, neatness, and order. Professor Rounds stressed the importance of clean and attractive schoolrooms in developing values for children. "It has been said," he repeated, "that a man never commits murder without a dirty shirt on." Professor Woolwine, in his lectures on school management, gave a fully rounded portrait of an ideal teacher: "just, honest, reliable, neat in person, and his clothes should fit him. He should carry himself erect; keep his nails pared closely, boots blacked, hair combed, and never use slang expressions." Other advice for teachers from Woolwine that students ought to emulate in order to become gentlemen and ladies included: "Do all things quietly; never draw even a chair, across the floor; speak in low tones . . . keep your feet on the floor; remember the chair has four legs; eat nothing in school; throw the ink from your pen back into the stand instead of on the floor."[31]

Discussions of better methods of disciplining students are invariably of interest to teachers, and Woolwine had a good deal to say on the topic. Some of his recommendations related to his emphasis on behaving quietly: "Reprove your pupils in a whisper," he advised. "Some teachers seemed to think they get the best results by using honeyed phrases and a specific amazing amount of kissing." But he warned that "If you adopt this plan, kiss all, beginning with the humblest and most unfortunate." He obviously didn't want teachers to get too involved in sticky-sweet methods, however, as he advised the teachers not to "dish out a lot of sentimental gush." He further recommended a common fraud perpetuated for generations on the young: "Develop a system of self-government and let each pupil think he is part of it." A later generation of behaviorists might oppose his counsel on extrinsic rewards ("neither offer prizes or have rolls of honor"); but, surely, everyone could accept his advice never to yawn during a student's recitation.[32]

Over the years of its existence, teachers remained enthusiastic about their experiences in the summer normal institutes. Newspaper reports commented on the spirited discussions among them as they competed for attention in order to get their opinions heard, and most seemed diligent in pursuing their studies; "Old ladies or gentlemen of sixty, down to young girls of sixteen," the *Chronicle* observed, "peg away and do not seem to think of it as work." The institute directors reserved the last days of a session for issuing certificates and for speeches and other expressions of opinion, perhaps orchestrated by the administration, in praise of every element of the institute. As examples, the 1880 session closed "amidst the upmost good feeling" after speeches by faculty, by students, and by visitors; and the 1881 session ended with "impromptu speech making" by guests, more or less distinguished.

"Hallelujah!" wrote J. L. M. Curry, general agent of the Peabody Fund, in his letter of congratulation to the students and faculty on the institute's success. Caught up in the spirit of the occasion, the *Chronicle* gushed, "The school has been a grand, a glorious success."[33]

By the turn of the century the age of the summer normal institutes was about over; the last in Knoxville was in 1898. In a number of unfortunate ways, they were a harbinger for teacher education. The academic requirements were low; for most of the history of the institutes all examinations were optional. Those who took examinations and could manage an average score of 65 percent received a teachers' certificate, valid for a year. The faculty promised to give much for little effort. In 1885 it was announced that students who completed a third summer's curriculum would "receive a diploma which will be good for life." And the institutes attracted students by promises of amusement and diversion—one historian of the Tennessee institutes characterized them as a "cross between a county fair and a political rally." In such historical experiences are found sources for the caricatures of teacher education.[34]

Land Grant Philosophy and Teacher Education

The campaign for teacher education in the University of Tennessee was part of the struggle between classicists and scientists or between the proponents of traditional education and of a more utilitarian education in the new land-grant college. In 1878 Hunter Nicholson, professor of agriculture and science who had championed the establishment of the summer normal institutes, argued education for modernization in a remarkable paper entitled "Relationship of the Science College to the Common School." In Christendom, he wrote, the most important movement in modern civilization for the "uplifting of the people" was the establishment of common schools, next was the application of machinery to industry. In the past, the forces of nature were studied and admired as abstract knowledge, but now they were studied "to conquer and domesticate." Science had become "the entire frame-work and running-gear" of civilization. Teaching the new science was imperative—it was the meaning of a practical education. Indeed, the demand for a more utilitarian, scientific education, he argued, was a continuation of the common school movement on a higher plane. To him, the moral was clear: there was a natural, organic relationship between common schools and the science college, and the most important question in education was "how to develop and strengthen the natural ties between the two institutions?"[35]

With this background out of the way, Nicholson was ready to tie the fortunes of the common schools and the science curriculum together, to the detriment of the classicists:

> The Classical Colleges were, one and all, built by the few, for the few. . . . What the Classical College never pretended to do the Science College seeks to accomplish. What the Science College offers is what the majority of men wish for their children and what their children will choose for themselves. As this fact becomes known the common school will become what it should be, a feeder to the Science College.[36]

Nicholson recognized that many of the college graduates taught for at least a time in the public schools, but that was insufficient. The university needed to teach young scientists how to teach science. Some things, he admitted, could be done in the regular classroom, such as occasionally selecting students to demonstrate how a lesson might be taught; but systematic teacher training "or normal teaching is perhaps the most effective way in which the science college can get at the common schools." Nicholson took the responsibility for teacher training seriously in his own classes. In his "Annual Report" for 1879–1880, he reported that he had formed a special class to meet the needs to "young men holding positions as teachers in the Public Schools where they are required to teach the geology of Tennessee." However the trustees and faculty did it, he insisted, the university had to get involved in teacher training to draw the common schools nearer, to supervise the quality of their work, and to make them "willing and powerful supporters and feeders" of the university. He had support from the trustees and from the state superintendent of schools who not only campaigned for more emphasis on developing agricultural and mechanical skills but specifically designated the state university, "situated in the beautiful metropolis of East Tennessee," with its "presentable faculty" as the natural institution to encourage and lead "the noble work."[37]

In May 1880, trustee Temple, as part of his continuing effort to pressure the faculty to move the university away from what he considered its classical and elitist mind-set and toward agricultural and mechanical education for the "industrial classes," submitted to each professor a long handwritten questionnaire designed to determine the extent to which each was carrying out the mandate of the Morrill Act and, not too subtly, to put the classicists further on the defensive. Question 48 on most of the questionnaires asked: "Do you give normal instruction, or instruction *specially* to qualify young men for teaching?" There was confusion, even at the time, about whether the university was providing such instruction.[38]

The small faculty gave surprisingly varied answers. Morton Easton prefaced his answer with complaints about his heavy teaching load: "I give instruction in French, German and Linguistics, assist in teaching Greek and Latin, and during the past year have taught Logic and Metaphysics." The answer to the question asked was no. He wrote that no department in the university offered normal instruction, but he declared that he was "in the habit of explaining my methods of teaching to advanced students, and consider that, in so doing, I am imparting such instruction." Chemistry Professor Brown also answered that normal instruction was not given, and he added that he believed that since the regular college curriculum was the best for all students, special courses to train teachers were unnecessary. English Professor Edward Joynes agreed that the university did not give normal instruction, as it would require more classes. He reminded Temple that the faculty had proposed a two-year course of selected studies for teachers that awaited trustees' approval. McBride answered that he "believed" that normal instruction was given and that there was a small class already enrolled. President Humes, feeling correctly that the questionnaire was an attack on his policies, was very much on the defensive and answered the normal school question and a number of others with: "I adopt the answer given by Professor McBride." The other professors agreed that the university provided a normal course.[39]

Temple seemed somewhat taken aback at the variety of answers and sent additional questions to several professors, asking, among other things, "Is the normal instruction spoken of in several answers, as being now given, *regular* instruction, or is it *special* instruction, given to two or three students for a special object?" The answers that were supposed to clarify the situation must have appeared quite unsatisfactory to Temple. Brown responded with: "There are no normal classes in this department." He did not indicate what was happening in the university generally. McBride replied that he could "only speak from information of others," but he understood that the normal students were "special." Nicholson and Lockett affirmed that the faculty had developed a normal course earlier in the year. Nicholson wrote that no student had elected it until the present term. He avoided labeling it regular or special but seemed to lean toward regular by replying that "the studies are the same ones as laid down in the Normal Course—heretofore submitted." Lockett, more positively, asserted that the course was regular "in that it is provided for, is well arranged, and adapted to the class of students who in the judgment of the Faculty will probably take it." He further confirmed that three students were pursuing it.[40]

Following the question on normal instruction, there was a related question that was a prologue to years of controversy: "What, in your opinion, would be the effect of admitting young ladies to the classes for normal instruction, if you have such?" Again the faculty lacked consensus. Brown, Easton, and Lockett were enthusiastic. Lockett wrote that admitting them would have a "most laudatory and happy effect—in elevating the tone, scholarship, and in improving the deportment of your young men." Easton would have admitted them to all classes. Nicholson opposed admitting them to any class whatsoever. McBride could "see no objection," and Alexander thought it inexpedient, although he suggested that they might be allowed to be examined for degrees and prepared for such examinations by the faculty "outside of the regular classes." "Such a plan is now in use at Harvard," the classicist reported. Joynes, a strong proponent of women's education, argued that with "the existing conditions of university discipline" and insufficient accommodations the effect would be "most disastrous." He added that: "Under better conditions, it might be highly beneficial."[41]

Temple asked particularly pointed questions of President Humes because of his earnest and consistent defense of the old system of classical education. Humes's responses were feeble and often evasive, and his days were clearly numbered. The agricultural and scientific advocates on the board were increasingly eager to rid themselves of "the most useless and at the same time the most expensive member of the faculty." Temple, Humes's chief critic among the trustees, had allies among the faculty. Indeed, Edward Joynes, who was hired after being dismissed for his drinking habits from Vanderbilt, still a good Methodist institution, acted somewhat as a spy-provocateur for Temple. The agricultural and some of the science faculty were generally also supportive of Temple.[42]

In December 1878, as the Temple faction increasingly voiced concerns about the university meeting the letter and the spirit of the Morrill Act, Joynes proposed another effort to offer normal instruction. In 1879, after lobbying by the modernists on the faculty, the trustees recreated a two-year normal course (and instituted the summer normal institutes). The proposal for the normal course provided for admission of men who had taught for at least one year in public or private schools as special students in the university. The 1879 catalog of the University of Tennessee, the first to bear the new and present name of the institution, required the endorsement of a county superintendent of public instruction or "some other known and competent person" before a normal student could be admitted. Upon successful completion of the program, the university would confer a teacher's certificate, but not a degree.[43]

Although suspicious of increasing pressure to depart from the classical curriculum, President Humes endorsed the new normal course: "The need of a larger number of competent Teachers for the Public Schools is obvious." He justified the university's competition with the State Normal School (later George Peabody College) by pointing to the distance from East Tennessee to Nashville; "It is desirable that opportunities of Normal instruction, such as the Faculty expresses their willingness to give, should be afforded here."[44]

The professors, always suspicious of the academic ability of prospective teachers, returned to the issue early in 1879, affirming that students in the proposed normal department would have to satisfy the faculty of their fitness to pursue college-level work. The faculty resolved to recognize students who performed "with distinction studies equivalent to the Sophomore Course" by awarding them a certificate, designating them Normal Licentiates of the University. The trustees accepted the faculty resolution the next month. In the midst of other fundamental changes taking place in the university, the press virtually ignored the re-creation of normal instruction. In a detailed story on the trustees meeting, the *Knoxville Daily Chronicle* simply reported that the course had been "authorized for the special education of teachers."[45]

By the Summer of 1879, a faculty committee had fashioned the curriculum for the normal program. The course, which did not include any training in pedagogy is reproduced below:

Normal Course
Certificate

SUBJECTS	HOURS
Mathematics	200
English	200
Latin	200

Chemistry	80
Physical Geography	80
Elements of Geology	80
Elements of Agriculture	120
Bookkeeping	80
Greek or Modern Languages	200
Total	1,240

(Catalog Note: "The hours are estimated for 40 weeks, or 200 days in the College year.")[46]

In their annual *Report* for 1881, the trustees attempted to ingratiate the university with the state lawmakers. They announced that the curriculum of the new normal school included "thorough instruction" in all courses required in the public schools of Tennessee and that teacher education was a major responsibility of a state university: "of the need for such work, in the present condition of the public schools of Tennessee, nothing needs to be said." The trustees expressed their hope that the efforts of the university to provide educated leaders for Tennessee's public schools would "meet with special approval of the General Assembly." The state superintendent responded positively, affirming that the addition of the normal department was "a new step in the right direction," placing the university "in line with other Universities in America and Europe." The faculty indicated its support to teacher education by including *Education* among the nineteen periodicals ordered for 1882; unfortunately, they suspended the order at the next faculty meeting because of uncertainty about funding for the library.[47]

In 1881, the *Knoxville Daily Chronicle* took notice of the establishment of a "permanent normal department," noting that the trustees accepted it without opposition or amendments. The newspaper prophesied that it would "be a growing, useful and beneficial branch of [the university], increasing in importance each year." It was a poor prophesy. The university immediately expelled the new course. On January 23, 1882, Joynes, chair of the Normal School Committee, introduced a resolution requesting the trustees to withdraw the teachers' course because such instruction was available in the university's summer normal institutes and because Tennessee was providing normal instruction in the State Normal College at Nashville. The professors agreed that it was important "that these two institutions should cooperate without conflict or competition." The trustees immediately concurred with the faculty decision.[48]

As usual, the death of a teacher education program was not permanent; the faculty resurrected it the next year as part of a general revision of the curriculum, without reference to competition with the State Normal College. The catalogs for 1883–84 and 1884–85 outlined a two-year Teacher's Course that included, for the first time since 1844 (excepting the summer institutes), a class in pedagogy: Theory of Teaching.

The Fiction of University African American Cadets

Land-grant status also created a possibility for early racial desegregation of the university, but the university administration was convinced that admitting black cadets would be *fatal* to the university. Tennessee legislators (including the twelve African American legislators who served in the General Assembly during the 1880s, before Jim Crow effectively ended the black franchise) were entitled to appoint three students to the state university. In May 1881, Representative T. F. Cassels wrote to President Humes inquiring about the possibility of "colored youths" attending the state university; other African-American legislators indicated that they, too, were interested in sending candidates. The Morrill Act that created land-grant colleges as well as the Fourteenth Amendment seemed to require the admission of black students.[49]

On August 16, 1881, trustee John Baxter precipitated what other trustees considered a crisis by proposing "separate instruction" for African Americans in the university: "When admitted they will be entitled to all the rights, privileges, immunities and advantages guaranteed to other students and we hereby pledge ourselves to protect them so far as we can in the enjoyment of these rights." The trustees defeated Judge Baxter's proposal by a fifteen to three vote. Baxter then moved a resolution to recognize the rights of qualified "colored" persons "to admission and instruction in the institution under our care." The chairman ruled the motion out of order; Baxter appealed the ruling, and, by a close vote, the trustees sustained the chair's ruling. In the Board of Trustee minutes, across the page in red letters and with a large X is written: "This Resolution of Judge Baxter's stricken out by order of the board at a meeting August 25 1881." UT agreed to pay $30 per student for "its colored cadets" to attend Fisk College. In 1884, the trustees turned to Knoxville College, a local African American Presbyterian institution, as the place for colored cadets. In

1890, after Congress passed the second Morrill Act, The trustees designated Knoxville College as the colored Industrial Department of the university. The arrangement continued until the Agricultural and Industrial State Normal School opened in Nashville in 1912. This fiction of African-American university students was the way the separate but equal doctrine played out in one southern institution.[50]

Teacher Education: Death and Rebirth

After a series of intrigues, Humes was finally ousted in 1883. The presidency remained vacant until Charles W. Dabney assumed the office in 1887. It was a time of troubles for the university: It was making do without a president, student enrollment and revenues were insufficient, professors were defensive and hostile, the press and the state legislature were increasingly critical, the trustees were badly divided, and acts of intrigue among all segments of the university community were a way of life.

Maneuvering for advantage, the faculty and trustees engaged in another basic curricular revision in 1886, and the agricultural interests under the vigorous leadership of Judge Temple won yet another battle. The teacher education program, however, was a casualty of this skirmish. Going back to the antebellum period, even when there was not a planned curriculum for teachers, the university catalogs described provisions for them with announcements such as the following:

TEACHERS

Holding the certificate of a County Superintendent, or other known and competent person, that they have taught successfully for one school-year, and intend to prepare themselves for further teaching, will be admitted without tuition fees, and will be allowed such special facilities as the Faculty may deem advisable.[51]

Even this notice disappeared with the new organization in the catalog for 1887–88. But the resurrection of teacher education came quickly; the catalog for 1889–90 announced that the university would "accommodate a large class of teachers who cannot attend college for a full session." The new program consisted of two five-month spring terms that met after the short public school year. Teachers who completed the course "to the satisfaction of the Faculty" were awarded a certificate. The teachers, who were designated "Special University Students," had to live off campus and were exempt from wearing military uniforms.[52]

Records of the persons enrolling in the normal or teachers courses prior to the 1890s are not extant, but the number must have been very small. A much larger group of university graduates taught, at least for a short time, in the public schools. The student literary magazines in their personal columns indicated that a good many former students, particularly during the 1880s, found their first jobs as teachers or school superintendents. The "Quads and Leads" column of the *Philo Star* was typical: "A great many of last year's students are pedagoging." The *Philo Star's* competitor, the *Chi-Delta Crescent*, was more specific about the good works in the public schools by Tennessee alumni. The persons mentioned below (including Philander P. Claxton, who was to become the university's most famous teacher educator) received A.B. degrees, indicating a classical curriculum; none were students in the normal curriculum:

> Two years ago E. P. Moses of the University of Tennessee left his position as Principal of the "Bell House" City Schools in Knoxville, to accept the position as Superintendent of the Goldsboro, N.C., Graded Schools. . . . In September last P. P. Claxton who had been assisting Prof. Moses was made Superintendent of a New Graded School at Kingston, and Prof. Johnson having gone to take charge of the School of Columbia, S.C. Price Thomas was elected Superintendent of the New Berne Schools, with R. F. O'Neal as Assistant.
>
> These young gentlemen are all well known in Knoxville as Knoxville boys, and we feel proud of them in their successful work in a new field.[53]

With such limited commitments to follow through, why did the university continuously begin programs in teacher education? In part it was simply a need for students in a small struggling institution. At the time of the first attempt to establish a teacher training program in 1844, the university had less than 100 students, and a third or more of them were in the preparatory department. In 1873 there were 65 students in the university and 206 in the preparatory department; in 1879 there were 126 in the university and 118 in the preparatory department; and by 1882 the total enrollment had dropped to 140, causing the faculty to request a committee to recommend ways of increasing enrollment. Suggestions included sending county superintendents self-addressed postcards requesting the names of parents of boys eligible for entrance and dispatching one or more professors to every part of the state to canvass for students. As late as 1901, the president sent letters to all students, giving them his Christmas greetings and suggesting that they bring a friend back with them after vacation. Thus, the university admitted prospective teachers free, not only out of zeal for the welfare of the common schools but out of a need for warm bodies on campus. Free tuition was also given for perspective ministers of the gospel, "Who shall bring a certificate to that effect from some church organization." There is little doubt that the university finally admitted women, in part, for the same reason.[54]

University officials also used promises of teacher education in politicking for state appropriations. Although the General Assembly charted it as a state institution as a result of the 1806 land grant and reincorporated it as The University of Tennessee in 1879, the university did not receive any state money for its support until 1903—$10,000 to buy a piece of land. Forays into teacher education often came after the state legislature appeared to be getting serious about supporting the common schools. As an example, the 1844 course was created after the state required the distribution of $100,000 for the common schools and $18,000 for academies in 1838. In 1839 Robert McEwen, Tennessee's first state superintendent, reported that under the new school act a school had to be kept at least three months by a qualified teacher in order to entitle a district to its share of the public fund.[55]

Similarly, the normal course of 1873 was a direct reaction to the enactment of a new school law, in the same year, establishing a public school system for Tennessee and creating a critical need for teachers. As the legislature increased its support for the public schools, the university trustees annually reminded the legislature that the university was the capstone of the public school system: "As the finishing school, and in this sense the head of the public educational system of the State, the University has a duty to discharge in regard to the public school." The way to fulfill their obligation and, in the process, to strengthen their case for tax dollars was to provide the children of Tennessee with competent teachers. In announcing the formation of the new normal course of 1879, the trustees said that they "should be glad to make such provision amply," and added they would be encouraged to do so "by a recognition from the State of the University as an authorized . . . instrumentality in the work of Normal instruction."[56]

In 1881 the trustees appraised the legislature of the success of the Summer Normal School and pointedly reminded the legislators that members of the faculty had volunteered their services and the university had provided buildings and apparatus. The hand of the university was clearly out: "But it cannot be expected that such work should be continued permanently at its own cost . . . it is therefore respectfully suggested that the legislature consider the propriety of a small appropriation out of the public fund for this purpose." The trustees suggested "not less than" $1,000 to come from the public school fund. Soon after the failure to gain state support, the Summer Normal School quietly folded.[57]

Chapter 2

The Teachers' Department

The phoenix of teacher education was reborn with great fanfare in 1891, when the university opened a new Teachers' Department. The establishment of the department was part of a national movement of establishing chairs of pedagogy in state universities and was everywhere, according to President Charles W. Dabney, Jr., "a tardy recognition" that the profession of teaching was based upon "fundamental principles" and a "system of educational doctrine" that could be taught as any other legitimate discipline in the university curriculum.[1]

There was also the continuing desire of university authorities to prove that they were of service to the common people of the state. In part, the establishment of the department was a result of educational change within Tennessee, particularly the passage of permissive legislation that allowed each county to establish public secondary schools. The coming of high schools would demand better-prepared teachers, and Dabney proclaimed that the Teachers' Department was "now fully prepared to train young men to successfully meet this demand." He saw, or pretended in propaganda documents to see, a bright new day in which the people of Tennessee would insist on employing only the best possible teachers, teachers who had been "regularly taught to teach" and in which teacher education institutions such as the University of Tennessee would have liberal appropriations. Indeed, he took the opportunity of the announcement of the new department to ask (unsuccessfully) for $10,000 from the General Assembly.[2]

The "Announcement" of the organization of the department was written with an eye to securing goodwill for the university from teachers, legislators, and the general public. It praised the struggles of the six thousand Tennessee public school teachers to earn a higher education:

> They form a large, earnest, and industrious class of students in all our higher schools, and among them will be found many leading spirits of the future. The history of popular education shows that no disadvantage of birth or station, and no measure of penury or destitution, can chain the young life down that has had the aspiration and the strength to lift itself out of the darkness of ignorance into the light of a liberal education.

The duty of the University of Tennessee was clearly to provide educational opportunities so that these young teachers could do wonderful things for the boys and girls of the state. The local press was enthusiastic about the establishment of the Teachers' Department. The *Morristown Gazette* of 2 January 1890 reprinted an editorial from the *Knoxville Sentinel* that described the new department and concluded that no other university in America was "making more earnest, intelligent and conscientious efforts" to promote quality schooling for the people of their state.[3]

The establishment of a Teachers' Department was minor compared to the other momentous changes that were taking place under the new president. Until Dabney's time, the university had been a military school patterned after West Point, with rules and regulations, drill, military government, and a required uniform. The faculty, except for the commander of cadets, enthusiastically supported Dabney's proposal to eliminate military government of the university, and they successfully instituted a new system in 1890. Of even more significance, the faculty and trustees voted to admit women to the university in 1892.[4]

The new department at first admitted only "male teachers" who had a teaching certificate or who had taught previously for at least ten months in a private school. Two years later, the university allowed men to enroll who had not taught with the provision that they had to take the military course. At first, the university announced that it could not admit women because of a lack of suitable facilities. The *Register* for 1891 listed 16 students in the teachers' course from a total university enrollment of 215 that included 14 in the subfreshman class and 16 African-American "State appointees at Knoxville College." One of the desirable side effects of teacher education from the faculty viewpoint was an increase in postgraduate students; 4 of the 13 graduate students were in the teachers' course in 1891. At the end of the next year, 16 graduate students were teachers, 14 were law students, and there were 6 other postgraduates.[5]

The teachers were assured of all the privileges of other university students, including the use of the reading room and library. They might join the literary societies, and they soon had their own organization as well. The 1893–94 *Register* announced the formation of a society for "the study and discussion" of pedagogy. Experienced teachers were free from military discipline and regulations, and they were not required to engage in military drill, but it was available for exercise if desired. A fine, new YMCA gymnasium was also advertised to meet their physical needs. The rules were "few and simple," only those necessary "to secure good order, prompt attendance, attention and faithful performance of duty." In short, they were expected to behave "according to the rules which govern gentlemen."[6]

The often poor, rural, and unschooled teachers were sometimes objects of derision by other students. Personal newspaper columns by students reported with glee the practical jokes that upperclassmen played on "the innocent fish" of the new Teachers' Department. While praising the earnestness of country teachers, the student magazine reported with pleasure a "metamorphosis" among them as time passed: "wool hats, celluloid collars and high top boots begun to give way to the more seemly derby, spotless linen and neat shoes."[7]

Tuition was free to teachers, and, unlike other students, they could live off campus; but the expenses for a term of twenty weeks on campus were quite attractive:

Matriculation	$7.00
Room rent and light	5.50
Board	40.00
Fuel, washing, use of furniture	10.00
Books, etc.	5.00
Total	$67.00

As late as 1895, the university assured students in the department that the cost of a five-month term "exclusive of traveling, need not go above $85.00 to $100.00."[8]

The trustees were adamant that the new program was in "no sense a Normal Department." They pointed out that teachers already had opportunities for "that kind of training." Universities were about advanced scholarship, not training: "For the easy ways, the short courses leading to long degrees, the mechanical methods, and the mere devices in teaching, we have no place here." A desire to avoid low-level instruction, not in keeping with the quest for recognition as a full-fledged university, was responsible for the similar warning that appeared in the *Register* for a number of years:

> This is not a normal course of instruction. Our teachers have already, in the various normal schools, teachers' institutes and State Normal College, opportunities for that kind of training. The object of the University is to promote higher education. The teachers who come to us want opportunities for improving their general education.[9]

The quality of scholarship remained a theme throughout the history of the Teachers' Department. At the 1892 commencement, Dabney introduced Daniel Albert Knapp, a student in the department, who gave "an able and eloquent oration" on professional teachers. Knapp compared the increasing standards for entering the legal and medical professions with that of teaching and concluded that "the day was not far distant when the standard of ability would be raised so high" that incompetent teachers could not enter the profession.[10]

The student magazine enthusiastically endorsed the new department and ventured that teachers should have more rigorous training than doctors, lawyers, or theologians, because "in truth a teacher should be to a certain extent all of these." A writer for the magazine asked a basic question about teacher preparation: "Is an academic education in a University better than training in teaching methods in a normal school?" With the assurance of youth, he explained the differences between the two and found a solution:

> The former has the foundation laid on which he can build, and he secured his training in the school room. The latter has what purports to be special training, but the foundation for special training is lacking. How can powers be trained that do not exist, never having been developed? How can preparation enable a man to teach something he has never learned? Why not acquire the mental grasp, and then take a course of special training, or make the special training one part of the college course? Short courses leading to long degrees are to be deprecated.

In words that echo issues of a century later, the editors of the student magazine also worried that, despite progress in curriculum and methods of teaching, moral education was in decline. They noted that public schools had "long since" been called Godless. While recognizing that the charge was often "groundless," they were troubled that, in avoiding sectarianism, schools were failing in their most important aim: "the development of moral character and true worth." A "Christian" but nonsectarian institution such as the University of Tennessee would give prospective teachers right moral bearings.[11]

Students enjoyed a modified elective system. They selected their courses, subject to the approval of the principal of the Teachers' Department, and providing that they took courses in mathematics, science, English, "or a language," and pedagogy. The new curriculum was on two levels: the first for a person who wished to prepare "for the profession of teacher in the public schools" (at the elementary level) and the second to prepare for positions as secondary school teachers, principals, and superintendents of schools.[12]

Since the common schools were in session only during the fall and early winter, the university offered courses in pedagogy for primary teachers in the spring term. If teachers were reasonably well prepared in the academic subjects at the freshman and sophomore level, they could receive a teaching certificate by attending only the Spring sessions for two years. The advanced teachers' course was an elective in the junior and senior years and led not only to a higher grade certificate but to a university degree as well. The faculty recommended this course for its "high culture value" even for those who did not intend to teach. Both certificates relieved one from teachers' examinations anywhere in Tennessee.[13]

The four-year, degree-granting curriculum for "positions of the higher order" included an elective in pedagogy in the senior year. The first semester of the course emphasized philosophy of education and, time permitting, "history of education, educational systems, theories, methods, and education psychology." In the Spring term, the principal's report indicated that he addressed more practical issues, including grading and discipline. The course in pedagogy could often substitute for required subjects in other curricula, and eventually it was offered as an elective with ethics and political science in the senior year of the general course. Beginning in 1894, the Teachers' Department offered first-year students a separate, special English course; contemporary documents do not indicate if this was for the purpose of making up deficiencies in their preparation.[14]

The Teachers' Department maintained a close relationship with Knoxville's "first-class system of graded city schools." Students visited each of the city schools. They were required to take copious notes on each grade, the management of each school, and on the administration of the system as a whole, with criticisms, "if any were to be made," on all they saw. Students read essays prepared from their notes to the class. The principal reported that this assignment gave the young men their first exposure to "the practical details of school-work."[15]

Local school administrators also came to the university to lecture prospective teachers. As an example, J. C. Ford, Knox County school superintendent, presented a "very practical" address in Spring 1894. Other local and imported speakers lectured the teachers. President Dabney gave a series of lectures on teaching science; and Chancellor Payne, of the Peabody Normal College, and J. L. M. Curry, Secretary of the Peabody Board, made presentations.[16]

The quality of students' work was, as it always is, a point of debate by the professors. In an 1892 faculty meeting the question of whether "the students were being worked too hard was discussed at considerable length." The professors did not reach a consensus. Two years after the establishment of the Teachers' Department, the principal declared that the standards for students' work had been "considerably raised." The two-year course for elementary teachers, he insisted, was the equivalent to the literary course with additional instruction in psychology and pedagogy.[17]

Principal Frank M. Smith, Agrarian Radical

Frank M. Smith, teacher in the summer normal institutes, former president of the state teachers' association, and outgoing state superintendent of schools was the first person to direct the Teachers' Department. He took charge of the department during the Spring term of 1891. In addition to his title of principal, he was also Professor of the History of Education and Pedagogics, the only faculty member to teach courses in pedagogy. He was probably appointed principal for political reasons, and he was an unfortunate choice.[18]

Smith provoked the university administration, his colleagues, and the wider community by openly engaging in partisan political activities. As a professor in the university he was given a double assignment (at the then sizable salary of $2,000 a year that many, including the *Knoxville Journal* editor, thought excessive). Since classes in pedagogy were held in the Spring term, he was to spend the rest of the academic year traveling the state speaking on behalf of public education and, what was more important, drumming up students for the university. According to his enemies, he spent the time hustling for the Farmers Alliance Wing of the Democratic Party. The Republican *Knoxville Journal* declared war on Captain Smith (for serving in the Confederate Army) almost immediately after his appointment as principal. The press campaign against him became a fierce battle in February 1893 after reports began to surface about a speech he had made the previous October in Columbia, Tennessee. According to

Republican newspapers, he had told his audience that his three brothers (and in some accounts, his father as well) had been assassinated in East Tennessee because of their politics, and the assassins (presumably Republicans) still ruled there.[19]

The East Tennessee press was properly outraged. The *Knoxville Journal* first declared unequivocally that none of Smith's brothers were assassinated in East Tennessee and then challenged him to give the names of any of his assassinated brothers, offering to give him free space "to vindicate himself" by telling the truth. The paper accused him of insulting much of the populace of the state with his "slanderous and wholly untruthful statements" and suggested that he was paid too much money to show such "bad taste and bad judgment" for partisan political purposes. The Republican press was particularly hard on Smith because he was not just a Democrat; he was leader of the radical left-wing Farmers Alliance during a period of agrarian revolt.[20]

After the state-wide uproar, the legislature's Education Committee visited the UT campus and attempted to determine what Smith had really been up to and to assess the damage. According to the *Knoxville Journal*, President Dabney told the committee that he considered Smith to have made a mistake in pursuing politics, "but that he was a politician and supposed he couldn't help it."[21]

To further muddy the water, on February 20 the *Knoxville Journal* reported that Smith, in testimony to the legislative committee, denied making the assassin charge. The paper editorialized that Smith made a mistake in not denying it before but that the editors were "glad" that he finally told the truth: "We give him the benefit of this first public denial and accept it as conclusive." In a letter to the *Journal*, members of the legislative committee immediately denied the paper's report on their meeting. According to the committee, Dabney had not said that Smith had made a mistake in actively pursuing politics, "nor did Professor Smith in any way whatever deny making the speech at Columbia . . . and that he had nothing to take back, but on the contrary, he said that under similar circumstances he would do as he did then." The *Journal*, in a somewhat misleading way, headed the column containing the committee's letter: "TAKES IT BACK. Professor Frank Smith Says He Didn't Make a Denial." The *Journal* followed the letter with a "Note" that said that its story about the testimony before the committee was based on "a thoroughly reliable source" and that the *Journal* did not intend to "misrepresent" Professor Smith.[22]

Journalists at the rival newspaper, the *Knoxville Tribune*, seemed delighted with the events, publishing the committee's letter to the *Knoxville Journal* and reporting that the *Journal* had given "a contorted report of what had occurred." The merciless press war on Captain Smith continued for months. The *Journal* accused him of using his position as principal of the Teachers' Department to campaign for state superintendent again as he had "a mad thirst for office":

> There is no doubt that Prof. Frank M. Smith, professor in the University of Tennessee (at an annual stipend of $2,000) is still a-heavin' and a-settin' at that position of superintendent of public instruction like a ram at a mill post. In one sense, he ought to get it. When a man is willing to be all things to all men—pig, puppy, red herring and dead ox—for an office he ought to have it. Few men want it that bad but when in the course of human affairs, one so peculiarly constructed appears, the office ought to seek the man even if it had to chase him across pig-sties and through the somewhat ghastly debris of an abattoir.

To be sure that he had exhausted all possible insults, the *Journal* editorialist suggested that if "Prof. Frank" didn't know what an abattoir was that one of his fellow professors who had been appointed to "sure-enough teach" could tell him.[23]

As it became apparent that Smith probably would be selected for a second term as state superintendent in 1893, the *Journal* "endorsed" him for the position or for any other office that would take him from East Tennessee "for the rest of his natural days." The paper darkly warned that it didn't want Smith "exposed to the risks of assassination for his politics sake" nor did it want the university's reputation further injured by Smith's activities, the paper piously concluded. But, of course, damage to the university, particularly to the Teachers' Department, had been done; and the university administration and faculty must have been relieved to see one of their most respected professors, Thomas Karns, appointed as principal after Smith left for Nashville to assume his coveted job.[24]

Smith continued to make trouble from Nashville, however. In 1896, as his term as state superintendent was about to end, he asserted to the UT trustees that the State Board of Education had the power to appoint the university's Teachers' Department principal. This intrusion into the internal affairs of the university appalled the trustees, and they appointed "a special committee of lawyers" to prepare a legal brief. On June 10, 1895, the trustees adopted the special committee's report denying Smith's claim.[25]

As Smith's term drew to a close, the *Knoxville Journal* saw renewed threats from this "scheming politician of a very low order." The paper blamed Smith for increasing criticisms of President Dabney, who was on leave to serve as United States Assistant Secretary of Agriculture. The *Journal* accused Smith of working behind the scenes to have Dabney dismissed because the president would not discharge Thomas Karns as principal of the Teachers' Department so that Smith could have his old job back.[26]

Principal Thomas Conner Karns, Genial Baptist

The resignation of Smith and the appointment of Thomas C. Karns as principal of the Teachers' Department was announced on June 9, 1893. Karns was to take "immediate charge" of the department and was to spend the summer visiting teacher institutes "for the purpose of laying its claims before the people." Karns, who had administered the department until Smith's first term as state superintendent had expired, was an obvious and fortunate choice. He was the first professor at the university with a preponderant interest in teacher education. In addition, he had enormous, perhaps compulsive, energy, a genial personality, and an imaginative mind. A prominent faculty member, he often performed the duties of the frequently absent President Dabney. One of East Tennessee's best known "scholars," the genial Karns was a popular speaker at teachers' meetings, farmers' conventions, and other rural meetings. He was the most popular professor in the summer normal institutes.[27]

Karns grew up on a farm less than ten miles from the university. Typhoid fever in adolescence, exacerbated by an infection in one of his legs, left him lame and often in pain throughout life. A reader rather than an athlete, Karns was salutatorian in the first graduating class of the university after the Civil War, an honor somewhat mitigated by the fact that there were only four graduates that year, all in the classical curriculum.

As was common in the nineteenth century, Karns pursued several occupations. He was a journalist both before and after his tenure as a school administrator and professor. Following college, he was a reporter (and sometimes editorial writer) on newspapers in Knoxville, Chattanooga, and Nashville. In his later years, he was agricultural editor of Knoxville newspapers, writing a farm column under the pen name Uncle Zeke. A rural-life enthusiast, he was always a part-time farmer. "Karns off in the country somewhere," Dabney grumbled to a correspondent in 1896.[28]

His career as an educator was also varied. He taught many unrelated disciplines and moved back and forth from administration to teaching and from lower to college levels. In 1873 the Tennessee Public School System was created, replacing school districts with a county system. Karns, at age twenty-eight, was elected Knox County Superintendent of Public Schools. From 1875 to 1877 he taught in the Preparatory Department of the university and from 1877 to 1881 at the Masonic Institute (a normal school) at Cleveland, Tennessee. He later served as a principal and city superintendent of schools in East Tennessee. An earnest Baptist, he was professor of English and modern languages at a local Baptist college, Carson and Newman, before returning to the university in 1886 as principal of the Preparatory Department. He joined the regular university faculty shortly thereafter, teaching, among other things, English, history, government, philosophy, and psychology before his election as principal of the Teachers' Department. He remained at the university until his resignation in 1899.

Because he had difficulty walking, Karns, who never married, was given a room in an academic building, South College, to use as a study-bedroom. Later he moved off campus. A racist account in the university archives describes his adjustment to his disability:

> As his crippled limb kept him from walking to the University he acquired a horse and buggy, also a young colored boy [sic] to look after horse and his owner. This horse, a beautiful, spirited by [bay], and Hurt, the darkey [sic], became almost as well known as Professor Karns himself. Hurt drove his master up to the University buildings in the mornings, came for him at noon, took him back, then called for him again in the afternoon.[29]

Karns was not an intellectual, and only by the liberal standards of the time in East Tennessee could he be considered a scholar. He wrote two books. *Tennessee History Stories* was written for children in the lower grades of elementary school. In the "great boys" tradition of history, it told inspiring tales of good boys doing great deeds. There is no reason to believe that the book's characters much resembled the actual persons of the same name. Neither original research nor scholarly interpretation is found in his book for older persons, *A History of the Politics and Government of Tennessee*.

Karns seemed to have great respect from the other members of the faculty and often represented them or the university in meetings of educational societies and other organizations. When President Dabney was on leave to serve as Assistant Secretary of Agriculture, the trustees placed him in charge of the president's office. He was also popular with school people throughout the state. His tastes, Baptist faith, and genial personality made him one of the most popular educators in the region. An examination of the state superintendent's *Reports* reveals that Karns conducted more summer normal institutes during the 1890s than anyone else, a circumstance that must have aided the university's fledgling program in teacher education. The student magazine recognized the strategy of using teacher institutes and the Teachers' Department as a means of gaining recognition for the university as head of public education in the state, "just as Michigan, Wisconsin, and also in Prussia, which is the prototype of the whole system." The magazine was particularly complimentary to Karns:

> Too much stress cannot be laid on the [Teachers'] Department of the University, having, as it has, Prof. T. C. Karns, who is considered one of the best educators, if not the best, in the State, at its head. Teachers desiring to prepare themselves better for their work cannot do better than attend this department of the University.[30]

He was a popular professor. Students and other audiences appreciated him for his humor and repartee. His reputation as a teacher was that he was easy but also effective. "He has the rare faculty," a local reporter wrote, "of making the most difficult questions, even in philosophy, perfectly plain." Karns's use of "progressive" methods of teaching antedated his teaching of pedagogy. The student magazine in 1889 described a mock United States Senate in his English classes "as a pleasant and profitable diversion from the regular work." Each student was a senator from a different state and, according to the student reporter, it was a "perfect imitation." Karns presided over the "whole affair," and "the rareness of it excited no little attention," with many visitors witnessing the proceedings.[31]

In teaching methodology, Karns was a Herbartian. His courses invariably included Herbart's five formal steps: perception, apperception, concept, interest, and laws of learning. Karns also taught the educational theories of Comenius, Pestalozzi, and Froebel in his history of education course. Despite his sometime forays into progressive methods, Karns, as was customary at the time in pedagogy as elsewhere, relied heavily on textbooks. He described the junior year in the advanced [degree] program:

Education doctrine, history, and practice. City-school organization, and supervision. Physical education. Manual training. Textbooks: Payne's *Educational Doctrine*. Spencer's *Education*. Painter's *History of Education*. Payne's *School Supervision*. DeGarmo's *Essentials of Methods*.[32]

Karns was eclectic, if not indiscriminate, in his philosophical and pedagogical views. Classically trained, he proposed that candidates for a degree in pedagogy should have three years of Latin and two of Greek. In his first year as principal, Karns assured Dabney that after an examination of education departments throughout the country, he was developing "an ideal course which shall embrace the entire science and art of pedagogy." To demonstrate that pedagogy was a science, he conducted experiments "from the scientific point of view" in educational psychology; unfortunately the nature of these experiments is unknown. As part of his devotion to science, he accepted Social Darwinism as a proposition "so evident as to demand no further argument." He explained to Dabney that all schools must adapt to their environments: "This principle holds in the evolution of culture as well as in the evolution of animal life." He insisted that his aim for the teacher education curriculum was a "strict harmony with both scientific theory and practical results."[33]

Some understanding of Karns's ideas concerning the work of public schools may be gleaned from a three-year model course of study that he devised for the Knoxville public high school in 1896. Karns constructed his curriculum shortly after the famous National Education Association Report of the Committee of Ten on the reorganization of the secondary curriculum that reaffirmed the desirability of a college preparatory curriculum, not just to prepare one for college but to prepare one for life. Karns agreed that a classical or traditional curriculum should be available for those who wanted it, but his interest was obviously in more utilitarian studies. Karns's curriculum included required courses in English, history, geography, mathematics, and sciences. Among a broad array of electives in business and "technical" studies were: freehand, "form study," mechanical, industrial, and architectural drawing; physical culture (female) and military tactics (male); single- and double-entry bookkeeping; household economy (females); shorthand and typewriting; commercial law; woodworking; cooking and "cutting and fitting clothes" (female). In the third and final year of his model high school, pedagogy was an elective; this course was devoted to the "theory and art" of teaching primary school. It included practice in teaching by having students serve as substitute teachers.[34]

Initial support for the department by Dabney and the enthusiastic commitment to his new duties as principal by Karns were demonstrated by the creation of a pedagogical museum. During the summer of 1894, quarters for Karns's department were papered, painted, and generally refurbished. He was given the entire lower floor of Old College, consisting of a "beautiful new lecture-room," reading room, and a library/museum—all "handsomely fitted up." Karns modeled his museum after that of the new Teachers College, Columbia University. By the end of 1894, he reported that he had a full set of materials from the U.S. Bureau of Education, including reports, circulars of information, and histories of education (probably the centennial state histories) and "a most excellent collection of maps." He collected photographs of model classrooms, teachers and students, rural and urban schools, and "noted educators." Among other material in the museum was a collection of students' work from schools of several states that consisted of "specimens of penmanship, number work, free-hand drawing, map-drawing, pretty [putty?] maps, work in clay, examination papers, and all kinds of school work which can be used as illustration in pedagogical training." Blank forms and specimens of school records, report cards, and class records were on display as well as sets of textbooks for various subjects and grade levels. In his annual report to Dabney in 1894, he insisted that "the value of such collections is plainly evident."[35]

He compared the need for an educational museum in training teachers with the necessity of "cabinets of minerals" in training scientists. He also recommended, not surprisingly, that he needed a special appropriation to support it. He promised other like exhibits for the future:

> Model libraries for primary work, for example, or for teaching geography, etc., will be collected. I desire, likewise, to show, by collected copies, chronologically arranged, the historical development and improvement of text-books. By these and other collections teachers will be enabled to make a concrete and practical study of the work in which they are to engage.[36]

The university magazine reported in 1896 that Professor Karns's educational museum was "one of the most interesting features of the Hill." Karns and Dabney used their influence to convince the national government to loan to the university much of the education exhibit of the recently held World Cotton Exhibition in Atlanta. Specimens of work done in American Indian industrial schools were on display as were material on the history of education, including "a number of old

relics that are interesting purely from an educational point of view."
The student editor opined that the exhibits "serve to give one a much
higher appreciation of the advantages of the educational system of
today over that of the past."[37]

Karns, a first-rate propagandist, campaigned for his department from
its inception. One technique was to publicize the demand for graduates of his department in public schools. He bragged that the
department's best graduates were hired quickly at good pay: "We recently sent a young man to the City High School in New Orleans at
$125.00 per month." He warned that while he could not guarantee
positions, graduates had no trouble finding teaching jobs. His first
report to the state superintendent commented on the job opportunities for the new certificate holders:

> Every one of the nine students who completed the course last June is now
> actively engaged in teaching. One is the principal of a county academy and a
> County Superintendent, one is president of a local college, another is the
> principal of a city graded school, three are principals of village schools, and
> the others have good positions in schools of the best class. Nearly all of the
> other students in the department are teaching in the common schools at the
> present time.[38]

Throughout the 1890s, the "alumni" column in the student magazine listed numerous appointments of Teachers' Department graduates as principals or superintendents of schools. However, in letters
to those actually seeking teaching jobs, Karns was more cautious:
"Teachers in the district schools here get $25 to $40 per month. With
proper energy you might get a school, though there is a great supply
of teachers." He acknowledged that teaching positions in a university
town were particularly scarce. He warned a prospective student who
wanted to teach while studying pedagogy in the university that the
Knox County elementary schools were "overrun with teachers," and
the chance of getting a job was uncertain.[40]

An enigma in Karns's professorship was his silence on one of the
most controversial issues of the early 1890s in the UT community,
the admission of women. At first the university admitted them only to
the Teachers' Department; yet he seems to have nothing to say, at
least publicly, on the issue.

"Lady Teachers" Admitted to the University

As in other southern state universities, teacher education provided a
back door by which women entered the university. In January 1891,

Dabney asked the trustees for authorization to request an annual appropriation of $10,000 for the Teachers' Department from the legislature. Trustee O. P. Temple moved that the request be granted on the condition that "lady teachers" be admitted to the department. The other trustees acquiesced, hoping that enrollment would increase and that the legislature would award scholarships in each senatorial district for the women. The university got the women but not the money. Nevertheless, the decision was widely thought to be wise. A local newspaper editorial endorsed the proposal, pointing out that most school teachers were women, including many of "the best teachers in the state." Women who had not taught were not allowed to enter the Teachers' Department until 1895.[41]

According to the student magazine, the university community gave "hearty support" to the proposal to admit "girls" to the department. Actually the reaction was mixed; some male students wrote misogynist poems, and professors debated the wisdom of the decision for years. From the perspective of a century later, much of the reaction seems sexist. The editors of the student magazine engaged in their usually juvenile clowning:

> We united in one fervent "Amen" to the project, and that it may mature and bring in the girls to the University, let us all earnestly pray. It is evident, also, that the Faculty are even as anxious, if not more so, than we to have the girls come in, for it is said that one of the members of that recondite body (whether one of the celibates or not, we were unable to learn, but we strongly suspect that it was) expressed himself as not only willing and anxious to throw open the doors of the University, but his arms, too, for the reception of the fair ones. All agree that "it is a consummation devoutly to be wished."

A couple of years later, the editors ventured that the "young ladies" had exercised a "very civilizing influence" on the Teachers' Department.[42]

The university admitted women to other curricula in the Fall of 1893, and before the academic year ended, forty-eight enrolled. The *Knoxville Tribune* argued that after their success in the Teachers' Department it was inconsistent to limit them to only that part of the university. The faculty wished to make it clear that women students would not be coddled, that they should not come to the University of Tennessee "to be polished or finished." "Not a single class was changed," the president proudly reported, "nor a new one started, for their special benefit." He further pointed out that the university did not even offer instruction in music or fine art or any of the so-called "accomplishments" and that women who wanted to study only such obviously feminine subjects as literature or French were not allowed to enroll. The president and faculty need not have worried; at the end of the first session, women had been awarded faculty scholarships as the best students in the freshman, sophomore, and junior classes.[43]

The university did not treat them exactly as they did men students; women had to be at least seventeen years old, although males were admitted at sixteen, and they were subject to special regulations:

1. They will have no dormitory or domicile on the University grounds, except in the families of the Faculty.
2. They will not board or lodge in any family in which male students board or lodge at the same time, and then only in families approved in writing by the Faculty, or by their own parents or legal guardians.
3. A building on the University ground shall be set apart temporarily for their use as reception rooms whilst awaiting their recitations.[44]

Women on campus took some getting used to and remained a curiosity for several years. At the formal opening of the 1894–95 school year, a reporter for the *Tribune*, attempting to capture the color of the ceremonies, described what appeared still exotic to him: "exactly twenty-seven 'co-ed' hats, and a very determined specimen of young womanhood beneath each one." According to James Hoskins, a student at the time and later president of the university, rather than "co-eds," the cadets often called the new women students "floozies." In the brave new world of coeducation (and in the Victorian era), reported relations between the sexes on campus appeared to be most innocent, but ideas of male rights of domination and conquest were clearly apparent: "'Co-eds' were seen here and there with head bent slightly forward listening with added color and a new sparkle of the eye to the warm greeting of a 'cadet' standing with hat in hand and gallantly making his prettiest 'opening' speech in the 'campaign' to follow." The women, however, adopted a yell that suggests somewhat more vigor on their part: "Rah! rah! ree! Come kiss me!!!"[45]

The Demise of the Teachers' Department

In keeping with the university's tradition of short love affairs with teacher education programs, the Teachers' Department was quietly dropped in 1896. President Charles W. Dabney, the young and energetic proponent of professional studies and later a prominent leader in the southern educational campaigns, gave Karns and the Teachers' Department strong initial support; but his enthusiasm waned quickly for reasons that are not completely clear from extant documents. In part, it was the failure of the legislature to support the department with appropriations. In their report for 1894, the trustees became insistent that "in view of the important work" that the Teachers' Department was doing for the public schools, "It deserves and should receive some direct state aid." The demands were ignored.[46]

In part, Dabney's disillusionment was related to academic quality and low standards for entering the program, and most of the other professors agreed with Dabney. Despite Karns's general popularity with the rest of the faculty, his Teachers' Department had few allies. Most professors had been cold from the beginning to the idea of becoming deeply involved in teacher education. In the previous twenty years, they had allowed two other programs in teacher education to die from lack of nurture.

Dabney's concerns about academic standards in the department were probably well founded. In response to letters from teachers inquiring about entrance requirements, Karns encouraged them to enroll by assuring them that the requirements were flexible and not too rigorous. He soothed one prospective student by assuring her that she would not have "to pass on the algebra" and that she should have nothing to fear from the entrance examination: "A little examination may be necessary to determine your scholarship, which as you see for the teacher's course embraces only arithmetic, English, grammar and composition, and geography and United States history. A grade of only 60% is required."[47]

Although based on genuine commitments, Karns used a tactic that was to become common for educationists in the university: He tried to gain support for teacher education by playing on the president's sense of the university's role as a service institution to the state. "Through the education and professional training of the thousands of instructors whom we may send forth to teach," he wrote Dabney, "our university may become a great power and an instrument for incalculable good." He also attempted to satisfy Dabney by increasing academic standards "in order that those who take the degree may meet creditably" the demands of teaching and so that the "foundations of their education may be well laid."[48]

Karns attempted to meet Dabney's demands for more academic rigor. After he had successfully negotiated curricular changes with the faculty and trustees, he wrote to Dabney, "You told me to do as I pleased about the matter. . . . In making these changes I have had in view a compliance with what I thought would be your wishes in the matter." Entrance requirements for those wishing to teach were made the same as for all other students, and course work was to be "equal in character" to that done in the other schools. The result, Karns assured Dabney, was to put teacher training on a "higher plane" so that the students in pedagogy would not be "segregated or made different from others." Dabney remained unconvinced.[49]

Another reason for the demise of the Teachers' Department may have been the loss of state certification for its graduates. The department had been able to bestow such a certificate, signed by the state superintendent, before 1896: "A certificate, with the title of Licentiate of Instruction, which licenses, without further examination to teach in the primary and secondary schools of the state" was granted upon completion of the teachers' course.[50]

In his continuing battle with Dabney and the university, state superintendent Frank Smith ended automatic certification of the Teachers' Department graduates. The university began issuing their own certificates in 1896, sometimes with the dubious assurance from Karns that "I think you will find this to serve your purpose about as well." In a letter to a complaining teacher, Dabney was more forthright. He placed the blame on "the politicians" and the State Board of Education who had ended the university's authority to grant certificates. He regretted that the state superintendent had "promised to get the State Board to give this authority again; but no action has been taken in the matter." A list of those awarded teachers' certificates last appeared in the Catalog for 1897–98. Ten students received certificates, not an insignificant number because at the same commencement only sixteen graduates of the Academic Department received bachelor's degrees.[51]

After the university abolished the Teachers' Department, Karns continued to argue that pedagogy should "be taught in a distinct school, or department of the university" but agreed that "for the present" it could become part of the Philosophy Department. In 1896 Karns prepared a seven-point proposal, quickly adopted by the faculty, that required prospective teachers to enroll in the regular academic program, although courses in pedagogy continued to be offered during the Spring term of each academic year. Karns also assured Dabney that he would drop his title of principal of the Teachers' Department and "retain simply that of Professor of Philosophy and Pedagogy."

Although he retired ostensibly to engage in more institute work and to write textbooks, continuing disagreements with Dabney caused Karns to resign from the university in 1899.[52]

A number of applicants for Karns's position wrote to Dabney, who put them off; apparently he was undecided about what to do about pedagogy: "It has not been decided when the position of Professor of Philosophy and Pedagogy will be filled. . . . I do not think any action will be taken this year, not perhaps until next summer." Early in January 1900, Dabney wrote William R. Dodd of Raleigh, North Carolina, that he wanted a "good man" for philosophy and pedagogy but just didn't know when money would be appropriated for the position. By the end of the month, he was a bit more pessimistic, writing Dodd that it wasn't "positively determined" that the position would be filled "at the present time." By March, he warned Dodd that an adjunct professor would probably be all they could afford and that the salary would be "a small one at first." In October, he regretted that they could not offer the position to well-qualified candidates: "for the want of means, and not for the want of interest."[53]

The Catalog for 1900–01 lists neither philosophy nor pedagogy, although it does promise that professional instruction was offered "in connection" with the regular academic courses. Faulty proofreading was probably responsible for the continuing provision that persons who had taught for at least five months could substitute pedagogics for military drill. The university catalog does not list a course in pedagogy again until 1903–04 after the establishment of the Department of Education.[54]

Chapter 3

The Department of Education and the Summer School of the South

For a few years at the turn of the twentieth century, the University of Tennessee was the most important southern university in teacher training and in the struggle for improved public education in the South. Under educationist Philander P. Claxton and President Charles Dabney, the university provided leadership for the Southern Education Campaigns, a coalition of conferences and boards that used money from northern philanthropists to crusade for improved public schooling in the South. (The campaigns are discussed in more detail in the next chapter.) The Southern Education Board (SEB), the propaganda arm of the movement, placed its Bureau of Information and Investigation in Knoxville under the supervision of Dabney. The interlocking General Education Board (GEB), which spent millions of Rockefeller dollars on southern education, bankrolled teacher education at UT.

Dabney brought Claxton to Knoxville to head the Bureau of Investigation and Information and to edit its journal, *Southern Education.* Dabney was convinced, despite his experience with Karns and the Teachers' Department, that pedagogy could be a scholarly university study. Both Claxton and Dabney were adept at securing funds from northern philanthropists, and they soon persuaded the GEB to finance a department of education at Tennessee that would rival the University of Chicago and Teachers College, Columbia University. They organized the Summer School of the South, making it the largest summer school in the United States and the source of thousands of workers in the southern educational campaigns. Claxton served as head of the Department of Education and superintendent of the summer school from 1902 until 1911.

Philander Priestly Claxton

Sometimes the influence of a particular person does make a crucial difference in the history of an institution. It is difficult to imagine that the University of Tennessee would have had a prominent place in early twentieth century southern teacher education without the powerful presence of Claxton. Called, with some justification, the Horace Mann of the South, Claxton was born in a log cabin on a Tennessee subsistence farm in 1862. Claxton attended several "cabin" schools within walking distance, spending three years at "Yaller Cat" school taught by his uncle. He later enrolled in a backwoods academy where at age sixteen he taught some classes for a remission of fees. He attended the University of Tennessee on borrowed money. A campus leader, he graduated from the classical curriculum in two and a half years, second in his class of sixteen.[1]

After graduation, he crossed over the mountains to teach in a new graded elementary school in North Carolina. The other first-year teacher was Edwin Alderman; they became friends and roommates. The school superintendent, E. P. Moses, introduced Claxton to the new science of pedagogy. Thus, early in his career, he became friends with two educators who in the early twentieth century would become leaders of the education campaigns to fund public schools in the South. He also began to study educational literature that led to his becoming one the most articulate leaders among southern progressives.[2]

After two years of teaching, he decided to attend a "real" university and entered Johns Hopkins, majoring in Teutonic languages. More important for his future career, he took a "most inspiring and informational" course in pedagogy from G. Stanley Hall. He immersed himself in the intellectual and cultural life of Baltimore, exciting stuff for a Tennessee farm boy. A six-month trip to Leipzig to study German schools was even more heady: "There are certain streets and restaurants where, I have been told, every other man was a professor, and author or critic more or less well known to fame." He served as a school administrator in several small systems in North Carolina, and from 1893 until 1902 taught pedagogy at North Carolina Normal and Industrial College.[3]

Dabney, recognizing his talents and ambition, invited him to Knoxville. Claxton was an indefatigable worker. He made hundreds of speeches a year, wrote extensively, administered complex institutions and survived on three or four hours of sleep a night. He had at least two "nervous breaks" early in his life, one while he was a student at Johns Hopkins, the other at Tennessee when the new university president, Brown Ayres, was reducing the size and influence of the Department of Education and Dabney was encouraging him to accept the deanship at Cincinnati.[4]

In the southern educational campaigns, Claxton spoke boldly for industrial education—the paramount tenet of orthodoxy in the movement. The General Education Board was paying for and expected propaganda on behalf of a "practical" education. His own philosophy of education was more balanced and eclectic. In 1911, Lucile Cole of Mississippi Women's College asked him directly which was better, a liberal or technological education. He refused to choose: "They both have their merits." He went on to argue his lifetime position that "It is very important that in every person's education there should be a good amount of attention to good literature, art and the things pertaining to the cultivation of the imagination, emotions and affections." As United States Commissioner of Education from 1911 to 1921, he championed foreign languages and art and music education, subjects sometimes slighted by progressives.[5]

Claxton advocated moral education in public schools and, like most educators of his time, seemed unable to entertain the notion that there might be conflicts between teaching values derived from a particular religious tradition and religious freedom. In response to a questionnaire from educationist (and later leader of the antiprogressive essentialist movement) William Bagley, Claxton argued that schools could give explicit moral instruction in most school subjects if teachers avoid too much preaching, which will "disgust the children." At the same time the ever-careful Claxton summarized his opinions to Bagley with advice that is generally consistent with later Supreme Court decisions:

> I doubt if a teacher should attempt to give systematic religious instruction, as this is generally understood in America, in the schools, nor do I believe it should be given in the school by visiting clergymen. I would, however, have large portions of the Bible read in the school for the sake of their moral and spiritual teaching, as well as for their literary value, but I would have this entirely void of the doctrine or teaching which could in any way be considered sectarian.[6]

While he made no original contribution to scholarship, he was a prolific writer of position papers and opinion columns in journals and pamphlets. In 1897, he founded the North Carolina *Journal of Edu-*

cation and edited it and its successor, the *Atlanta Educational Journal*, until 1903. His *Practical Fonetic Alfabet Drill Book* was popular with elementary teachers early in the century, and he coedited a series of elementary school readers in the same period.[7]

Claxton was a complex personality who left people with quite different impressions. His detractors charged that he was arrogant, conceited, and self-seeking; his admirers found him modest, unselfish, and unassuming. He was a passionate advocate. He was neutral about practically nothing. When asked for information for a college debate on the need for compulsory education in Tennessee, he responded, "There is no negative side to the question." He was often aggressive in stating his opinions yet was an effective lobbyist and back-room negotiator. He was courageous in defending his opinions but left little evidence of introspection. Occasional self-doubts might have been more becoming for a scholar but would have been a handicap for Claxton's role as a crusader.[8]

The Department of Education

On July 22, 1902, Trustee Judge Temple moved that the university establish a department of education "upon the receipt of sufficient funds for its maintenance and that the President be authorized to accept subscriptions for this purpose." The resolution passed the Board of Trustees unanimously. The department was modeled after Columbia's Teachers College, "acknowledged to be the finest of its kind in America." Dabney wrote, "Are you ashamed of your god-child?" on a newspaper clipping about the new department and sent it to Teachers College Dean James E. Russell. Russell responded graciously that he was "not ashamed to stand sponser [sic] for so good an undertaking." Comparisons with prestigious Columbia continued. In negotiations for financial support, Dabney bragged to George Foster Peabody that "ours is undoubtedly the best department of Education and the best faculty outside of the Teachers College."[9]

As it had with the Teachers' Department a decade before, the university stressed that the new department was for the academic and professional education of teachers; it was not a normal school. The goal of the new department was not simply to train local teachers or even Tennessee teachers, "but is intended for the whole south, and is free alike to all students." The local newspaper bragged that Tennessee was the first southern university with a department of education. Students in the department were not charged tuition, even those who were preparing to teach in other states. The university sent announcements and advertisements about the department to newspapers and other periodicals across the South, including thirteen state education and teachers' journals.[10]

The need for teacher education in Tennessee and throughout the South was great. Less than 15 percent of Tennessee's public school teachers had as much as a high school education, and Claxton argued that teacher education was the most important element in improved public schooling. Claxton despaired that the legislators and other custodians of the public purse wanted to improve the quality of teachers by more rigid examinations rather than by quality teacher education. Claxton scoffed at their solution: "Examining teachers does not give them more knowledge or skill any more than weighing boys makes them heavier." Nothing else mattered much if teachers were ill prepared; he explained that it all revolved around children in a building "and a man or woman called a teacher in the house with them. The whole thing can be photographed with a kodak."[11]

With great optimism the department opened in January 1903 with sixty-five students and five full-time professors, which was soon increased to seven. This was the largest education faculty in American universities with the exceptions of Chicago and Columbia. In addition to Claxton, who taught the art and science of teaching, the original faculty included Wickliffe Rose, professor of the history and philosophy of education. After leaving the university, Rose was appointed to important positions on the Southern Education Board and the Peabody Board, and he eventually became president of the General Education Board and the International Education Board.

Not only did Dabney and Claxton copy Teachers College, Columbia's curriculum; Dabney, on one of his frequent money-raising trips to New York, recruited faculty from Teachers College. Ever conscious of southern sensibilities about Yankees, he was cautious about how effective "outsiders" might be. He recruited Burtis B. Breese, born in New York and educated in Kansas, to teach educational psychology and ethics. Breese was a former student of Edward Lee Thorndike's at Teachers College, who highly recommended him:

> In a university position he will attract the attention and win the confidence of school men and women, but at the same time hold the esteem of his university colleagues and of psychologists in other universities. Very few university teachers of psychology can do the former. The men trained in school work who do the former, universally fail to do the latter.

But Dabney asked Albert Shaw, SEB member and editor of *Review of Reviews*, to investigate if Breese "is the kind of man who can get along with these southern people?" The answers were satisfactory, and Dabney strongly and successfully recruited him.[12]

The department of education brought two women to the male-dominated faculty of the university: Anna M. Gilchrist, a graduate student in Teachers College and a middle-westerner, to train domestic economy teachers. And a Memphis native, Lilian W. Johnson, a former instructor in history at Vassar College and the recipient of a new Ph.D. in history from Rutgers University to teach American history and methods of teaching history. Because she was a woman, Dabney saw special roles for Johnson. "I believe Miss Johnson would take pleasure in working up the women of the city schools," he wrote Claxton. Dabney also assigned Johnson to assist with the work of the Southern Education Board, particularly in attempts to organize women's clubs in the southern educational campaigns.[13]

Elevated scholarship is a continuing theme in the university's history of teacher education, and the faculty of the new department of Education in 1903 stressed an academic imperative in preparing successful teachers—"without it no amount of professional training will avail." Knowledge of subject matter, they argued, was paramount. They proposed a teacher education graduate program that would not be realized until 1988:

> But, above all, the department wants graduate students who have taken a bachelor's degree at this University or another college of good standing, and have attained such maturity of years . . . as will engage them to do the advanced professional work to the best advantage. Only with students of this kind can it become the real university department of education for which it was established.[14]

In addition to the usual pedagogical courses of the time, the new curriculum reflected the southern education movement's emphasis on industrial and homemaking education and the northern philanthropists' promotion of it. In 1902, the president of the Nashville Board of Education wrote to Ayres complaining that the South lacked teacher training for women in manual training, including cooking. Ayres responded that the university had tried such a curriculum in the past, "but our girls were too high toned to take it up." The next year, after George Foster Peabody made generous donations, including $1,000 to support domestic science in the new department, Claxton gave

Anna Monroe Gilchrist responsibility for training domestic science teachers. She reported that the first two years of work was equivalent to the high school curriculum of the progressive Horace Mann School of New York City and included "such knowledge as will tend to the making of good house wives rather than teachers of domestic science." She endorsed a strong academic, rather than a "sugar-coated" science curriculum for domestic arts teachers, including required courses in bacteriology, biology, chemistry, and physiology. Yet, her report on the work in her sewing class did not seem to be intellectually challenging: the teacher candidates "had drills in using thimbles, threading needles, and cutting with scissors—means necessary in the teaching of primary children." As class projects, the prospective teachers made: "a pincushion, needle book, emery bag, button bag, scissors case, etc., they have cemented their knowledge of basting, running, gathering, shirring, backstitching, stitching and hemming."[15]

The department depended on financial support from the GEB for its existence. Dabney had his fingers in the pockets of the northern philanthropists, and for several years he campaigned for larger donations and more systematic giving to the Department of Education and to the Summer School of the South. The GEB granted $5,000 a year for the department, provided the university would raise an additional $4,000. These were sizable funds at the time; in 1903, the University of Tennessee had a total "handsome" income of $85,000 a year, which included the appropriation for the Agricultural Experiment Station and the GEB grants.[16]

Dabney used his close personal relationship with some of the northern philanthropists to solicit additional funds, and he was not above appeals based on sympathy. In a five-page letter to GEB member Walter Hines Page, he complained that he was "in a wretchedly worn out condition" all of the time that he was soliciting funds in the North: "You know how straitened we are and how the failure to get this entire fund for three years would demoralize the Board [of Trustees] and discredit me with faculty." Dabney had initial successes with northern benefactors. In 1903, his "Confidential Report" on the results of his trip to New York reported pledges of $10,000 a year for three years for the Summer School of the South, $5,000 a year for three years for the new Department of Education, and $8,000 for other university needs. The changing whims of the General Education Board and misunderstandings about how the money was to be spent created problems for the administration and unease among the faculty.[17]

The major misunderstandings developed over the terms of financial support from the GEB that insisted that the gifts had been conditional on securing a practice school under the control of the Department of Education. (Lack of a practice or laboratory school was a source of frustration for the faculty throughout most of the history of teacher education in the university.) Dabney insisted that such a laboratory school had been planned from the beginning, but he disagreed that money to support the department hinged on establishing it immediately: "I never knew anything about the pledge by which it is now said I am bound until recently. No copy of it has ever been supplied me and I had no way of knowing that the immediate organization of the practice school was a feature of the pledge which I was supposed to have agreed to."[18]

In June 1903, Dabney attempted to persuade the GEB to drop the appropriation requirement for the immediate establishment of a practice school. A special committee consisting of John D. Rockefeller, Jr., George Foster Peabody, and William H. Baldwin, Jr. considered and then denied the request, insisting that the denial would help the university secure a practice school from the Knoxville school system and, in typical bureaucratic fashion, indicating that they were receiving many requests for modifications of terms of conditional gifts and needed to consistently deny them. Dabney argued that even without a practice school the department had quickly accomplished much, including stimulating other southern universities to create similar departments.[19]

Dabney was especially embarrassed because George Peabody, in addition to the $1,000 to support a school of domestic science, had given $2,000 of his own money to equip a practice school. In the summer of 1903, Dabney was a house guest of Peabody. Things had obviously not gone well; and Dabney, after returning home, wrote Peabody, apologizing for "brain fag" caused by hard work and worrying:

> It has pained me deeply to see that you thought that I had failed in doing anything expected of me. I had supposed that every step in the process was fully understood by you and that you approved of our postponing the school until we could get into a new building. It seemed to me wise in the mean-time to use the fund for the education of teachers and this has been done with, I believe, fine results. Every dollar of the money has been expended or promised, and all of it for our cause.[20]

The university attempted to honor its commitment to establish a practice school. The trustees entered into an agreement with the Knoxville Board of Education to use the nearby three-teacher Rose Avenue School as a "Model and Practice" school. The school had five grades and approximately 120 students. The university supported a manual training teacher, Amanda Stoltzfus, for the school and offered the use of books and apparatus, "manual training tools, natural history specimens for nature study, etc." for the use of the practice schools with the understanding that "if any loss occurs by breakage or otherwise, it shall be made good by said professors and instructors." University authorities seem to have exaggerated the importance of the Rose Avenue School, calling it "the central feature" of the new department and indicating that it served teacher education in the same way that a laboratory serves departments of chemistry and physics: "It is hoped that it may soon become a model for the study of school officers and teachers throughout the South."[21]

The reports on Rose Avenue School proved too optimistic. Even before the 1903 school year started, Dabney admitted to Buttrick that Rose Avenue was not working out as a practice school. He reported that the education professors found the building in "very unsatisfactory" condition, and the Knoxville Board of Education pressured the department to retain teachers that were unacceptable models for beginning teachers. He explained that the legislature had been expected to approve a bond issue to build schools in Knoxville and the Board of Education had agreed that the university would get the use of one of those as a practice school. Unfortunately, he explained, "Republicans aroused factious opposition to the plan based wholly on political grounds," and the bond issue failed.[22]

The education faculty was already uneasy about the uncertain financial support from the North when, in 1904, Dabney resigned to take the presidency of the University of Cincinnati. They quickly bailed out, leaving only Claxton, who was tormented for weeks as he tried to decide if he should accept Dabney's offer to become Dean of Education at Cincinnati. At first, Claxton was optimistic about the new president, Brown Ayres, a physicist who had taught in the Summer School of the South. "I think Doctor Ayres has a very good spirit about things," Claxton wrote to Dabney, writing that he would avoid "any extreme narrowness." But Ayres had a strong bias against pedagogy and within a few months of taking office wrote to other university presidents across the country, asking them about the advisability of teachers' colleges in such institutions.[23]

In September 1904, in view of changed conditions, including the resignation of most of his education faculty, Ayres asked the GEB to release the university from the requirement for a practice school. Once more, the GEB denied the request for modification of the conditions of the grant. Failing that attempt, Ayres then requested a smaller amount, $4,000, to keep the department operating; again the GEB refused any support unless a practice school was established. After failing to secure additional funding to support the department (Peabody contributed $500 from his own pocket), Ayres recommended to the university trustees that any plans for the practice school be discontinued, and that only Claxton, whose position was secure because of his popularity with politicians, businessmen, and educators outside the university, be retained.[24]

Teacher education languished for the rest of Ayres's tenure. The university established a Department of Education in part because the southern school campaigns seemed to promise that at long last the southern states, including Tennessee, were going to create systems of public schools equivalent to those in the North, with an accompanying need for trained teachers. Of course, there was also the money. Not only would the new department give the university yet another opportunity to verify its worth to the people of the state to justify increased appropriations, but the big-hearted philanthropists on the General Education Board seemed eager to help provide decent schooling for the poor children of Tennessee. The legislature proved to be no more generous than it had been in the past, and the northern captains of industry were demanding about how their funds were spent. Again, the commitment to train teachers proved to be halfhearted. The pattern of false hopes for a strong teacher education program in the university quickly reemerged. "Our educational department would have grown very rapidly, and would have been one of the largest in the country," Claxton wrote in disgust, had it not been "for the coldness and opposition with which it was received here."[25]

The "School of Education"

Following its heady beginnings, the Department of Education became little more than a professorship in the College of Liberal Arts. Although it was upgraded on paper to a School of Education in 1911, the catalog for that year lists only one professor of education and nine courses in pedagogy. Rather than an administrative entity, the School of Education was a curriculum in the College of Liberal Arts, leading to degrees of Bachelor of Arts and Bachelor of Science in Education. The admission and degree requirements (including a major and minor in an academic discipline) were the same for all students in the college. The students followed a literary or scientific liberal arts curriculum except for eight one-year courses in education in the junior and senior years. The catalog for the School of Education listed a number of liberal arts professors as faculty members; they were to prepare potential high school teachers in methods of teaching their disciplines. In 1915, the Tennessee Department of Public Instruction granted teachers' certificates to thirty-two of these professors so that they might legally prepare teachers. The creation of the "School of Education" was a response to the opening of state normal schools to train elementary teachers, a topic I discuss later in this chapter.[26]

In 1911, Claxton left to become U.S. Commissioner of Education, further weakening the status of teacher education in the university. Robert Morris Ogden, professor of philosophy and psychology, taught the education students until Claxton could be replaced. Ayres appreciated Ogden, in part because he was not an educationist: "He is a fine scholar, not at all the narrow kind of man that one often finds especially interested in educational psychology, though he is taking quite an active interest in our work of teacher preparation so far as it has been developed."[27]

Soon after Claxton's resignation, D. S. Hill was appointed to the education professorship, but he was immediately released from his obligation to accept a position at Tulane University. Ayres then interviewed and offered the position to Frederick Eby, a distinguished education professor at the University of Texas. Eby didn't accept, but he strongly recommended a younger Texas colleague, E. E. Rall. In negotiations, Rall wrote Ayres that he would not be interested in the position unless he was appointed head of the department. In response, Ayres frankly discussed the somewhat misleading organization of education in the university:

> So far as there is any organization in the department of education he will be the head of the department, but we have not organized our educational work as an independent department as has been done at the University of Texas. We consider it as included in the College of Liberal Arts. We have, however, outlined certain courses in education and have published a circular in which we speak of these courses as constituting a "school of education."[28]

Rall was a native Iowan, educated in the Iowa State Normal School and the University of Iowa. His Ph.D. was from Yale and he had a year's postdoctoral work at Teachers College, Columbia. Despite his northern background, he was hired for the position. His strong evangelical religious views (even if tinged with a social gospel theology) helped make him acceptable to the Knoxville community. Rall soon became superintendent of the Sunday school of Church Street Methodist Church, the largest and most prestigious Methodist church in Knoxville. He gave his "talk" (the "Boy and Religion") in a number of mainstream churches. A mix of muscular Christianity and the social gospel, his speech was particularly popular with the elders of young men. Rall's litany of social problems was common to the social gospelers and other progressives of the time: immigrants, long hours of labor, child labor, industrial accidents, public health, class conflict, and graft and corruption in business and politics. In addition, as an educational progressive, he saw injustice and promise in public schools as well as in churches. He denounced particularly the low pay for teachers, who receive less for teaching children than janitors for sweeping out classrooms. Social justice in society should begin with justice for teachers and quality education for children in public schools, and Christian men, he argued, must furnish the leadership for reform.[29]

Rall supported a much more traditional liberal arts curriculum in public high schools than did southern progressives and their northern philanthropic supporters. He proposed a study of English as "the backbone" of the curriculum, one or two foreign languages for "most, if not for all students," American history as well as mathematics, and at least two years of science. He called vocational training a difficult issue and recognized its class bias, and he suggested limiting vocational subjects to one course a year. He particularly opposed separate vocational schools, calling them undemocratic and tending "to produce objectionable class distinctions."[30]

In a 1916 general faculty committee, President Ayres angered Rall, a member of the Committee on Degrees, by indicating that Rall favored the education degree option in advising students and that changes in certification requirements had "slipped" into the catalog. In a closely argued four-page letter, Rall disputed Ayres, indicating correctly that the requirements for the degrees and for certification had not changed since he was hired and that despite "your statement to the contrary to the faculty" the thirteen to fourteen students taking the education degree were indeed preparing to teach.[31]

Shortly thereafter, in the summer of 1916, Rall resigned to accept the presidency of Northwestern College (later University). In his gracious acknowledgment of Rall's contributions to the university, Ayres specifically mentioned his work on university committees.[32]

The Education Curriculum

In the early years of the department, except for Gilchrist's courses for training domestic science teachers, the curriculum emphasized a scholarly and theoretical study of education. Breese taught psychology for teachers and an advanced seminar in educational psychology. Johnson offered a course in teaching history: "Some period of American History will be chosen and practical exercises in research, criticism, and interpretation will be required of each member of the class." A photograph in the university's collection shows Johnson's attractive, well-furnished library and seminar room in Old College.[33]

When only Claxton was left on the faculty, educational history was the paramount discipline. History of Education was a survey from ancient cultures to the then present. Textbooks were: Laurie's *Rise and Early Constitution of the Universities*, Quick's *Educational Reformers*, and Russell's *German High Schools*. A class in Education Classics included Plato's *Republic* and readings from Quintillian's *Institutes of Oratory*, Plutarch's *Morals*, Comenius's *School of Infancy*, Locke's *Some Thoughts Concerning Education*, Rousseau's *Emile*, Kant's *Ueber Padagogik*, and Froebel's *Education of Men*. For the 1905-06 academic year, Claxton adopted Paul Monroe's newly published *A Text-Book in the History of Education* and Laurie's *Historical Survey of Pre-Christian Education,* and more emphasis was placed on history of education in the United States.[34]

The other two courses were Science of Teaching and Art of Teaching. The Science of Teaching course was described as a study of the "fundamental principles of teaching" without further elaboration or bibliography. The Art of Teaching was a methods of teaching course that included material on school management, curriculum, and teaching the common school subjects. In 1904, Claxton combined the two courses into the Science and Art of Teaching which emphasized educational psychology, curriculum, and methods of teaching. Over the Fall and Winter terms, Claxton assigned McMurry's *General Method*, Lange's *Apperception*, DeGarmo's *Interest and Education*, Thorndike's *Principles of Teaching*, and McMurry's *Method of the*

Recitation as well as "leading articles in the magazines and school journals." Enrollments were small: ten in History of Education, four in Educational Classics, and four in the Science and Art of Teachers, but Claxton reported that most of the students were "earnest and faithful, and are doing good work."[35]

From the beginning, Dabney had urged the education faculty to vigorously recruit local teachers to attend courses, particularly Saturday classes offered especially for them: "It is going to be difficult to get them to understand a new thing like this and to appreciate the great benefits to be derived from it. You will have to lay it down to them line upon line." Throughout the period, the education faculty continued to offer after school and Saturday courses to local teachers. In Fall 1915, as an example, Rall offered two special courses: one on school supervision and administration for principals and a course in the history of modern elementary education for elementary teachers. These special courses were a way of circumventing an agreement with normal schools that the university would not teach elementary education courses. University administrators supported such courses out of a concern with enrollment numbers and with a commitment to "service" teachers in local school systems; but Harry Clark, appointed professor of secondary education in 1912, saw a stronger reciprocal relationship: "keeping alive in the university the public school point of view." In addition to the courses for teachers, local papers throughout the period were replete with stories about educationists speaking to community groups on schools and child rearing. From 1902 to 1918, the education faculty claimed that they served an average of nearly 2,000 persons a year in some sort of teacher and parent training.[36]

Science enchanted Americans, and educationists across the country increasingly claimed that pedagogy was becoming a science. Science, they hoped, would give education an esoteric knowledge and an accompanying status that it had previously lacked. Educationists at Tennessee shared the promise. Harry Clark "admitted" that, in their beginnings, schools of education had to base their teaching on theory and ideas borrowed from psychology and philosophy; but now, he claimed, pedagogy was becoming an "exact science": "The most interesting feature of this is the effort to discover uniform tests by which exact measurements can be made of the work in the elementary and high schools so that any school principal may determine whether his students are measuring up to a national standard."[37]

But innovations were expensive, and education facilities and materials were inadequate. The faculty continually lobbied for more resources. A practice or laboratory school remained their top priority. Their ideal was a laboratory school on campus directly under their control. Lacking that, they pleaded with Ayres to make arrangements with the Knoxville Board of Education for an assigned school for "observation and practice." In similes that Tennessee educationists would use for decades, they pled for a school of their own.

> Such a model school is to the school of education what the laboratory is to the school of chemistry or physics, the work shops to the schools of mechanics or engineering, or the farms to the schools of agriculture. It is no less essential and should be considered as much an integral part of the University. . . . I believe every successful University department or school of education in America and Europe has such a school connected with it. . . . A training school without such a model school under its direction and for its use is a swimming school without water.[38]

The library's education collection was old and woefully inadequate. Hyperbole in university publications about new programs is expected, but the claim in the "Announcement" of the Department of Education that the excellent university library contained "the most important books" in teacher education was misleading, if not disgraceful. When the department opened, Dabney spent some of the philanthropists' money on the library, and the Summer School of the South allowed education students to use their collection, which was finally donated to the University Library. But Claxton continued to complain that the collection was "very incomplete" and lacked even essential publications: "I have to constantly supply students with books from the rather meager collection of my own private library."[39]

Rall, in his job negotiations with Ayres, wrote that Professor Eby said the library was "quite inadequate" in pedagogy. Rall insisted that it would have to be improved if he were to take the position. His appeal seems to have had some success because shortly after he arrived, the *Orange and White* reported that the library had added new educational periodicals: *Education*, *The School Review*, *Teachers College Record*, and *School Science and Mathematics*.[40]

Claxton also lobbied for an educational museum (soon to be called curriculum laboratories by the new scientific educators); Karns's extensive museum for the Teachers' Department seems to have disappeared. Claxton's description of the contents of his model museum gives a further sense of the teacher education curriculum:

(a) Of school work of all kinds and grades, especially of industrial work, manual training and drawing; also of examination papers and such other papers as will show the character of work done in urban and rural schools in all parts of the United States and in foreign countries.
(b) Photographs and prints of buildings, grounds, recitation rooms, laboratories, work shops and of pupils at work.
(c) Maps, charts, desks, apparatus, and all school appliances.
(d) Catalogues and reports of schools, including courses of study, programs of recitations, etc.
(e) Textbooks on various subjects of the elementary and high school curriculum.

Claxton suggested to Ayres that they could get much of the material free or at little expense if freight and space were available. He also broached the possibility of securing the educational exhibit of the 1904 Worlds Fair in St. Louis as the foundation of the education museum.[41]

Throughout the period, the chief extracurricular activity for prospective teachers was the Education Club, one of the most active student organizations on campus. Its predecessor, the Teachers' Literary Society, disappeared with the disbanding of the Teachers' Department. In March 1903, shortly after the establishment of the Department of Education, the faculty and students organized a new Education Club. Rall re-created it as the Educational Journal Club and devoted its meetings to student discussions of education journal articles. The *Orange and White* reported that many students engaged in the discussions even though attendance was "entirely voluntary" and no credit was given. In 1914, it was reorganized with more emphasis on outside speakers; membership was limited to education students, but teachers in local schools were invited to become honorary members.[42]

Programs varied widely. Professor Ogden spoke on higher education in Germany ("at one time . . . aristocratic students devoted the first two years of their college life almost exclusively the various activities of the dueling club"); Miss Ambrose, in support of industrial and home-making education, spoke of the work of Tomato Canning Clubs for girls. In November 1920, the Education Club opened its membership to any university student interested in the "welfare of the state of Tennessee." According to the student newspaper, the policy change resulted from of the passage of the Nineteenth Amendment: with women voting, every citizen needed to be informed about educational issues.[43]

Education Students

In the first decade of the new century, teaching was the most common occupation of new college graduates; more than a quarter of them entered teaching. And even without a specific program in teacher education, the university continued to produce many teachers. In November 1903, just as the university established the Education Department, the *Tennessee University Magazine* reported that over half of the Spring graduates of that year were teaching.[44]

Enrollment numbers in the new department are difficult to establish because most students who enrolled in education courses followed the regular Liberal Arts College curriculum rather than the B.S. in Education. In December 1906, Claxton responded to a survey on teacher education conducted by Frederick Bolton of the University of Iowa. Claxton reported that there were eighty students in the department and that all were undergraduates (there were only three graduate students in the university). He estimated that about half of the students taking courses in education, particularly in history of education and psychology, did not intend to teach, and most who planned to teach were preparing for high schools and normal schools; only a few intended to work in elementary schools.[45]

In 1913, Clark bragged about "remarkable" growth in teacher education, from one professor to three and a few students to a "third of the Liberal Arts department." To schools with vacancies, he offered thirty young teachers prepared to teach high school, including young women in domestic science and young men in agriculture. Yet the number of students actually taking their degrees in education remained low. Of the 956 students in the university in 1915, only fifteen were officially listed in the School of Education, including five special students.[46]

The "Alumni Notes" of the September 23, 1914, *Orange and White*, gave the occupations of twenty-one graduates from the 1913 class. Eleven were teaching in public schools (six of them women) and seven (all men) were practicing law. Miss Mirian Glasser, the paper reported, had given "up her much-talked of teacher's career to become Mrs. Alex Klienberger of Knoxville." Except for marriage, the paper gave no occupation other than teaching for women.[47]

On gender, as on many other issues, Claxton was a southern liberal (by no means a feminist) of his time. In answers to question from New York City's Commission on Teachers' Salaries, he responded that 25 percent of public school teachers should be men, including half of high school teachers, but that men should also be an important presence among elementary school teachers, even in the early grades: "Women as a rule can sympathize better with little children and are more tactful, but men have a different point of view and many men are very sympathetic and tactful." He indicated that "at least" half of principals should be men, but that they should also be experienced teachers. He assured the woman secretary of the Commission that he did "not like the man boss and woman servant idea." The questionnaire referred to the "equal pay for equal work controversy" but did not specifically ask Claxton's opinion on it, and he did not take the opportunity to comment on unequal pay for teachers, which was extreme in Tennessee. He could make strong eloquent pleas on behalf of women teachers ("women of good brain and purpose, noble enthusiasm and sweet culture, but as a rule not . . . women of means"). These southern women of "scholarship, culture, training and experience," he lamented, often taught even in city schools for less than $500 a school year:

> For board, lodging and laundry they must pay not less than $250. They can scarcely be expected to dress on less than $100 a year. They are fortunate if their medical and dental bills are less than $25 a year and if $25 is spent in books, contributions to church, charities, etc., little is left to apply to the college debt.[48]

When the new Department of Education opened, Claxton feared that even with free tuition, women teachers would simply be unable to afford the cost of college, depriving them of "a fuller life," and children of better instruction. He campaigned unsuccessfully to raise $30,000 for a proposed Tennessee Hall where women preparing to teach could stay for only the cost of heating and maintaining the building. Claxton also harbored popular prejudices of his time toward women: "This is the trouble with women, especially young women teachers, they will swear by anybody. . . . I find, for instance, that Miss West is swearing by modern vagaries of Herbartism as worked out in Teachers College."[49]

In 1908, Ayres asked Claxton for enrollments by gender. The numbers were small: three men and three women in History of Education; five in the Science and Art of Teaching, all women; four men and one woman in a course in Secondary Education; and one man and one woman in Educational Classics. In addition, Claxton offered two one-credit hour special classes for Knoxville city teachers; thirty-six women teachers and one man enrolled in the science and art of teaching class and four women and one man in the special class in secondary education.[50]

Low salaries was a perpetual reason that fewer men entered teaching; they had occupational choices that women did not, and each generation of educationists condemned low teacher salaries. In 1914, Harry Clark wrote a long column for a Knoxville newspaper, "Get Thee to Mop and Broom for Profit," showing in some detail how even lowly paid women in occupations that required much less schooling were paid as well as and often more than teachers:

> In comparing salaries, you must remember that a teacher must dress better than her sister in other occupations. She must go to lectures, travel, attend summer schools, buy books, buy tickets and magazines from her pupils, spend money to fix up her room, travel half way across the state to an annual educational gathering, and give money to the many hungry, half-clad waifs that drift into her room.[51]

President Ayres was much more matter-of-fact about public school salaries. He thought it was not surprising that male university graduates didn't become teachers but taught as a "temporary expedient until they can get into something else." The absence of men would make teaching a female profession; he hoped that the Smith-Hughes Act, which gave a stipend for vocational and agriculture teachers, might influence boards of education to increase the stipend for male teachers generally.[52]

Despite a crucial need for black teachers, all of the faces in the education department, and in the university generally, remained white, although education professors often held meetings and in-service training with black teachers. The fiction that African American students enrolled in a "separate industrial department" of the university continued as federal land grant-funds were shared with all-black, church-related Knoxville College. In order to comply with the separate-but-equal decision of the Supreme Court in *Plessy v. Ferguson*, Tennessee law required equality for all races and colors in public schools from elementary to the university; but, as Dabney explained to U.S. Commissioner of Education William T. Harris, Tennessee law also required "that the accommodation and instruction of persons of color shall be separate from the white." The university president nominally administered the industrial department, which primarily trained teachers, in Knoxville College, but:

Colored students have their entirely separate buildings, separate teachers, etc. The state having provided a certain number of free scholarships for the students in the college of agriculture and mechanic arts, these are open to colored students as well as to white, but when appointed they are sent to their own department.[53]

The education law of 1909 established state normal schools, including a black institution. Because of white opposition to literary or academic education for African Americans, the school was originally named the Agricultural and Industrial State Normal School. It opened in 1912; the following year, the university's responsibility for black education ended, and land-grant funds from the Morrill Act were withdrawn from Knoxville College and given to the Nashville school.[54]

Relationships with Other Teacher Training Institutions

In the turn-of-the-century South, teacher training institutions were numerous and distinctive for their variety as well as their easy standards. Segregated by race, there were a bewildering assortment of institutes and normal schools. Many were proprietary. In Kentucky, thirty-four private schools received state charters and engaged in teacher training before 1905. The privately owned Southern Normal School at Bowling Green claimed to be the largest normal school in the South, with 683 students enrolled in 1897–98, and Jasper Normal Institute trained more teachers than all the public institutions in Florida in the late 1800s and early 1900s. The private Holbrook Normal School of Knoxville trained more teachers than the University of Tennessee in the late 1890s. To further indicate the variety, Knoxville also had a Masonic normal school in the same period.[55]

For decades, the university's major competition in Tennessee was the Peabody Normal College. Established by George Peabody in 1875, from 1881 to 1905, Peabody received state appropriations and was under partial control of the new state board of education, making it a quasi-public institution; it was sometimes referred to as the State Normal School. In 1909, the Peabody Fund trustees used the remainder of its assets to endow the renamed George Peabody College of Teachers. Although it became clearly a private rather than a public institution, for many years university administrators complained that officials of the state department of education continued to favor Peabody College over the university. In the first two decades of the twentieth century, Peabody trained from 100 to 300 teachers annually, many more than UT.[56]

One of the final acts of the Peabody Fund trustees, before they granted the residue of their assets to the college, was particularly galling to university officials. They awarded $40,000, then a significant sum, for the erection of a university school of education building in most southern states. The chief condition to the gift was that the universities would have to spend at least $10,000 per year on their school of education. Because the George Peabody College of Teachers was located in Tennessee, the university did not receive such a grant. Ayres and the trustees were outraged at this "injustice"; they were particularly exasperated at their impotence since Wickliffe Rose had recently left the education department to become General Agent of the Peabody Fund. The university trustees beseeched the Fund's officers but they remained adamant, and Ayres and other university officials remained resentful.[57]

In 1914, Ayres was a tad harsh with a University of Virginia professor of secondary education who was conducting a study of what southern universities were "able to do" with their $40,000 gift and how they were spending their $10,000 annual appropriation. He innocently asked Ayres how the University of Tennessee was spending their funds. Ayres replied that the university didn't get the money, that he didn't agree with the attitude of the Peabody Fund, and that the university was not spending $10,000 on the education department "for the good reason that we have not the money."[58]

By 1900, state normal schools were the common institutions for training teachers in the North and West. First established in Massachusetts in the late 1830s, by 1875 they were as ubiquitous as community colleges are today, except in the South. Particularly for women (most normalites were women), they often served much the same purpose as present-day community colleges, a place inexpensive and close to home where youth could continue their schooling beyond high school. In the beginning, the curriculum consisted of a review of elementary school subjects in addition to some art and music, scriptural reading, and lectures on schoolkeeping, followed by practice teaching. They were not scholarly institutions. In a recent study of the history of teacher education, Jurgen Herbst writes that "academic requirements were intentionally kept low."[59]

Although there was a legislative struggle to establish a normal school in Tennessee in 1855-57, such schools were not authorized until the

General Education Act of 1909. In 1911 and 1912, a school opened in each "grand division" of the state—at Memphis on the banks of the Mississippi River, Murfreesboro in middle Tennessee, and Johnson City in far East Tennessee as well as the "colored" [sic] Agricultural and Industrial State Normal School in Nashville. (In 1925, the legislature renamed them teachers colleges.) Although they provided competition for the education department of the university, Claxton wrote the law establishing normal schools and led the educational campaigns that made passage possible (see chapter 4 for his role in the campaigns).[60]

Ideally, Claxton argued, teacher education for elementary as well as for secondary teachers was best achieved in colleges and universities, but he worried that many liberal arts professors saw the training of public school teachers as beneath them. He feared that universities were unable to "descend from the freezing heights of dignity on which so many of them live (or die), and can understand that he who would be greatest must be the servant of all." He despaired that southern college and university professors, in particular, were too aristocratic, having "little real sympathy with the people" or sense of obligation to universal public schooling.[61]

In a 1906 Society of College Teachers of Education survey, Frederick Bolton asked Claxton if he favored normal colleges for preparing high school teachers. Claxton responded:

> If the departments of education in universities could have such liberal support as to enable them to do all the work for training teachers, I think they would be better for this purpose than advanced normal schools. The association of teachers with men and women of liberal culture preparing for other professions cannot fail to have a broadening tendency which is much needed by a teacher, whose greatest danger is becoming narrow in thought and sympathy.[62]

In the minds of educationists and presidents of the university, the role of the normal schools was clear: they were to restrict themselves to training elementary teachers. In February 1911, shortly after the establishment of the normal schools, Claxton answered a questionnaire from Moses E. Wood of Clark University: "I do not believe that the state normal schools can do much to help toward better supervision in the cities. Their large problem must be the preparation of teachers for elementary schools." Ayres echoed the response a few months later: "We propose to limit our educational work in the University proper to the preparation of high school teachers and superintendents, leaving to the State Normal Schools the work of the preparation of teachers for the elementary grades."[63]

Conflict between the university and normal schools began immediately after the normals opened and continued well beyond the period under consideration in this chapter. Arguments included much unseemly name-calling, particularly between Sidney Gilbreath, president of East Tennessee State Normal School and former state superintendent of public instruction, and Ayres. In 1911, the Tennessee Board of Education published a *Bulletin* that announced that normal school graduates were entitled to a teaching certificate valid for any of the state's public schools. Ayres was outraged at what he perceived as a direct challenge to the proper roles and function of the university and the normal schools. He wrote to the presidents of the normal schools naively urging them to pressure the State Board of Education to deny the normal school graduates the privilege of secondary school certification. Among other arguments, he indicated that high schools taught by normal school graduates would lose their accreditation from the Association of Colleges and Preparatory Schools of the Southern States.[64]

The normal school presidents took umbrage at what they considered the arrogance of Ayres. Seymour Mynders, president of West Tennessee State Normal School and another former state superintendent, called Ayres assertions "a wholly indefensible position" and insisted that Tennessee authorities would not be dictated to by "some self-constituted" body like an accreditation association. Gilbreath was more combative, charging Ayres with being opposed to normal schools from the beginning as attested by his "violent" opposition to high school certification, making "absurd academic generalizations," and leading the university beyond the functions for which its funds had been appropriated. He wrote that he "did not care to discuss, at this time," Ayres opinions on the education of teachers or on other educational issues; he urged Ayres to "seriously and deliberately" reconsider his protest.[65]

Ayres four-page response to Gilbreath was generally conciliatory, but he could not avoid intimating that Gilbreath had been a bit hysterical: "The trouble with us Southerners is that we are too much inclined to work our emotions and not sufficiently inclined to work with our reasons." Ayres assured Gilbreath that he had misinterpreted his attitude toward normal schools, that it was "extremely friendly and cooperative," and that, indeed, he was "most enthusiastic" about them. Taking the high ground, Ayres wrote that it was not a "personal matter" with him but he did have special legal responsibilities as the university was "head of the public school system" of Tennessee. And, he insisted, he did not threaten accreditation by the university of high schools that had normal school graduates as teachers, but he stood by his warning that such high schools were in danger of losing their Southern Association accreditation. He observed that such accreditation was standard in the North and that the South would have to follow the practice if it was to escape its inferior position. He also quoted Section 7 of the General Education Act of 1909 that established the normal schools to the effect that they were "*solely* for the education and professional training of teachers of the elementary schools of the State."[66]

The combative Gilbreath fired back that he rather enjoyed Ayres "sermonette" on reason and emotion: "A school teacher should always be willing to pardon a fellow teacher who sermonizes. It is a habit we sometimes unconsciously form and while it seldom results in any good the weakness of the habit leaves it impossible that any lasting injury should be done." He asserted (correctly) that Ayres had indeed said that the university would not accredit high schools with normal school graduates as teachers. If this statement was not a threat, Gilbreath wrote, "I am unable to properly translate plain English." At any rate he was glad that Ayres disclaimed his previous regrettable statement. He also reiterated a charge that the university was exceeding the functions for which state funds were appropriated. Ayres asked for particulars or examples to support such a charge. Gilbreath response was murky: "I beg to suggest that if you will study closely the definite purpose for which your appropriations both State and National are made and the actual results achieved in the University it may throw some light on the question that is likely to be interesting." Ayres called the response incomprehensible. Although agreements were made that the normal schools would not train high school teachers and the university would not train elementary teachers, both sides chafed under the agreements, remained resentful of the other, and continually experimented with ways of exceeding the spirit of the accords.[67]

The Summer School of the South

In the first decade of the new century, the Department of Education was sustained by the nationally famous Summer School of the South. The summer school was, in part, an attempt to bring Yankee dollars (captains of industry had many to give away, and they seemed eager to spend them on southern schools) to the University of Tennessee. In addition, Dabney and Claxton were energetic and personally ambitious, eager to play in larger arenas; they could make national reputations from this kind of activity. Dabney and Claxton were first-rate grantsmen, and they created a school that seemed irresistible to the philanthropic boards. Teachers from all over the South would be professionally educated in pedagogy by visiting experts from Teachers College and Chicago, indoctrinated in an industrial education philosophy, and trained to be political agents on behalf of public school campaigns.

Between 1902 and World War I, the Summer School of the South instructed and propagandized tens of thousands of public school teachers from the southern states; 22,000 students attended during the first ten years. The school (a mixture of university, normal school, political rally, and religious revival) was an integral part of the southern educational campaigns to "modernize" public schools in the South. It was held under the auspices of the Southern Education Board (SEB) and initially financed by the interlocking General Education Board (GEB). The members of these philanthropic boards not only wanted to "awaken the people" but to educate the teachers, "who were the best of them already sufficiently awake"(the southern educational campaigns are treated in chapter 4).[68]

A school to train southern teachers seems to have been Dabney's idea—or as one propaganda piece put it—he "heard the call" for something far more consequential than the "little summer normals" that dotted the southern states. Claxton, its long-time superintendent, accepted credit for the name—Summer School of the South. When Dabney went to Claxton with the idea in February 1902, he had only a promise of $5,000 from George Foster Peabody to support the school. For the first session, Dabney raised $1,000 in Knoxville, and the SEB, the Peabody Fund, Robert Ogden (of the Wanamaker department stores of New York and Philadelphia and president of the Conference for Education in the South) and other "private individuals, here and in the East" supplied additional funds. Dabney spent much of his time courting funding sources. In 1903, after a trip to New York, he reported pledges of $10,000 a year for three years to support the summer school.[69]

On behalf of his good causes, Dabney took advantage of his close, personal relationships with some of the northern philanthropists. His formal request for funds to railroad magnate William H. Baldwin, Jr., member of the SEB and the GEB, is an example: "We must have ample lecture rooms and laboratories, and an auditorium to contain 2,500 to 3,000 people, a dining room and public comfort building and, if possible, new dormitories. Our architect reports that it will take at least $25,000 to provide the ordinary facilities upon a substantial and modest scale." A personal second letter to Baldwin typed the same day makes clear that the previous one was for propaganda purposes: "I enclose the letter which you were kind enough to ask for. If it is not in correct form or does not suit you in any way, return it to me with your comments and I will try to make it right."[70]

Dabney tried to endear himself further by naming temporary buildings (constructed to meet the needs of summer school students) after southern education movement leaders. As examples, He named the exhibition building Ogden Hall for Robert Ogden and Curry Hall for J. L. M. Curry, general agent of the Peabody Fund. In the latter case, the ploy did not work. Supporters of Peabody Normal School in Nashville complained about an initial gift of $1,500 from the Peabody Fund, and Curry, bowing to the pressure, asked Dabney for the money back. Finally, after angry recriminations, half was returned (which George Foster Peabody replaced from his own pocket). Until his death in 1903, Curry refused to contribute any more from the Peabody Fund and argued against any of the philanthropic boards supporting the Summer School of the South. Textbook companies subsidized the stipends of some instructors, particularly for authors of their books. The American Book Company, for example, contributed about half of the salaries ($150.00 with an offer to increase the amount by $25.00 each, "if necessary") of three instructors in 1903.[71]

Dabney had to use his considerable powers of persuasion to convince the always conservative university trustees to allow the campus to be invaded by teachers—mainly women. He argued that the school would improve the common schools throughout the South, especially in Tennessee, and would further the interests of the university. The board reluctantly approved, providing that it didn't cost the university any money for maintenance, including utilities, that the building be properly cared for, and that "the university assume no responsibility for the instruction given . . . and have no connection as a university with the school."[72]

As a result of the roaring (and to many in Knoxville, surprising) success of the school and the accompanying national publicity in magazines such as *Outlook* and the *Independent*, the Board became much more enthusiastic, expressing "its profound appreciation of the great success and beneficial influence of the Summer School of the South" and authorizing the use of the campus for 1903, 1904, and 1905. Throughout the early years of the Summer School of the South, however, both institutions acknowledged the separation of the summer school from the university.[73]

The Summer School of the South was a huge undertaking. Before the first session one hundred thousand circulars were distributed, and Claxton, hustling students from throughout the South, kept warning Ayres that hundreds, perhaps thousands would attend. Ayres was suspicious of Claxton's "unbounding optimism" but continued to hire additional faculty, finally borrowing $1,500 on his insurance policy "to pay those fellows." Although only about 350 students attended UT during the regular academic year, 2,019 persons finally registered for the first session. The writer of a report at the end of the session was conscious of his bragging: "We Americans are often warned that our darling virtue is bigness. We love it. We roll numbers under our tongue." But he felt that the leaders of the school should be excused "for the innocence of their joy" in these statistics.[74]

Claxton carefully organized for the arrival of the teachers. Railroads gave special rates for teachers on their way to the Knoxville summer school (although there were complaints that others, who were not teachers, took advantage of the rates to visit summer resorts in the mountains nearby), and streetcars, hacks, and carriages met the trains. Police were stationed on campus to protect the students' baggage, a bootblack was available on the hill, "ice-water was kept in barrels" throughout the campus, free Knoxville newspapers were distributed, and the "white caps" were everywhere. Everyone connected with the Summer School of the South from clerk to officer was require to wear a white cap "to distinguish him from ordinary mortals" so that anxious teachers would know whom to ask their "multitude of questions" and could solve their problems.[75]

Famous Faculty and Other Celebrities

For many rural and small-town southern teachers, a major attraction to the Summer School of the South was the opportunity to meet celebrities. The faculty were famous and near-famous, and invited speakers were often persons whom one only expected to see in pictures in *Harper's Weekly* or *World's Work*. Speakers in the first session (many returned for future sessions) were a who's who of the southern education campaigns: E. A. Alderman, president of the University of North Carolina; J. L. M. Curry, general agent of the Peabody and Slater Funds; Charles D. McIver, president of North Carolina Normal and Industrial School; Albert Shaw, editor of *Review of Reviews*; Edgar Gardner Murphy, secretary of the SEB; William J. Baldwin, railroad executive and member of the GEB; and Walter Hines Page, editor of *World's Work* and a chief propagandist of the campaigns, who stayed to teach English usage.

A list of faculty who lectured in following years (some returning summer after summer) is impressive. The best known from Teachers College, Columbia, included President Nicholas Murray Butler and Dean James E. Russell. William Heard Kilpatrick taught philosophy of education and Paul Monroe history of education. Charles A. McMurry expounded on Herbartian methods. Edward Lee Thorndike lectured in psychology and spent a good deal of time sitting on benches on campus, chatting with students. Wisconsin was well represented. Richard Ely taught economics and U. B. Phillips history. Phillips's interpretation of southern history must have been comfortable to that generation of southern white teachers.

G. Stanley Hall, president of Clark University and pioneer in educational psychology and child study, was one of the most popular professors and returned to Knoxville summer after summer. Seaman Knapp, Liberty Hyde Bailey, and C. Hart Merriam, head of the U.S. Bureau of Biological Survey, taught agriculture and nature study. John Dewey received $800 for five lectures in the session of 1904, even though the normal stipend was $200. William T. Harris, U.S. Commissioner of Education, and Jane Addams lectured; Booker T. Washington and William Jennings Bryan gave major addresses (Washington's off campus, of course).[76]

A popular feature of the Summer School of the South was the entertainment. In early planning for the school, Dabney promised that there would be "a full program of platform exercises of a highly stimulating and entertaining character," and public school teachers were attracted to Knoxville with assurances that they would have a good time. Concerts and plays at the summer school garnered much publicity in the local press; as many as 3,000 persons attended some performances. (The critics of the summer school, most notably Ayres, condemned the "chautauqua features," calling them frivolous and un-academic.) But much of the entertainment included nationally known serious artists. For music week in 1908, as an example, the local newspaper announced that among the artists secured were Maud Powell ("the greatest violinist in America and the greatest woman violinist in the world"), Herbert Witherspoon ("the finest concert Basso in America"), and Elizabeth Dodge ("who is among the very best concert sopranos before the public today"). The newspaper, perhaps needing to apologize for her not being *the* greatest soprano, added that "She has a glorious voice." Max Schulz brought the forty-piece Cincinnati Symphony Orchestra assisted by "well-known vocalists Miss Ruth Welch, soprano, and Miss Emma Noe, contralto." Students were also encouraged to bring their own "musical instruments, tennis rackets, and other apparatus for music and sports."[77]

The entertainment sometimes got in the way of academics. After faculty complaints in the first session, Claxton decided that the male quartet would not sing before the lectures because it wasted valuable lecture time and that the mornings should be more serious with lighter entertainment in the evening. A popular activity was the daily boat trips on the Tennessee River, "especially the moonlight cruise, which was the subject of much rumor" among the teachers. Weekends were free for more extended educational excursions, short ones to "the most beautiful suburbs of Knoxville, Fountain City, Lyons View, Island Home . . . for enjoying exquisite scenery and for breathing in pure air" and longer ones to Mammoth Cave, Kentucky; Chickamauga Park near Chattanooga; and the new Biltmore House near Asheville, North Carolina. At the end of the session, students could take advantage of special group rates for cross-country trips to Niagara Falls or to the World's Fair in St. Louis.[78]

Claxton helped historians by carefully preserving the papers of the school, a collection that exceeds one hundred boxes. He, the faculty, and students were self-consciously convinced that they were making history with a movement that "bears the hall-mark of being one of those great historic waves of feeling and action that later generations name epochs." Yearbooks included photographs of students by states, faculty pictures, and scenes of the campus and East Tennessee. Documents from the school were carefully preserved, including numerous lectures, outlines of activities, daily notices, and even lists of persons with unclaimed mail.[79]

Dabney and Claxton were not wont to hide their school under a basket. Prizes were offered for the best student essays on "The Summer School" to be published in hometown newspapers, resulting in the publications of hyperbolic reports throughout the South of the goings on in Knoxville. The leaders searched for similes to indicate the importance of the school. One report called it an educational West Point, training leaders for southern schools. Another said that teachers going to Knoxville were like "enterprising merchants" who go to New York trade fairs at the beginning of the season "to see the newest and best things that are on the market. . . . In like manner, teachers go to the Summer School of the South to learn the newest and best methods of teaching." A third preferred a comparison with a frontier camp meeting where Christians meet "to have their spiritual strength renewed. The newspaper observed that the summer school sessions were intellectual camp meetings." The competition for prizes may have caused a bit of excess in columns sent to hometown newspapers, such as the one of Lily Johnson, published in the *Tupelo Journal*: "God made University Hill (Knoxville, Tenn.) and left it for man to utilize in his own way. . . . O! I had no idea teaching was so beautiful till I came here. I shall be so happy in my work after this and I'm coming back to dear old University Hill next year to get more inspiration." Professors were also asked to offer testimonials for the school. Publicity circulars often quoted Hall's testimony that "the best training school for teachers in America" was the Summer School of the South: "To be so rated by Dr. G. Stanley Hall is no small thing."[80]

Dabney was particularly concerned with avoiding negative publicity. He ordered (his memorandum said "requested") that faculty and staff refuse to be interviewed except by arrangement with the Director of the Press Bureau. "This is the only way," he argued, "to furnish reliable information and to prevent the circulation of wild stories which might be prejudicial to the school."[81]

Educational Rallies

Much of the publicity was not aimed directly at enhancing the Summer School of the South or the University of Tennessee but at furthering the southern educational campaigns. The Summer School of the South was an institute for change agents. It trained educational campaigners, whipped up enthusiasm for a southern progressive gospel of public school support among the teacher/students, and staged elaborate demonstrations replete with inspirational propaganda of a type that would later be called a media event. The 1908 yearbook of the school claimed that it "served as the most important center of the educational propaganda for this section, and its influence has been felt in city and county schools, public and private, and in the halls of legislation in every Southern State."[82]

The most direct way that the summer school campaigned was through the elaborate Fourth of July educational rallies—a fixture throughout the school's existence. An observer of the 1902 rally who saw "a look of almost boyish delight" on the leaders' faces explained that they knew that they were going to win the battle for better schools in the South: "It is the delight in the game, the tingling of the blood, the perfect assurance that everything is going to turn out all right."[83]

The leaders of the school attempted to maintain state identity. There were state meetings, rallies, and excursions with the state superintendents of public instruction often in charge. State delegations, sometimes with members in outlandish costumes, marched together behind their state flag to the campus pavilion for prayers, songs, yells, and orations, confessing past educational sins of their state, testifying of their recent successes, and exhorting one another to do better. In the 1914 rally, the parade marshal on horseback, wearing "a gay purple sash," organized the state delegations in alphabetical order. The women teachers from Mississippi wore white dresses with red tomatoes pinned to the hems of their skirts, dangled green tomato plants from their belts, and wore red tomato caps. The Kentucky women wore garlands of bluegrass around their hats and green girdles, and, at the head of the column, two men "carried a framework, adorned with hemp," perhaps helping to explain the madness of the occasion. In a rare bit of humor in the summer school, the faculty and the few students from northern states banded together in one delegation and named themselves the barbarians; "one would never have thought that they were the dignified and sedate instructors transformed into a wild and warlike band of beings."[84]

Despite the hoopla, the leaders and the participants in the Independence Day rallies were uncompromisingly serious. "The value of the work here is inestimable," Mrs. S. C. Lattimore wrote to her hometown newspaper in Dublin, Texas; "Today Dr. Dabney quoted to us pres. Roosevelt's personal commendation, 'Dabney the work you have undertaken in your Summer School is the greatest event since the Civil War.'" The President of the United States could not be counted on to send a message of approval every year to the summer school students, but, in the early years, many of the southern governors were prevailed on to send telegrams of congratulations and support.[85]

Willis A. Sutton, who later became president of the National Education Association, reminisced about his attendance at the summer school in 1911 and 1912. He declared its greatest contribution was as "a great rallying inspirational center." It was also a place for interest groups to organize and meet. Among the groups that either formed at the summer school or met there regularly were the Southern Kindergarten Association, the National Storyteller's League, the National Guild of Play, the Southern Association of College Women, the Association of Collegiate Alumnae, the Interstate Association for the Betterment of Public School Houses, the School Improvement Conference, and the Southern High School Conference.[86]

Curriculum

Students were overwhelmingly enthusiastic, wanting to experience everything. Beginning in 1903, the administration restrained students by limiting them to four classes each day, and charging them an extra $2.00 for taking more subjects, which cut overloads considerably. They were allowed, however, to have "visitors' tickets" for limited visits to classes in which they were not enrolled.[87]

Some of the lectures smacked of the "chautauqua features" that exasperated Ayres. As an example, Henry Oldys, "the bird specialist," lectured on bird music. But the northern philanthropists who bankrolled the Summer School of the South and the southern progressives who organized and administered it agreed that the most desirable kind of education was agricultural, industrial, and domestic science for girls and young women. Indeed, this kind of education was an article of faith in the southern educational crusades of the period, and the Summer School of the South was to prepare teachers to teach the preferred curriculum. The prominent guest speakers, including the "education governors," extolled the virtues of agricultural and industrial education for the rural South. The publicity photographs often depicted teachers becoming knowledgeable in such studies, and there was interest in "practical" courses. Claxton assured a corespondent that the summer school would teach cooking classes, including "bread making, biscuit making, baking, broiling, and pastry."[88]

President Charles D. McIver of North Carolina Normal and Industrial School was one of the summer school instructors who urged manual and handicraft education. In the process, he also reflected the stereotype of the shiftless poor southern white: "In the South in the winter a home [sic] when we have nothing to do, we have nothing to do and we do it." But the situation was no better in the summer, "when the hot air first dances on the wall, and the butterflies flit by the windows, and everybody gets drowsy and frequently does go to sleep." The solution was to teach the children handicrafts so that they could make wise use of their time regardless of the season. And elementary methods courses often stressed manual training. Generally, however, the Summer School of the South was less an industrial and agricultural school than its publicity indicated, although efforts to stimulate such offerings continued for years. In 1910, the school offered free scholarships to four teachers in each county of Tennessee if they would take four prescribed courses in agriculture.[89]

An examination of the school catalogs gives a more accurate understanding of the actual curriculum than does the rhetoric of the reformers. Many of the 150 to 200 courses offered each summer were traditional college courses: Latin, Greek, and German; trigonometry and calculus; physics, geology, and astronomy.[90]

After the first session, elementary teachers lobbied for more courses in teaching methods. Kindergarten instruction was prized particularly as this innovation was making its way south. The apostles of modernization in the New South saw a special need for it in "the mills and factories where children run free all day"; in addition, it developed the right character traits such as "courtesy, promptness, industry, neatness, helpfulness, as well as respect for others and their turn." The model kindergarten with real live children was a popular place to visit and observe:

> There were three little tables holding from six to eight children of three different ages, or grades of advancement. At each of these tables, with the children, was a teacher, a young girl, of eighteen or twenty, so interested in them, so gentle, so fully the center of their interest, that to the spectator there came at once a realization of the beauty of the mother-idea in the kindergarten.[91]

G. Stanley Hall was a mainstay in the study of pedagogy; he returned to lecture on child development year after year. His lectures on the psychology and pedagogy of Jesus and on the "recapitulation theory" must have seemed a weird blending of incongruous systems of thought to many small town Christian teachers. According to recapitulation theory, children in their development mirrored the evolution of the species. Hall told the teachers that one of the first fears of infants was of being eaten. A Knoxville newspaper summarized his lecture:

> He said that it had been demonstrated that an infant shuddered when it touched fur, when it saw teeth, and when it saw large eyes. This fear he said, it is claimed descended from a time, he would not say when, when the ancestors of men had as one of their first necessary instincts the preservation from death from animals.[92]

The summer school tried to stay abreast of educational innovations; and, in the 1912 session, it introduced instruction in Montessori methods (popular in "Paris, New York and other cities"), although a local reporter, reflecting its original intent in Italy, indicated it was for "mentally defective" children. The Montessori "didactic apparatus" was available for use by the summer school students, and Miss Alice Damon, who had studied for a year with Mme. Maria Montessori herself, demonstrated and lectured.[93]

For the most part, the curriculum reflected what the teachers who attended wanted—a predominance of traditional liberal arts courses and offerings in pedagogy such as found at Teachers College. The Summer School of the South reflected the southern education movement in its vigorous and colorful political rallies on behalf of public schools rather than in most day-to-day classroom activities.

The Summer Students

Between 1902 and 1918 some 32,000 students enrolled in the Summer School of the South. Nearly all of them were teachers and all were white. The school attracted teachers from more prosperous rural areas, villages, and mid-sized southern towns. Comparatively few students were really "country" teachers, who were so poorly paid that even the modest cost of the school ($5 registration fee, good for all classes, lectures, and concerts; and $3 to $5 a week for room and board; and the special railroad rates) was too much to allow them to spend six weeks in Knoxville.[94]

The students were overwhelmingly women. The large number of women was itself an indictment of the summer school in the minds of some male professors and administrators in the University of Tennessee. (And in other universities as well; a 1909 article in *The Nation* condemned summer schools for bringing women to the universities: "though zealous far beyond the zeal of the average undergraduate" they gave the campus "too much of the air of a summer normal school.")

The photographs of the summer school illustrate the predominance of women. The only extant photograph of classrooms or other scenes of Summer School of the South students in which women did not outnumber men was a physics class, illustrating the longtime bias against women in the sciences. Physical accommodations were made for the women, most notably the women's restroom—in the original sense of the term. It was a comfortable carpeted "apartment" in East College with "all kinds of conveniences, such as toilet-rooms, couches, and easy-chairs." The restroom was popular with women and highly appreciated.[95]

In the midst of the first summer session, "an old alumnus" of the university visited the campus; a local paper claimed to record his reactions verbatim. He said that he could see nothing but "a crowd of women," and he wondered why they just didn't call it "the women's summer school":

> They had a nonchalant and very independent air, and seemed perfectly at home. There was something jaunty and self-sufficient about them. I remembered when only cadets held sway in that quarter, and I was somewhat abashed by the immense aggregation of the aggressive sex. A few mild-looking, quiet men passed to and fro, or sat apart on the benches, meekly eyeing the women out of the corners of their eyes.
>
> The women gathered here and there or walked boldly up and down the walk, engaged in animated conversation. They laughed much among themselves and regarded visitors critically and with immense self-complacence.

Looking for safety from the disturbing scene of "intellectual women," he approached a "rather elderly gentleman" sitting on a bench. The man turned out to be G. Stanley Hall, and the alumnus reported that he felt "relieved and safe" in his company.[96]

In his column for his hometown newspaper, student T. S. Stribling of Florence, Alabama, saw a greater variety of types among the women students, even if his eyes were no less clouded by male presumptions:

> Women? A myriad! Long and short, stout and slim, grave and gay, fair and fairer; sweet, sweeter, sweetest; from those shimmery creatures in whites and pinks, trimmed in bows and beaux—who eat ice cream at the University restaurant and quote poetry at times, to the "dear old maids" with kindly eyes and gentle bearing.[97]

The women students and men faculty contested the curriculum. The men instructors usually championed a gender differentiated-curriculum. Some women students and faculty advocated an equal academic education for females, while others wanted more practical

courses in how to teach. Hall, "the champion of masculinity in education," worried that sexual distinctions were endangered and argued
that the curriculum should strive to "make boys more manly and girls
more womanly." He told the summer school students that women had
slower logical thought than men, that they talked too much, and were
given to "giggling spells." In 1913, a popular speaker in the summer
schools, Albert E, Winship, lectured on "Making Girls Womanly" and
on "Rescuing Girls."[98]

On the other hand, a group of eighteen women founded the Southern Association of College Women and the Association of Collegiate
Alumnae at the summer school in 1903. Their leaders, such as Ellen
Richards and Celeste Parrish, lobbied for a strong academic curriculum for women: "We have not invented a woman's grammar or a
woman's arithmetic. The laws of astronomy are the same to women
that they are to men."[99]

All of the students and faculty in the Summer School of the South
were white. Only in the last year of the summer school did black persons appear in Jefferson Hall, and they were the Jubilee Singers from
Knoxville College, offering a program of "old-fashioned negro [sic]
songs." In 1902, Dabney and President McGranahan of Knoxville
College proposed a summer school for African-American teachers,
reasoning that speakers and faculty from the Summer School of the
South could lecture for little additional expense at Knoxville College.
They solicited $1,500 from the General Education Board to help sub-
sidize the idea. Opposition came immediately from H. B. Frissell of
Hampton Institute and Booker T. Washington of Tuskegee Institute,
who wanted philanthropic support for their summer schools. The GEB
gave $500 but indicated that future aid would go to Hampton and
Tuskegee, and Dabney abandoned plans to share his visiting faculty
with Knoxville College after the first session.[100]

On race, the summer school leaders reflected the attitudes of the
broader southern education movement. First, they believed that their
success depended on not raising the wrath of "Negro-baiting" politicians and journalists who were constantly alert to any hint of racial
tolerance on the part of educational reformers. And, second, they
thought that they had learned well the lessons of Reconstruction: even
though most of the money was coming from northern philanthropists, there must not be even a suggestion of carpetbagger interference in racial policies. "The beautiful harmony that existed between
northern and southern men," Dabney wrote to Walter Hines Page,

was chiefly responsible for the success of their work. "The success of the movement in the South," he continued, "has been due to the fact that southern men were permitted to formulate a detailed policy and do most of the actual work."[101]

The major strategy that Dabney, Claxton, and the faculty of the Summer School of the South used to avoid criticism on racial issues was to say as little about African Americans and their education as possible. An evaluation of the first session concluded that race "is one subject that has never been brought up in the public addresses at the school." Edgar Gardner Murphy of the Southern Education Board exhibited much the same attitude when he wrote to Claxton about possible titles for his lectures. "Negro Taxes and the Negro Schools" was one topic that Murphy suggested, but he quickly added that such a subject should not "be announced in the programme." After the 1903 session, Dabney warned Page:

> We shall have to be more careful in the future than in the past. We are to-day farther from the time when we can push the question of negro [sic] rights and negro education than we were two years ago. I do not despair by any means. Our Board has done and is doing more than any other agency in the country to heal these sores. Other people started up the present troubles but we must be all the more careful not to put salt on the wounds, but balm.[102]

Closing the Summer School—Politics and Aesthetics

The Summer School of the South survived until 1918, but Dabney's move to Cincinnati in 1904 and Claxton's appointment as U.S. Commissioner of Education in 1911 left it without powerful leadership. The General Education Board ceased direct financial support in 1905, bringing on a financial crisis. Other southern universities provided competition by creating summer sessions. The southern education campaigns that nurtured the school were over by the First World War, and the war reduced enrollment.

Because of these factors, the summer school might not have survived anyway, but President Brown Ayres hounded and finally executed it. In part, his campaign against the school exemplifies the liberal arts and pedagogy animosity that is a fixture of twentieth-century university culture. Ayres had allies from the liberal arts faculty who "raised their academic noses" at the summer school, although many had taught in it. In 1911, with Claxton's departure for Washington imminent, Ayres declared war on the summer school. He argued

that it was an embarrassment to the university. The chautauqua features were in direct conflict with serious scholarship; and the emphasis on kindergarten and primary methods filled the school "with elementary teachers, mostly women," driving "more seriously minded
persons" to northern universities.[103]

Ayres complained that the wear and tear on the buildings and
grounds by the summer school students, who were "practically an
unorganized mob," was intolerable. And the appearance of the temporary buildings, little more than large open sheds, was "exceedingly
unfortunate." He continually harassed Claxton about the summer school
property. In 1908 and 1909, when Claxton was traveling the state
campaigning for better schools, Ayres demanded that he "make suitable arrangements to have all of the summer school property moved
to some storage warehouse." Jefferson Hall, a large temporary pavilion, and the outdoor stage were particularly irritating to him. In an
outburst of aesthetic indignation, he protested that he didn't believe
that "any other university in America would have consented to have its
campus disfigured for ten years by a structure of this character. It
makes an exceedingly irritating feature of our landscape." "Can you
not have the flooring taken off so as to allow the sun to get to the
grass?" he asked Claxton; "It could be put back in a little while."[104]

In Fall 1911, after the largest enrollment (2,529) in its history, the
trustees accepted Ayres's recommendations to make the Summer
School of the South the regular summer term of the university. But it
survived with surprisingly little change (silent movies even supplemented
the "chautauqua features") and Jefferson Hall continued to desecrate
the hill until the summer school closed in 1918. But with money
troubles and without faculty support, it was in deepening trouble. In
1914, the Knoxville Board of Commerce guaranteed $5,000 to help
subsidize the school but asked to be relieved of the responsibility in
1916. During World War I, enrollments dropped to 1,500 in 1916,
1,290 in 1917, and to a low of 902 in 1918. Its time had clearly
passed. The legacy is so strong, however, that a half century later, the
College of Education tried to revive the name for its Summer
session.[105]

Chapter 4

The Educational Campaigns: Professors of Secondary Education

In the first decade of the twentieth century, the University of Tennessee was the most influential southern institution in efforts to improve public schooling in the South. Reconstruction legislatures had passed legislation providing for public school systems in the southern states following the Civil War, but, at the turn of the century, such "systems" still existed only on paper. Public schools in the South lacked popular and, as a result, financial support. Those that existed were often miserable places. At worst, they were little more than shacks that were heated by fireplaces and taught by semiliterate teachers who often had but months of elementary schooling themselves. In most communities, regardless of how bad schools were for white students, they were worse for African Americans. Conditions were a result of poverty, of cultural attitudes about schooling and public expenditures for social purposes, and of racism.

The southern educational campaigns to improve conditions began with a series of meetings, primarily of southern educators and northern ministers, from 1898 to 1900 at the Capon Springs Hotel in West Virginia. Originally called the Conference for Christian Education in the South, at a meeting in Winston-Salem in 1901 the group broadened its membership and changed its name to the Conference for Education in the South. The General Education Board (GEB) was formed to spend large sums of Rockefeller money that flowed South. The interlocking Southern Education Board (SEB) was established as the executive board of the Conference and was given the responsibility for organizing its propaganda efforts.[1]

The primary purpose of the southern educational campaign was much the same as that of the common school crusade of a half-century before in the North: to propagandize for free, tax-supported systems of schools for all children. In the extravagant language typical of the campaign, Edwin A. Alderman, president of Tulane, promised the Conference in 1902 that "This educational crusade shall not cease until every child in this nation, high or low, white or black, bond or free, shall be emancipated from the great, black empire of ignorance and of night." These southern educational progressives also campaigned for school consolidation, state financial aid for equalization, establishment of county high schools, improved teacher training, and, of major consequence, industrial and agricultural education.[2]

Philander P. Claxton, one of the most effective of the campaigners, gave his assessment of the success of the movement in 1914, the last year of the Conference: Illiteracy among white youths ages ten to twenty decreased by more than 50 percent, the average school term increased from 105 to 130 days, total school expenditures increased 256 percent, and the total value of school property grew by 337 percent.[3]

The University of Tennessee was at the center of the educational campaigns, in part because of the quality of leadership in the university. Charles Dabney, with a patrician Virginian background, got on well with the movement's northern benefactors. An agricultural chemist, he had also been a true believer in technical and agricultural education even before northern money was available. He was an effective campaigner and knew how to appeal to the Christian religious sentiments of southerners. His address at the end of the 1903 Conference for Education in the South in Memphis compared the education crusade with Jesus' concern for little children:

> This campaign commenced over 1,900 years ago. It commenced on some hill in Palestine, overlooking the waters of Galilee. Our Master brought a little child and sat him in the midst of the wise men. He said "suffer little children to come unto me and forbid them not, for of such is the kingdom of heaven." . . . We must go as Christians if we would succeed in this campaign. . . . Let us enter this campaign with this spirit. Nothing else will bring us the success we seek.

The *Memphis Commercial Appeal* reported that the applause was long and many eyes were dimmed with tears when Dabney finished. P. P. Claxton, whose extraordinary talents as a campaigner I will discuss below, and Wickliffe Rose, later president of the GEB, were on the education faculty.[4]

According to Dabney, the southern educational campaigns began with an address in 1901 by the Rev. Edgar Gardner Murphy, executive secretary of the SEB, to "a large audience of Knoxville's best people" in Staub's Theater. The SEB soon established its Bureau of Information and Investigation at Knoxville under the supervision of Dabney and appointed Claxton to administer the Bureau and publish its journal, *Southern Education*.[5]

The General Education Board Supports Professors of Secondary Education

It was obvious that the Bureau of Information and Investigation in Knoxville could not organize educational campaigns throughout the South; they needed a campaign manager in each state. But neither the southern state departments of education nor the state universities had the funds to conduct state-wide campaigns. In 1903, Dabney made a request of Wallace Buttrick, administrator of the GEB, that anticipated the state-by-state organization of the campaign. The GEB was supporting the new Department of Education, and Claxton was teaching pedagogy, administrating the SEB's Bureau of Information, and working in the Tennessee campaign. Dabney proposed that the GEB pay the salary of an associate professor of education in order to free Claxton for full-time work on the Tennessee campaign. Buttrick did not support that request, but, in 1905, the GEB started supporting an education professorship at the University of Virginia to campaign for the establishment of high schools. Dabney, now president of the University of Cincinnati, wrote Claxton that the "old mossbacks" at Virginia would find proposals for modern education quite a pill to swallow. "But then it is sugar-coated with so many of Mr. Carnegie's and Mr. Rockefeller's dollars I am sure they will swallow it gracefully." He hoped that the GEB was planning to give such a professorship to each southern university.[6]

The GEB established the professorships in North Carolina, South Carolina, Georgia, Alabama, and Tennessee as well as Virginia in 1905. Other southern states followed; the last was Kentucky in 1910. The Board ended the program in June 1925. In its final report, the GEB called its plan "direct, disarmingly simple, and in the end extraordinarily successful." Although the GEB stressed that the professors were employed by the universities and answerable to them alone, the professors were primarily school evangelists rather than teachers and researchers; they were to "inform, cultivate, and guide professional, public, and legislative opinion" in each southern state. They were all native sons of the South; the GEB announced proudly that "no carpetbaggers were to be found among them." The GEB reported that they were remarkably able and fit: "The men were young, hardy, and enthusiastic—pioneers in physique as they were evangelists in spirit." In the early years of the campaigns, the professors of secondary education directed much of their efforts at creating faith in public schools generally; later more energy went to campaigning for the establishment and supervision of county high schools.[7]

Philander P. Claxton, Tennessee's
First Professor of Secondary Education

The first two professors of secondary education at Tennessee were men of extraordinary ability. In leadership, energy, and force of his personality, Claxton, the first to hold this position, overshadowed most other members of the university faculty. His supporters periodically campaigned for him behind the scenes, and occasionally in the press, for state superintendent of schools or, when the job was open, for president of the University of Tennessee. The university has had a longtime tradition of low faculty salaries and the influential and highly sought-after Claxton, never a person to underestimate his own worth, presented a special problem. President Ayres took credit for the idea of giving Claxton a double salary "so he would be able to remain here," paying him both as a regular university professor and as an agent for "high school propaganda in this state . . . [using] such part of his time as will not seriously interfere with the discharge of his duties as professor of education in the University." Claxton, whose regular professorial salary was $2,000, agreed to lead the educational campaign for an additional $1,500 in salary and $500 in expenses from the GEB. He also initiated a perpetual source of contention between professors of secondary education and their administrators when he indicated that the university would provide stenographic services. Claxton organized his schedule to meet classes and other university responsibilities on Tuesdays through Thursdays, leaving the rest of the week and vacations available for the campaign. In an exchange of letters with the GEB, Ayres argued that although the "double work" would be taxing on Claxton, he was "convinced that no one known to us can do the work you wish done as well." The GEB at first refused the arrangement, arguing that the salary of the professor of second-ary education should not be more than that of a regular professor. The Board eventually agreed, deciding by the next appropriation that they had made a good bargain as Claxton's work was "beyond praise." Ayres agreed that his work was "phenomenal; my only fear is that his various duties may over tax his strength."[8]

A couple of years later, however, when the university was in worse than its usually grim financial circumstances, Ayres caught wind of the fact that Claxton was receiving yet a third salary as campaign manager of the SEB. In an angry four-page letter ("The fact that you have heretofore drawn a double salary has not been uncriticised, but I have in all cases defended it."), Ayres repeated the rumors about Claxton's large outside salary and made a blunt request: "I would like now to ask you whether this is true and to say that if it is true I think that you should be willing to give up as much of your University salary as you receive from the Southern Education Board, even up to the full amount of the salary." Claxton ended his paid work with the SEB, but the troublesome relationship with Ayres continued. Claxton resigned as professor of secondary education in 1911 to become United States Commissioner of Education.[9]

Claxton and the Educational Campaigns

Grueling demands were made of the professors. "I only wish there were two or three of me," Claxton complained in 1906 as he contem-plated his several roles in the university and in the field. Walter Hines Page, then editor of *The World's Work* and a member of the GEB, warned Claxton against overwork in 1908. At the bottom of his letter Page sketched a grave with the comment, "If you don't rest. This is a mound where the daisies grow!"[10]

The university administration expected and received more than just the salary of a professor of secondary education and the accompany-ing good will of public school teachers and administrators. The pro-fessors of secondary education were propaganda agents for the uni-versity as well as campaigners for the establishment of high schools. The agents of the state Department of Public Instruction and the uni-versity administration lobbied for each other before the professors of secondary education became involved. State Superintendent Mynders wrote Dabney in 1903 that he was not only endorsing the Summer School of the South at educational rallies, but had "undertaken a work

on behalf of The University of Tennessee and has succeeded in getting some influential country papers to begin the agitation of State
help for The University of Tennessee." Claxton made increased state
funds for UT a plank in the education reform platform of 1909, the
chief educational campaign document.[11]

The initial state-wide educational campaign lasted for four years,
1905 to 1909. In the first years of the campaign, a missionary effort
to convert the citizens of Tennessee to a faith in public schools was
the primary goal. Claxton and other leaders understood the power of
camp-meeting revival techniques and made good use of them. In 1906,
Tennessee state superintendent S. A. Mynders reported that speakers
for better schools had appeared at nearly all occasions when citizens
congregated: "Education and public schools have been preached from
the pulpit, the bar, the stump; at picnics, barbecues, circuit and county
courts, school commencements, county fairs, race tracks and even at
a wedding ceremony."[12]

Claxton conducted educational rallies in each of Tennessee's counties; sometimes as many as 5,000 persons attended a single rally.
Citizens attending the county rallies voted on resolutions in favor of
school reforms. Claxton later claimed (outrageously) that of the more
than 100,000 citizens who attended the rallies over a four-year period, "only one person voted against the resolutions." Many of the
rallies were all-day meetings with local supporters claiming that half
of the adults of the county were in attendance. In the Maynardville
Courthouse, as an example, "every seat was taken, and the people
stood in the aisles and adjoining rooms, eagerly listening to the doctrine of education." The *Memphis Commercial Appeal* reported that
Claxton's talk at the Hickman County rally "did much good, and it
was worth coming twenty miles through the rain, as many did, to hear
it." According to the *Knoxville Sentinel*, a rally crowd protested
Claxton's attempts to limit his speech to half an hour and he gained
strength as he was urged on, and when he finally satisfied the audience the applause "was as sincere as it was lusty." As at religious
camp meetings, a basket dinner was commonly served on the grounds,
often under the shade trees of the county square, followed by more
speaking in the afternoon.[13]

In 1908, Claxton reviewed his campaign strategy with the Conference for Education in the South:

> We began a campaign which lasted for ninety-six working days and . . . we
> went to every county in the State and appealed to more than 100,000 people.

Frequently half the voters of the county were present. We had all-day meetings. The people in the Southern States were raised on camp meetings, and
when they go and carry their dinner with them it is an offense to them to
speak a half hour and dismiss them. The man who has come twenty miles to
hear a speaking wants to hear a good deal of it.[14]

Claxton was an astute politician and an effective organizer. He carefully plotted the details of each county rally, instructing local organizers to make sure that ministers announced forthcoming rallies in their
churches, county papers printed notices, leading citizens were invited
to appear on the rally platform, and all teachers were required to attend. In organizing the campaign, Claxton sent letters of instruction
to each county superintendent of schools, urging them to consider
carefully the best location for the rally and advising them to hold the
rally in a town other than the county seat if the change would attract
a larger crowd. He especially urged the superintendents to have county
politicians present and visible. Do all you can, he implored Superintendent Farmer of Rutledge, to have "as many as possible members of
the county court, school directors, leading tax-payers. . . . I do hope
Judge G. McHenderson can be with us and make an address." Claxton
also brought his own entourage of "leading men" as headliners to
draw crowds, often including Governor John Cox, State Superintendent Seymour Mynders, UT President Brown Ayres (who was often
unenthusiastic), and assorted state cabinet members and other digni-
taries more or less famous. Only the northern benefactors were invis-
ible; perceptions of Yankee carpetbaggers were still too fresh in the
minds of southerners to allow the philanthropists and their agents to
attend the rallies. Wallace Buttrick, administrator of the GEB, confirmed the policy with Claxton: "I wish it were practicable for me to be
with you and Mr. Mynders at some of those educational rallies, but I
am convinced that I must be a silent partner in all these matters. The
propaganda must be the work of Southern men."[15]

The enthusiastic support of the press was indispensable to the success of the campaign, and it was unreserved in Tennessee. In the early
years of the campaign, the state's newspapers were full of hyperbolic
reports on the rallies. Claxton was conscious of their power and used
the newspapers effectively, including the organization of press committees "in order to get a better hearing in the public press." He also
tried to increase attendance at rallies and cut down on the expenses
of campaigning by cajoling railroads to offer special rates, sometimes
successfully: "A special rate has been made from all points on the

Louisville and Nashville railroad." Occasionally, special trains were organized to make "rally runs."[16]

The campaign offered something to everyone. In order to get as wide a support base as possible, it was carefully apolitical; and, to the degree possible, it tried to appear nonideological. A variety of women's clubs endorsed the educational resolutions, including the United Daughters of the Confederacy, the Daughters of the American Revolution, the Women's Christian Temperance Union, and Mothers Associations. Claxton reported that throughout the South thousands of women were working for school improvement with "zeal and enthusiasm." Harry Clark, who would become Claxton's successor, sometimes traveled with him gratis to garner continued support from club women. Claxton sent campaign propaganda to "all" Christian ministers in Tennessee, requesting that they "preach one or more sermons" on public schools during the following year. Chambers of Commerce and commercial clubs endorsed the educational resolutions, but so did labor unions and the Farmers Union.[17]

There was, of course, opposition. Claxton recognized a social class differential in support of high schools: the prosperous and "men of affairs" usually supported them (after all, their children would be able to attend high schools) whereas the poor more often opposed them. Local politicians were often afraid to raise taxes to support high schools. And, behind the scenes, Claxton maneuvered to elect more responsive officeholders. "A good deal can be done quietly toward getting liberal men in office," he wrote Ayres, "which is very important."[18]

The leaders of the campaign unabashedly used teachers and students in their propaganda efforts. In 1905, the first year of the campaign, Claxton urged the state superintendent to authorize county superintendents to close their schools on rally day in order to increase crowd size. The next year teachers were informed that they were required to attend by state law—"a certificate of attendance will be issued to each teacher and director, and a valid excuse must be rendered for non-attendance." Before rallies, he reminded county superintendents that the state superintendent had authorized the closing of schools on rally days and urged them to make sure that all teachers attended. Administrators expected teachers to bring as many other persons with them as they could cajole. "Let us not fall behind other counties in attendance and interest," the Sullivan County superintendent urged, and he reminded teachers to bring their own lunches.[19]

The dreadfully underpaid teachers were also expected to contribute to the cost of the campaign. In 1907, the Cooperative Education Association of Tennessee was organized with Claxton as Chairman of the Executive Committee. To raise funds Claxton immediately solicited $1.00 from all city public school teachers and 50 cents from rural teachers. "Rural teachers receive more direct and greater financial benefit from this campaign than any other class or people in the State," he wrote in his circular letter, "and the committee hopes they will respond to his appeal promptly and liberally."[20]

On at least one occasion, a teacher and her students saved the rally day. Despite exhaustive preparations, an all-day rain was ruining the 1906 Williamson County rally. An especially heavy downpour disheartened the small crowd of the faithful when "Miss Mary Bennett from Rock Hill marched in with almost her entire school, some of the little tots being barely of school age." A Nashville newspaper reported that the heavy applause that followed restored good feelings for the "admirable" address that followed.[21]

The message of the campaigners was a clear reflection of southern progressivism, a brand of reform that educational historians sometimes refer to as administrative progressivism. The paramount goal of schools was to aid modernization, and education was to pay off where it really counts—in dollars and cents: "The poor widow's son may be capable of developing his county if he can only get a chance for an education." The establishment of high school was only a part of a campaign that included school consolidation, pupil transportation, school libraries, "professional" school supervision, better attendance, improved school buildings, better educated teachers, and "the adjustment of the courses of study to meet the demands of modern life" (i.e., more industrial education).[22]

A basic platform of the southern educational campaigns was the belief that industrial and agricultural education would enhance the productivity and the prosperity of the region. Historians such as Henry Bullock and James Anderson, who accused the campaigns of leading to a special industrial education for African Americans, give an incomplete picture. If the leaders of the movement, north and south, were racists, they were also class biased as well. They wanted an industrial education for most southerners—all blacks and poor whites. The professors of secondary education in Tennessee supported industrial education enthusiastically. It is the idea of the campaigners "to fit the pupils for work," Claxton insisted, "not for graces." Modern society demands that men work, he insisted, and a man "who fails to do his part must be made to understand that he is a parasite and entitled to little consideration." The schools must teach that "donning overalls" and doing the work before him raises rather than lowers a person's status.[23]

In his standard campaign speech, Claxton's arguments for the necessity of better attendance were a prelude to a propaganda blitz for a compulsory attendance law. "Irregular attendance is the greatest evil," whereas compulsory attendance laws were "just, right, and democratic." In the name of democracy, Claxton was willing to engage in a considerable amount of compulsion. "Old nests of illiteracy," he argued, can be eliminated "only by laws compelling ignorant and indifferent parents" to send their children to public or to quality private schools. And he added, for good measure, that communities that did not provide adequate school buildings and equipment may "need a little of the same brand of compulsion that the parents need."[24]

Professionally trained teachers was another important plank in the progressive platform. Although not necessarily in the best interest of the fledgling education department of the university, Claxton urged the establishment of state normal schools. He also championed standardization of teachers' certificates and more rigid examination of teachers. According to state School Superintendent Mynders, results of the campaign for better teachers and higher standards became apparent immediately. He wrote to Claxton in November 1905 that "about twelve hundred incompetent teachers" had already been dropped from the teaching force.[25]

The initial campaign was a success. Claxton wrote the bill that passed the Tennessee legislature with only two amendments, one insignificant, the other changing the share of the state's gross revenue to be earmarked for education from one-third to one-fourth. The law led to the first significant financial support for public schools by the state. Among other things, it provided an equal per capita distribution of state funds for elementary schools, partial state support of county high schools, school consolidation, aid to school libraries, establishment of three normal schools, the first general state appropriation for the University of Tennessee, and support for one agricultural school in each congressional district.[26]

Much of the success and the rejoicing came at the local level. In a letter to Robert Ogden, president of the Conference for Education in the South and a member of the GEB, Claxton bragged about the success in Rhea County, and described "a sight that would have pleased you": After every member of the court had voted for a sizable increase in the school tax, "the crowd of citizens present in the courtroom broke into applause, and the members of the court joined with them, applauding their own action." Claxton, ever the good politician, assured Ogden that all who knew the history of the campaign know its success was "due very largely to the work of the General Education Board."[27]

Conflicts Between the General
Education Board and the University

Much of support for teacher education in the university came from the interlocking Southern and General Education Boards. Claxton, Dabney, and Ayres were always full of public praise for the unselfishness and broad vision of the northern philanthropists. Even a hint of public criticism is difficult to find. But there was a gulf between public utterances and private attitudes. An exchange of letters between Dabney, after he became president of the University of Cincinnati in 1905, and Claxton reveals some of their reservations and hints at self-serving motives.

In 1906, after a trip to New York to meet with the GEB, Dabney wrote of his frustrations to Claxton. "It pained me much to find the affairs of a great educational trust in the hands of such inexperienced, unphilosophical, and emotional, though good, people," he complained. Later in the seven-page letter ("Please consider this as confidential"), he called them "fickle and passionate" and complained that he was distressed with their "changeable spirit and the passionate way in which they take up every new thing." Dabney was particularly indignant about the influence of Seaman Knapp, former president of Iowa State University and famous leader of agricultural education for youth and father of the corn clubs for boys and tomato clubs for girls that eventually became ubiquitous in rural America. Knapp, "a good talker [and] a great promoter," had committed the GEB to support cooperative agricultural experiments and model rural schools rather than to continue supporting departments of education and summer schools for teachers. "I had quite a talk with each one of them" about continuing support of the Summer School of the South, Dabney assured Claxton, "but without avail. They will absolutely not give you a cent." Dabney's advice to Claxton is familiar to those who survive on grants: "[T]hey have found a new fad and are booming it for all they are worth. . . . Perhaps you can find some way to catch on the schemes. It looks as if one will have to catch each one of their fads or he will get nothing." Claxton, ever ready to dip his hands in the pockets of the wealthy, took his advice and received GEB funds to help establish Farragut School, a "model rural school," in Knox County that received national attention and which the Summer School of the South used as an observation school.[28]

The GEB's new policy of endowing small colleges, particularly Peabody at Nashville, also concerned Dabney. In a prophecy that was not fulfilled for more than seventy years, Dabney predicted that "Vanderbilt University will annex the proposed Peabody College and make it its teacher college." This takeover, in his mind, was the first step in making Vanderbilt a state university and destroying the University of Tennessee, a plan "frankly avowed by [Methodist] Bishop McTyeirs as their policy."[29]

President Brown Ayres, Charles Dabney's successor and a physicist, had a much more traditional liberal arts point of view, but the GEB provided a good deal of money and the university was poor. Pressed by Claxton to speak at rallies, he responded that he had already communicated "verbally and in writing" his objections to parts of the campaign platform, particularly those related to agricultural education in high schools. He wrote that he could not "heartily enter" into the campaign and that it would "be very awkward and undesirable for you and myself to be arguing for different things from the same platform."[30]

The financial arrangement between the university and the GEB was not without conflict. There was the usual squabbling in joint enterprises about territoriality and control. As already indicated, Claxton, with his close personal ties to the university trustees and members of the GEB, presented special problems for Ayres, who was sensitive about his prerogatives. Shortly after taking office, Ayres complained to Wallace Buttrick about the GEB making "arrangements with Prof. Claxton direct." Buttrick assured Ayres that in all states a uniform policy of dealing directly with the universities rather than with professors on personnel policies would be followed.[31]

The relationship between the salary of the professor of secondary education and general university salaries remained an issue, but the GEB was amenable to redistributing the relative amounts of their appropriation between salaries and travel expenses to meet the needs of the university administration. In negotiations with Harry Clark, who replaced Claxton in 1911, Ayres increased the salary offer from $2,000 to $2,200 by reducing the expense money, whereas in 1920 President Morgan didn't want to pay Clark the $3,500 appropriated by the

GEB because the other university professors were receiving $3,250, so he asked to divert the extra money to Clark's travel account.[32]

Throughout his presidency, Ayres continued his sensitivity to any implication that the professors of secondary education were employees of the GEB rather than the university. In 1916, after complaints by Clark that he was having to pay his traveling expenses out of his own pocket and wait for reimbursement, Buttrick sent Ayres a detailed reminder that expense money was to relieve the professor "of the burden of advancing money himself." Buttrick's "suggestion" was that upon receiving the expense check from the GEB that Ayres "turn it over promptly" to Clark. The next year, the auditor of the GEB asked Clark to sign a receipt for his expenses. Ayres dashed off a two-page letter of protest: "Professor Clark is a professor in the University; he has been appointed as such by the Board of Trustees of the University. . . . We cannot look upon Professor Clark as the direct employee of the General Education Board, which would be implied in his signing a receipt directly to you for his expenses."[33]

Harry Clark Replaces Claxton

After the resignation of P. P. Claxton in 1911, Ayres hired Harry Clark to replace him. He had pursued Clark from the time of Claxton's resignation, but Clark was under contract with Middle Tennessee State Normal School and made much of his "pride" in keeping his commitments, despite the willingness of the superintendent of the normal school to release him. Ayres refused to fill the position until Clark was available in the Fall of 1912. Clark served as Professor of Secondary Education for nearly a decade. Another native Tennessean, he was a Yale graduate (A.B. 1903, M.A. 1915) with a powerful constituency outside the university, especially among the innumerable Tennessee Baptists. He, too, was a powerful public speaker ("one of the best in the South") who was often invited to address state teachers conventions elsewhere and was pursued by lyceum boards. He claimed to make over 200 speeches a year. He was literate, perceptive, and the possessor of a lively sense of humor—a trait that Claxton lacked. The student newspaper called him the "Disciple of Sunshine" for his happy smile" which would chase away the clouds "no matter how dark they seemed."[34]

Like Claxton, Clark was a perpetual candidate for other jobs, including the presidencies of Baptist colleges (both Carson-Newman and Cumberland made offers), superintendent of the Middle Tennessee State Normal School, and executive secretary of the Knoxville Board of Commerce "at a large salary." The local newspapers seemed starved for news and often heightened anticipation by making a guessing game of whether he would accept each position offered.

After appointing him professor of secondary education, Ayres gave Clark a daunting charge:

> the working up of interest in the various counties in the establishment of high schools, the speaking before county courts, educational, and other gatherings in the favor of such an establishment, and the advantage of the educational interests of the public school system of the state in general. His duties will also include the visiting and inspection of the public high schools of the State, as well as the other secondary schools and of influencing these schools in the direction of better and more perfectly taught courses of study, primarily on account of the importance of such good high schools to the respective communities, and secondarily of their relationship to the normal schools and the University.

Ayres assured Clark that he was to be in "no sense a drummer for the University," but in reality he was expected to sell the university as well as public schools generally. Since UT was often considered an East Tennessee institution, Ayres urged him to campaign throughout the state and "not be too much localized." In addition to his other duties on the road, he prepared the list of accredited schools for the university (he also represented the university with the Southern Association of Colleges and Secondary Schools; he was a longtime secretary of the Association); and he kept an eye open for bright pupils, teachers, and principals to recruit as students for the university.[35]

Clark and The Progressive Agenda

In the spirit of southern progressivism, Clark preached the gospel of a more practical education throughout rural and small-town Tennessee, admonishing those who toyed with the liberal arts in general and with the classics in particular. Selling industrial education to secondary educators across Tennessee was often a difficult assignment. Camden High School was revising its curriculum when he visited, and he protested against a course in the history of English and American literature. Suspicious of the school at Waverly, he examined the students' notebooks, finding Latin assignments rather than something "useful"; he blamed the problem on the classical-minded principal. Sometimes he was rightfully indignant about educators giving only lip service to industrial education, as when he reported to President Ayres that there were no industrial courses in the Huntingdon Industrial Training School. In West Tennessee he tried to convince an uninterested high school principal that agricultural education should be the core of the curriculum only to discover that the principal was a cotton buyer, devoting all of his energies to a scheme to force down cotton prices in the county. "Oh for a Moses to lead the benighted county out of Egypt!" Clark cried, and added that he hoped that "he'll start on the hotel where I theoretically dined."[36]

He found the same miserable conditions in the Cumberlands of East Tennessee:

> I ran over to the county seat, Jacksboro, to visit the high school, which I found very weak. There was a course in domestic science taught out of a book with no equipment and taught, *mirabile dictu*, by a man. I went into the seventh and eighth grades room, taught by a man with a hickory switch longer than a buggy whip and said switch was very much frayed at the end. No one knows how long it was originally. When I entered, he dismissed the class and tried to get me to speak. I declined on the ground that I wanted to hear a recitation. He at once went to studying his next lesson like mad. I sat there 15 minutes and discovered I was wasting time. So I went into the high school rooms, where I found a very small class in Agriculture going through a *book* recitation. I went back into the seventh and eighth grade room. Immediately the class was dismissed! So I accepted the situation and spoke to the room on corn judging, illustrating by the 12 little books I had brought with me to put in the school library. I went down town after school to ask the county superintendent about that teacher, but I found he was in another county at a political speaking. Poor county! Requiescat in pace![37]

Females as well as males needed a more practical curriculum that would pay dividends in prosperity. Recent historians of the female high school experience in the early twentieth century have been critical of industrial and homemaking or domestic science education and of different curriculums for males and females. These historians argue that the administrative progressives' advocacy of separate curriculums based on gender led to a separate, anti-intellectual experience for young women. Clark, however, praised such differentiated curriculums. In 1914, as an example, he found a much improved high school in Milan, Tennessee, where chemistry classes had been divided into boys' and girls' sections with separate subject matter.[38]

Like industrial and agricultural education for boys, Clark advocated domestic science for girls. His assurances about the consequences of such curricula seem a mite extravagant: "We have 1,500,000 deaths in the United States annually, one third of which is preventable. We have 4,200,000 constantly sick causing anxiety to probably 20,000,000 friends. This constitutes a tax on this nation just as much as if it were collected by the county trustee." Since teaching proper methods of sanitation and food preparation could prevent many of the deaths, according to Clark, a domestic science curriculum was in reality an investment in health and prosperity. Cleanliness was a cardinal virtue for the southern progressives; they believed that filth and crime had a centripetal relationship, and disease caused by lack of sanitation was rampant among southerners at the time.

> Tuberculosis, smallpox, hookworm, typhoid, diphtheria, and a host of gastrointestinal ailments struck young people down regardless of where they lived. Physicians and educators blamed much of that suffering on "ignorance" and on "filthy" habits of personal hygiene. They pointed especially to the failure of rural families to build and use outdoor toilets.[39]

Clark was a veritable crusader for sanitation—outhouses were a symbol of civilization for him. In 1914 he visited a school where one of his former students was vice-principal. When he asked for the outhouse, he "*mirabile dictu*" received the staggering reply: "Why we did have one until we admitted girls to the college. Then the girls took the privy and the boys go out there in the woods." Clark reported that he discussed that shameful state of affairs "very warmly" with his former student, reported the situation to the state health department, and announced that we would vote against the school's request to be rated a junior college by the university. No wonder, he stormed, under such an example the teachers in small mountain rural schools instruct their pupils at the beginning of the year: "At recess, the boys will go East and the girls go West. . . . No wonder these mountain homes have no privies! No wonder that county is full of hookworm!"[40]

Clark complained continually about the physical condition of school buildings, especially poor lighting. Always alert to the possibilities of discovering a cause that might appeal to the GEB, Clark proposed in 1916 that the Board would make a "magnificent investment" if it would pay for five years the salary of a state architect in each southern state to oversee the construction of a school building. He would be "one of the greatest savers of public property, one of the surest guarantors against graft," Clark claimed.[41]

Clark had increasing reservations about the GEB's supposition that Tennessee was to remain rural and that agricultural education was the best curriculum to prepare Tennessee students for their futures. In a 1916 letter to GEB member E. C. Sage, he took great pains to show that he was a true believer in agricultural education ("I have made rural sociology and rural economics the predominating feature" of my work). After all, he knew the expectations of the board that paid his salary. Nevertheless, and with "all due respect to the policy of your board," he insisted that the future of East Tennessee was to be urban not rural: "the New England of Tennessee, or the Alsace" of France. Thus the need was for industrial and commercial education and a "very very different" kind of agricultural education for the small truck farms that would be created to meet the needs of an urban population.[42]

Administrative progressives sought continually to expand the role and scope of public schooling. Schools should teach children from kindergarten to community college; they should school the mentally and physically disabled as well as youthful criminals and the emotionally disturbed. They should have responsibility for the recreation, health, and testing of the young. By 1916, Clark was urging a similar expansion of education for Tennessee, as urbanization was underway and "our people" must understand that:

> City people cannot live like country people. There must be play grounds and parks and planning for the "City Beautiful." The school nurse and the school luncheon and medical inspection, to a greater degree than we shall ever need in the country, must be provided. There must be detention homes and schools for the defective, the delinquent and the cripple. . . . A conviction of the necessity of school gymnasium in urban surroundings must be stamped upon our people.

In his report for the next year, Clark, always looking for new ways to spend their money, informed the GEB that he had become "very much interested" in the problems of mental defectives, and he campaigned for funds to build a school for delinquent girls at Tullahoma and was urging the use of "Binet-Simon tests." He cautioned that the results "of this propaganda . . . will have to be seen in the future."[43]

In many ways Clark was a quintessential southern progressive; he, too, feared radicalism. Following the First World War, his speeches were filled with the rhetoric of the Big Red Scare, although to what degree he was using the scare as a campaign tactic to gain support for school funds from businessmen is unclear. In 1920 he addressed the Kiwanis, telling them that he stood with them for conservatism and against radicalism but that their tight-fisted attitudes were not helping: "We are sitting on a volcano. If you do not come to the rescue these teachers are going to see red and you are going to see the seeds of incipient bolshevism sown in the minds of your children." The Kiwanis heeded the warning. Demands for raises in the salaries of local school teachers were "greeted with prolonged cheers," and the club passed a resolution supporting a substantial increase in teachers' salaries.[44]

Clark's Campaigns

In language similar to Claxton's a decade before, Clark wrote: "I wish I could split myself into a dozen men because I could set everyone of them to work." Clark was as indefatigable a worker as Claxton. He spent most of his time on the road, for months at a stretch, conducting rallies and otherwise politicking for increased local taxes and bond issues to support establishment of county high schools. In December 1915, as an example, the *Orange and White* reported that he was leaving for an educational campaign in eighteen West Tennessee counties. He often had to beg correspondents to excuse him for not being available to speak at their rallies because he would be in another part of the state for several months. In addition to the trips, he corresponded with officials and political candidates in every county that did not have a high school; much of his correspondence from across the state concerned general university business, a point he often made to the university president in his reports. Clark also published regularly to keep the "scholar's attitude." In his report at the end of the 1918–19 academic year, he listed an impressive number of journal articles in the *High School Quarterly*, *Progressive Teacher*, *North Carolina High School Journal*, *Florida School Room*, and the *Southern Agriculturist*. He was also associate editor of the *High School Quarterly* that year. In addition, he taught in the Summer School of the South and six hours in the Spring Semester: "I point with pride to the fact that I have missed very few of my classes on account of my field work, although that has necessitated my going several times from one train to my class and from my class to another train." In his 1917 report to the GEB, he directed attention to the fact that he had not had a vacation since they had appointed him in 1912 and that he had worked half of the Sundays in the previous year.[45]

In the hills of Appalachia and in rural Tennessee generally, physical deprivation and distress were common for the traveling professors. In mid-December 1919, Clark complained of sleeping for four nights in a room without heat and having to break ice in his pitcher every morning to shave. An earlier report, with somewhat of a Dickinson flavor, described Christmas week on the road ("I had to forego my Xmas"). He wrote that he had to spend one night "in an 'accommodation house,' so called because of its lack of accommodations." It was so cold he slept in his clothes, and he reported that it was a mistake not to wear his gloves. This extended excerpt from one of Clark's field reports in 1916 gives a feeling for the grueling work and deprivation of the traveling professors of secondary education:

> We left the Valley country and took horses because the mountain districts to which we were going were too steep for buggies or automobiles. We went right into the back woods for a week's campaign. We had to abandon our razors, let alone our collars, and go as unshaven as this necessitated. However, this is the very way to gain votes for the object of our campaign, because the back district people are very suspicious of overdressed people. Their teachers are nearly all men and teach in overalls. Practically every school house that we visited was untenable, and it would have been forbidden in Massachusetts for such a building to be used as a schoolroom. We found three children seated on one seat in practically every school that we visited. In some places the children sat on the floor. . . . We went into one regular hornets nest of opposition. . . . At one place rowdies tried to break up our meeting with pistol shots and yelling and they ran a doctor's automobile down the hill and into a rock fence while he was inside helping boost for the bond issue. Into one town which we went there was so much opposition to the bond issue that many citizens refused to reply to our salutations. Women were bare footed as a general proposition and some of the men were the same. I felt as if I had paid a visit to the Eighteenth Century with its intensity of partisan feeling, and its backward home conditions. I had no mishaps during the week other than having to ride for two days on horseback through a drizzling rain and having my horse mire up in the mud of a cattle pond. We did a lot of good on that trip, had a lot of fun and won a lot of votes.[46]

No one could know the difficulties that the professors would encounter in the hinterlands. In 1914 Clark tried to rally the citizens of Hixon County, but many of them were engaged in a bitter factional fight that had begun as a quarrel in the Methodist church and that had "led to the burning of the courthouse, the abolition of the high school, the voting down of bond issues for roads and schools." Clark abandoned his school speech and urged the citizens to forsake their "hatreds and partisanship." He reported that his talk was a success as each side said that the other needed it. Sometimes the local controversies went in the other direction with their origin in school controversies and then moving into the churches. Clark reported that the fight was so bitter in the Methodist church in Monteagle that all members of one faction in the congregation would stay home if an organist from another side played at Sunday services.[47]

There was so much local opposition to raising taxes or supporting bond issues to establish country high schools that politicians often resisted the appeals of the charming Clark. After a long struggle to get a "flicker" of interest from one county superintendent, who was more interested in reelection than anything else, Clark reported with disgust that the superintendent dreaded supporting the high school campaign as a child hates castor oil. Occasionally, the conflict between Clark and county superintendents became personal and bitter. He reported that one superintendent actively opposed the rally in his county but attended to make sure that Clark was not abusing him, sat in the front, facing the audience, fell asleep, and snored. The superintendent refused to provide Clark with transportation, and he had to walk on the railroad tracks for four miles to the next town. He wrote Ayres that after what he said about the superintendent there, "We are even."[48]

An organized campaign of letters to the editor was a part of the campaign effort. Harry Clark urged the high school teachers to:

> Sit down and write an article of 50 to 100 words on WHAT THE HIGH SCHOOL HAS DONE FOR YOUR COUNTY. If you have some magistrates who opposed the creation of the high school but who are now converted after seeing their results, PLEASE GET A LETTER from them stating that fact. A dozen such letters read before a county court would do more to persuade the magistrates to vote for a high school than a two hour speech; and you know it.

Newspapers also gave space to proponents of the campaign for articles, including maps and illustrations, that went beyond mere letters to the editor. Both Claxton and Clark wrote such signed articles, Clark by the dozens. He particularly liked to indicate how outsiders were impressed: "The commissioner of education reports that it is the most remarkable educational development of recent years and the secretary of Yale, after a southern trip wrote his surprise at our wonderful advance."[49]

As the campaign succeeded and most counties established high schools, Clark spent most of his time inspecting them as well as private "colleges" and normal schools, many of which were offering work only at the secondary level, attempting to cajole or shame them into improvement. After Tennessee appointed a high school inspector in 1914, Buttrick indicated that the GEB would probably end appropriations for a professor of secondary education because the responsibilities of the two positions were similar. Ayres lobbied Buttrick strongly, arguing that the role of the high school inspector was more routine: assuring obedience to the rules and regulations of the state Department of Public Instruction. Whereas much work remained in stimulating "general uplift" of quality high schools, work of a wider scope that Clark was doing effectively. The GEB continued to fund the position at Tennessee until it ended the program throughout the South.[50]

Nevertheless, school inspections rather than political rallies took more of Clark's time in later years. Clark commented with sympathy and humor on schools with little substance and great pretensions. He described Bethel College where the Cumberland Presbyterians trained preachers as "seven windows wide, three windows high, six windows and wood-shed deep." He spoke at a new "Cambellite" college build high on a river bluff. After listening to dubious claims by the principal, he wrote that he didn't know if the river or the principal had the higher bluff. He attended a class in a school where nine ministerial students were passing around two books to read and expound. He verified that "they were great expounders." He reported that the head of one of these colleges had an imagination and a sense of humor "in inverse ratio." When he started teaching, he claimed undergraduate work from Union University at Jackson, Tennessee; later he printed an imaginary masters degree in the catalog. "His imagination waxed as his sense of the ridiculous waned," Clark recounted, "and he conferred a doctor's degree on himself." During Clark's visit, he asked how long it would take him to get a bachelor's degree from the University of Tennessee.[51]

He visited a school in Union City that was sadly deficient in discipline and teaching methods. He wrote that he tried tactfully to offer some suggestions, but since the principals were recent college graduates, he "soon perceived that they were above advice, so [he] spent a pleasant half hour hearing them talk." He gently chided the GEB, contending that if they would stop sending money to such institutions and "let the law of survival work," in a few years Tennessee would no longer have "eight more colleges than the German Empire has universities."[52]

African Americans and the Educational Campaigns

How did the educational campaigns affect African Americans and their separate schools? Late twentieth-century historians agree that the campaigners supported a separate and unequal education for black southerners—there is no other way to read the historical evidence. Yet, forty years after the campaign, Dabney asserted somewhat plaintively, and perhaps defensively, that they were not racists. And, if racism is relative, *perhaps* some of them were not, but Dabney voiced the social Darwinist views on which turn-of-the-century liberals justified a separate and unequal society. In a 1903 address in Carnegie Hall, he insisted that whites were natural social and political leaders, and that would and could not be changed by education:

> The white race is, from the standpoint of evolution, from two to five thousand years ahead of the negro [sic] in development. This is a fact in nature which we cannot change in a decade or a century. The white man is the natural leader, industrially, socially, politically, and no amount of education, literary or industrial, is going to put the negro above him.[53]

At the turn of the century, many southern whites still keenly felt the grievances of Reconstruction, and politicians and newspaper editors often aggravated the painful memories (real or imagined) for their own purposes. Shared myths by southern whites included despicable villains: northern carpetbaggers who came south to rub Confederate noses in their defeat and, even worse, scalawags, southern whites who, Judas-like, aided the carpetbaggers in their nefarious activities. Carpetbagger Yankee teachers had opened schools for blacks throughout the South, and scalawag state legislatures had created state-wide systems of public schooling. At the beginning of the twentieth century, white southerners usually viewed black education and state-financed and state-controlled public schools with suspicion. Leaders of the educational campaigns were keenly aware that the educational campaigns would fail if reactionary politicians and the conservative press could convince white southerners that northern philanthropists were the new carpetbaggers and southern campaigners were the new scalawags.

Southern whites who wanted to keep African Americans in a separate, inferior, dependent place were just beginning to feel comfortable in 1900. Laws and court decisions had effectively disenfranchised southern African Americans; in 1895, the white-appointed leader of southern blacks, Booker T. Washington, at the Atlanta World's Cotton Exhibition, had asked "his people" to accept social inequality; and, in 1896, the Supreme Court of the United States in *Plessy v. Ferguson* allowed state-mandated racial segregation. The leaders of the Conference for Education in the South sought to reassure southern whites that they too supported racial segregation. At Capon Springs, the first president of the Conference, the venerable old Confederate, J. L. M. Curry, settled the issue: "The white people are to be the leaders, to take the initiative, to have the directive control in all matters pertaining to civilization and the highest interest or our beloved land. History demonstrates that the Caucasian will rule." In return for accepting the lowest position in a stratified society, African Americans were to receive an "appropriate" education. The most important question is not if blacks will be educated but how, President Edwin Alderman of Tulane University told the Conference. Industrial education as found at Hampton and Tuskegee was the answer, for they had "something to teach to the whole world in the way of training for freedom a backward, child race."[54]

But many white southerners remained suspicious of the racial attitudes of the campaigners. The Bureau of the Southern Education Board in Knoxville collected and saved newspaper clippings from throughout the South that questioned the racial policies of the campaigns. The most racist of the editors opposed the movement because they didn't want schooling for African Americans at all. The Columbia (South Carolina) *The State* denounced the "Ogden Movement" for promoting black education. Black schooling was the "hobby" of the leaders, according to the paper, although the editor hinted of even more sinister but unnamed aims: "something further to which the south is opposed." The something further was racial equality or even racial "mixing," and the campaign leaders were ever anxious that they not appear to promote it. In January 1901 southern newspapers reported that Dabney and Alderman had espoused racial equality at a dinner with northern philanthropists at the New York City Waldorf-Astoria Hotel. Dabney immediately denied the charge, blaming the inflammatory reports on the New York yellow press. The next year, newspapers from throughout the South picked up a story by the *Baltimore Sun* that blacks had dined with members of the Southern Education Board at New York's Unitarian Club. Editorials followed, suggesting that "the red flag" of social equality was waved. Again, members of the SEB denied the charge: "The two negroes [sic] came in after dinner, two of them, to hear the speeches. They were not invited to the dinner, neither did they sit down to dinner on [the basis of] social equality." Controversy over the dinner caused Buttrick to reemphasize that the northern leaders of the campaign recognized "that the Education of the negro race [sic] is in the hands of the white people of the South, and must ever remain there."[55]

In Tennessee, campaigners sometimes held racially segregated school rallies on the same day "on different grounds," with the same "able white speakers." But more or less benign neglect of African Americans was typical of the leaders at Knoxville. Some members of the SEB criticized Dabney for ignoring African Americans in his propaganda efforts as director of the Bureau of Information and Investigation. Dabney was mindful of the problem of hundreds of thousands of illiterate African Americans on one hand, but a more serious issue, for him, was the illiteracy "of scores of thousands of the purest American stock in the country upon the other."[56]

Even in the shadow of the University of Tennessee, some local school officials held even more extreme racial views. In an open discussion at the 1903 Conference of Education in the South meeting, the school superintendent of Loudon County, Tennessee, said that:

> It was frequently the case that it was necessary to use a club to make the negro [sic] honest and to use a rope to make him moral. . . . The negro will steal. We all know he will steal. I do not mean to say anything against the negro (great laughter), but the leopard cannot change his spots, and we know the negro will steal. We should give him in the way of education only what he can take, and see to it that he takes it.

When possible, Tennessee campaigners found it easier to avoid discussions of black education.[57]

Northerners were also often tired of hearing about the educational plight of southern African Americans. In 1905 Claxton took a fundraising trip to the North, staying at Chicago's Gertrude House at the invitation of his long-time admirer and correspondent, Amelia Hofer. She provided audiences of the literati for Claxton but warned him to "clear away the notion that you speak for blacks or mountain whites—or what not." He promised not to talk much about Appalachian whites or blacks.[58]

At the beginning of the Tennessee campaign, state Superintendent Mynders paid the traveling expenses of F. G. Smith, the African-American principal of Nashville's Pearl High School, to campaign in West Tennessee. "I know that he accomplished good," Mynders wrote. Claxton replied that he thought it "very well to give some attention" to black school improvement. Claxton's personal attitude toward blacks is unclear; it seems to have been a fairly typical southern progressive blend of racist paternalism toward African Americans on one hand

and a self-righteous dislike of extreme white bigots on the other. He indicated that educational opportunities for African Americans were assured because southerners "with their blue eyes and soft hearts" were compassionate. To an inquiry from G. Stanley Hall on research concerning southern blacks, Claxton responded with a short list of researchers and publications, including those of Atlanta University, and the following satirical observation:

> People of the South know very little about the negro [sic]. What little we do know we have learned from Northern people who have never seen the South, or write learnedly, at least dogmatically, on the subject after having spent two or three days, or probably a week, in this section. Tons of matter have been printed as editorials and contributions in our newspapers, but, like the negro's thunder storm at night, there has been much more of noise than light in them.[59]

Claxton strongly supported an increase in the poll tax but insisted that he did not wish to use the tax to disenfranchise blacks: "It is nothing but just that people who do not pay tax on real estate or other property which is taxed in this State, should pay their part for the support of schools." Yet, in a discussion of compulsory education before the East Tennessee Education Association the same year, 1904, he recognized that the poll tax disenfranchised African Americans but explained it on the basis of freedom and democracy. Southerners were "doing this largely in the belief that there is only freedom where there is education." He called it "state treason" to allow ignorant people "to act as citizens."[60]

Clark, too, was uncertain about his responsibility for African-American education. After four years as professor of secondary education, he reported that he woke "with a start to the fact" that he had responsibility to black schools as well as to white. In 1916 he confessed that before then "it never dawned on my mental horizon that I owed any obligation" to black schools. He assured the GEB that, in the future, he would be an "attorney for the negro [sic]," acting as an advocate for him with school boards throughout Tennessee.[61]

A year later he reported that "one of the significant things" that had happened to him was an "awakening on the subject of negro [sic] education." He wrote that teaching rural sociology has been very broadening as it had compelled him to study the relationship between black labor and black education. Yet, in the same report, he indicated that he visited only the most significant African-American schools (such as Turner Normal School) or made "fill-in" trips, occasions when train schedules gave him some extra time after visits to white schools.[62]

In January 1916, Clark feigned ignorance about the proper type of secondary education for blacks: "I feel a little bit confused in my own mind." In seeking to find answers to his dilemma, he visited Europe to study their "peasant schools." Not surprisingly, he decided the most desirable type of education to prepare African Americans for their futures and to allay "anti-negro demagoguery" was industrial, home-making, and agricultural education. In an awkward but apt phrase, he called it conservative progressiveness. His denunciation of classical studies was not simply racial prejudice; an evangelist for industrial education for whites was unlikely to testify for another type of schooling for African Americans. After visiting a black college in Rogersville, he complained of the lack of industrial classes, but fumed that forty were enrolled in "beginning Greek!!" And he was as critical of substandard, pretentious, free enterprise black schools as he was of those run by whites. He complained about the principal of the Henderson Colored Business College who had disguised his ownership of the college and was seeking large grants from northern philanthropists. He "modestly advertises himself The Super-man," Clark reported.[63]

Clark exhibited the racially naive and insensitive attitudes of southern white moderates of his day. It is black peoples' "nature," he explained, to do better work for whites who are sympathetic but keep their distance and demand respect. He recognized his "prejudices as a Southern white man" when he condemned white teachers in black schools who stayed in black homes while traveling or attending conventions. His report on an educational rally in a black church further demonstrated these prejudices as he attempted to show African Americans as amusingly primitive. He reported that when he arrived with the black high school inspector at 9:00 in the evening the church "was just getting in good, shouting trim after an hour's session!" He wrote that they had to wait another hour before the congregation got out of breath from shouting and jumping up and down: "They extended the jungle of Africa with all its night of ignorance." Clark, however, refused to accept other stereotypes. Presumptions of black promiscuity, as an example, annoyed him. It saddened him, that at the dedication of a new black normal school, the administrator introduced each teacher with the statement that "no one had ever questioned her VIRTUE AND THAT NONE OF HER SISTERS HAD EVER GONE ASTRAY!!!"[64]

The attitude of African Americans as the United States entered the First World War concerned Clark; he worried that they might be "caught by German propaganda." Informants told him that there was no question that blacks had been "tampered with." And he "found a very sullen attitude" by leading black educators toward their responsibility in the War that caused him to have "a very earnest talk with some of my negro teacher friends." He worried about the decline of African-American population in East Tennessee and the border states generally because of the great migration to the North during and following the War, hoping it would be a "temporary decline." He, and other white southerners, feared that "migration fever" could shrink the supply of cheap labor.[65]

Clark Resigns

In 1919 President Ayres died unexpectedly, "called into the great beyond," the student newspaper reported. Claxton was the leading candidate to replace him but wished to finish his term as U.S. Commissioner of Education. Sidney Gilbreath, Ayres old adversary, was popular with public school interests but opposed by the university faculty, who supported the dean of agriculture, Harcourt Morgan. There was some concern that Morgan dressed like the farmers with whom he worked, but the trustees appointed him, deciding that they could dress him up to look the part of a university president.[66]

Clark resigned in 1920, shortly after Morgan's appointment, in part because he felt a lack of support and appreciation from the university administration. Over the years, one of his most bitter complaints was that he lacked secretarial help; it became a symbol of his resentment. He pointed out that he had a heavy correspondence on school matters, and "it is hard on a man without a stenographer." In an oblique threat, after fussing repeatedly about the problem, he wrote that if he were to leave the university, he advised the administration to give his replacement "proper clerical aid." When he finally resigned, a lack of secretarial support was on his mind:

> It is with great regret that I leave the University, which I have served to the best of my ability for nearly nine years. During all of this time I have taken no vacation, have been absent from home on University work four Christmases and seven Thanksgivings. I believe I am the only High School Visitor in the nation who has worked without a stenographer.[67]

Morgan seemed to have little anxiety about overworking his professor of secondary education. In 1919, after eight years on the job, Clark asked to have August and early September to attend summer school at Harvard. He pointed out that it would be his "first vacation" since he had been at the university and that the president would have to concede that his request was reasonable. Morgan responded that he was "sure" that Clark was due a vacation, but it was, of course, "a most unfortunate time" for him to leave his duties.[68]

Clark sometimes used job offers in blatant attempts to improve his circumstances and to assure himself job security when the GEB ceased support, originally scheduled for 1920. In 1918 he wrote President Ayres that he "would probably" decline other offers if the university would keep him on the faculty without a decrease in salary, "insuring me a place so long as I satisfactorily discharge my duties." Not only was he a person with other offers, he reminded Ayres of what a hardworking, valuable employee he was:

> I have worked seven years day and night, Sunday too, with no vacations, even on Saturday afternoons. You would not be likely to get any one who would work as hard as I have done. Moreover I have been in a place that called for tact, where slight indiscretions on my part could have seriously embarrassed the University. In the midst of difficult school politics and bitter factional fights, I have proved that I can protect the good name of the University. Hence I feel that I may say that any new man must invest another seven years of service to get to the place where I stand today. Each year's work now is worth any two years' when I first took up my work.[69]

Clark asked for job security from newly installed president Morgan in 1919: "President Ayres in his lifetime assured me that he would continue me at the University, as long as he lived." Clark suggested that the GEB might continue to pay the salaries of long-time professors during a transitional period as the Board had promised "to look after its boys." But he hinted that if he left (to accept the presidency of Cumberland College "at $3,600 a year with a furnished house") the university might not secure any additional funds at all. Regardless of any assurance that he may have secured, he left the university in February 1921 to become Secretary of Christian Education for the Southern Baptist Convention of Tennessee.[70]

The GEB Ends Support of Professors of Secondary Education

The official mission of the professors of secondary education changed after November 1919 when the southern state superintendents of public instruction and university presidents met with representatives of the GEB at the Congress Hotel in Chicago and declared the educational campaigns a success: "High schools exist in considerable abundance."

According to their memorandum, the urgent problems of southern high schools were "qualitative rather than quantitative." In clearer words, the major role of the professor of secondary education was to change from a political campaigner to a teacher educator. A month after the Chicago meeting, Abraham Flexner wrote to the newly installed UT president about the implications of the meeting. The professor of secondary education should now be considered

> the nucleus of a department of the fundamental training of prospective secondary school teachers in the methods, subject matter and objects of high school work. While it was understood that in a limited way the professor would remain in contact with the high schools particularly in the vicinity of the university, it was believed that the time had come when his main thought and energy should be given to the training of high school teachers.[71]

The GEB announced that it would cease supporting professors of secondary education in 1920. After pleas and resolutions by southern university presidents and superintendents of public instruction, organized by Presidents George Denny of the University of Alabama and Morgan of Tennessee, the GEB agreed to continue support of the professors for five years, ending June 30, 1925. The Board was very firm that there would not be any extensions beyond that date. Nevertheless, with time running out, the presidents and state superintendents met in Atlanta in December 1924 and adopted resolutions begging the GEB for reconsideration and more opportunities to present their case in detail. The officers of the GEB refused adamantly to consider an extension.[72]

The administrators of some universities, including Tennessee, tried an end run. They argued unique and critical circumstances and requested individual appropriations. No exception was the response of the Board: "The offices have no discretionary power." The General Education Board file in Morgan's administration papers ends with a note from him to the GEB on 15 January 1926, reporting that the university was continuing to support its professor of secondary education.[73]

Chapter 5

The College of Education:
An Uneasy Resident of the University,
the 1920s and 1930s

By the early 1920s, teacher education at UT was once more on its sickbed, ready for one of its periodic, miraculous recoveries. There were only two faculty members, a professor of the history and principles of education and a professor of secondary education whose salary was subsidized by the General Education Board. In addition to the usual antieducationist sentiments characteristic of most state university campuses, teacher education had a special nemesis, long-time university administrator James Hoskins. He was irascible, thin-skinned, and enthusiastically antieducationist; and, by the time he retired, it seemed to the education faculty that he had been around forever. He was a nineteenth-century alumnus of the university. In 1900 he joined the faculty as assistant professor of history and became dean of the College of Liberal Arts in 1911. Appointed acting president in 1919, he served as dean of the university (provost) thereafter until he was appointed president in 1934. He retired in 1946.[1]

Hoskins kept the educationists on the defensive. In 1923 he fired professor of secondary education Jesse Sprowls for insubordination, primarily for making fun of him. He then terminated the contracts of professors who came to Sprowls's defense. A censure from the American Association of University Professors (AAUP) moderated Hoskins's authoritarian behavior toward the faculty but left his hostility toward educationists undiminished. In private letters to university trustees, he warned against professors of education: "aggressive men" who "have played havoc, or you might say hell, with the program of education as it is carried on today." In 1932, Hoskins proposed the elimination of the undergraduate teacher education program, which would have ef-

fectively destroyed the college. With the aid of public school supporters, the education faculty barely managed to hold on to the undergraduate program. In the 1940s, Hoskins went on the offensive with
widely publicized attacks on progressive pedagogy.[2]

"The Great Professor Trial" provides a context for the tribulations
of the educationists in the 1920s. In April 1923, Hoskins ordered
Sprowls and John Thackston, Director of the School of Education, to
his office, where he terminated Sprowls for the next year. Sprowls
immediately began telling his startled colleagues that he had been fired
because he had ordered James Harvey Robinson's popular *The Mind
in the Making*, which contained evolutionary themes, for use in his
classes. A new daily newspaper, the *Knoxville News,* took up the
cause. "Give Sprowls a Hearing" read an editorial headline. "Thinking
people will look with scorn upon an institution which would not permit one of its professors to use *The Mind in the Making. . . .* If Prof.
Sprowls's head can be chopped off, what is to save the next fellow
from similar summary action?" Within a short time five professors
from other departments, four of whom were suspected of supporting
Sprowls, were also fired, including some professors who had national
reputations as scholars.[3]

There were a number of conditions that led to the controversy,
including a rigid and pervasive fundamentalist religious climate, authoritarian administrators, and an almost complete lack of due process in faculty personnel matters. Neither President Harcourt Morgan
nor Hoskins seemed to be able to take criticism. As a later sympathetic president of the university put it, "Morgan could not take criticism. It hurt him—he simply couldn't stand it."[4]

The *News* wrote that Sprowls was not rehired because he wanted
to tell his students the truth about science and that the real issue was
"the existence of autocratic control of the university led by the "Mor-
gan-Hoskins-Thackston regime." When Philip Hamer, the head of the
history department and a friend of Sprowls, told the editor of the
News that the Robinson book had nothing to do with the firing, the
editor responded, according to Hamer's diary, "that he didn't give a
damn about that but it made a good issue." What Sprowls did not tell
his colleagues until much later was that the reason given by Hoskins
and Thackston for his firing was his failure to do field work with the
public schools, especially to promote secondary education throughout
the state. He followed the magnetic, extroverted Harry Clark as professor of secondary education. Clark was remarkably successful in
working with public school teachers and administrators. The 1924

AAUP report suggested that Sprowls was his antithesis: "a retiring scholar, an ineffective speaker and a poor friend maker and promoter." Nevertheless, there was an uproar among some members of the faculty, including a letter to the AAUP asking for an inquiry—which was seen by the administration as outside meddling.[5]

At a time of statewide agitation over the firings and its aftermath, the official student newspaper, the *Orange and White*, never mentioned the controversy, indicating the complete control of the administration over student publications. The best it was able to do was to leave a blank space in one issue where an offending editorial had been censored. Hoskins was horrified when an underground student newspaper appeared. The students called their paper *The Independent Truth* and claimed that it was a paper for "college MEN not mollycoddles." Actually it was quite mild, assuring its readers that "a radical in our estimation is about the worst kind of person in existence." The basic complaint was that the university administration was anti-intellectual, a criticism with an element of truth. Hoskins's autocratic ways were the major target of the *Truth*, and he was determined to find and punish the students and, especially, faculty allies who had anything to do with the paper. As a Knoxville newspaper understated it, there is "quite a bit of speculation as to those responsible for its publication." After graduation, and with diplomas in hand, a good part of the senior class admitted taking part and absolved "professors from all connections with it." Calculated to protect their professors, their denials were not true. According to Hamer's diary, several of the suspected professors contributed money or wrote for the underground paper.[6]

The most disquieting events in the controversy followed. After receiving assurances from President Morgan that he would "back him up," Hoskins conducted formal hearings in his office on the loyalty of a number of professors to the administration. In the hearings Hoskins acted as both prosecuting attorney and judge. In several cases he demanded that professors squeal on each other and on students. Facing an angry dean and without job security, some professors were obviously badly flustered. In order to save their hides, some indicted their colleagues. Hoskins's formal summary of the testimony of each presented to the Board of Trustees was often quite prejudicial, and refusal to name colleagues was among the charges brought against professors.[7]

The controversy was played out against the backdrop of the reactionary and fundamentalist Tennessee of the 1920s. Not only was it unlawful to teach evolution, but a city as large as Chattanooga did not allow public school students or teachers to attend dances on their own time, even in private homes; in 1922 a high school teacher was fired because he attended a dance. The University of Tennessee during this period was often called a Christian institution, and professors were expected to be visible church leaders. Sunday schools and congregations throughout the area adopted resolutions praising President Morgan. As an example, the Central Avenue Baptist Church unanimously endorsed the action of Morgan, Hoskins, and Thackston "in refusing to permit the teachings of unsound doctrines" in the University of Tennessee. The Chamber of Commerce condemned criticism of the University of Tennessee and expressed confidence in Morgan as "an able educator" and "Christian gentleman." The East Tennessee Farmers Convention not only praised Morgan for his stand against the teaching of evolution, but the delegates became so excited after the vote that they rose to their feet and cheered. A local newspaper summed it up: "Nothing in the history of the state university has ever served to arouse such enthusiastic and pronounced support in his favor . . . as has President Morgan's attitude with reference to the teaching of evolution."[8]

When Morgan received letters condemning his actions as abridgments of academic freedom, he always responded with a return letter carefully spelling out that Sprowls had been terminated for his failures to perform his duties, especially in field service, not for teaching evolution. In one of the more unlovely aspects of the case, when Morgan responded to the numerous letters praising him for ridding the university of modernists, atheists, or infidels, he simply thanked the writer for his support, without repeating the disclaimer as to why Sprowls was fired. Of course Morgan also received letters from further right, suggesting that the ungodly university was reaping its just harvest. The most frequent complaint was allowing dances:

> I am wondering why you allow those noble young men and sweet young girls to have those wicked degenerate dances which I know and you know is grieving the Heart of Christ.[9]
>
> And just seen the other day where you pulled off a Big Dance in your Summer School see where your pupils pulls off Big Dances at Whittle Springs Hotel ever once a while training them for the Devil.[10]

The report of the AAUP investigation was mild and evenhanded. It criticized particularly the procedures used in terminating the professors and the form of tenure: It "is neither just or compatible with the dignity of the professor of University teaching." Shortly after the great professor trial, a Primitive Baptist legislator, George Washington Butler, introduced the evolution bill that resulted in the Scopes Trial that so entertained the nation.[11]

Organization and Reorganization of the College of Education

In 1921, President Morgan asked Thackston for a plan for reviving teacher training in the university. Thackston responded with a seven-page letter that expressed the attitudes and aspirations of the educationists. He began the letter with defensiveness about the significance of their work: "The University of Tennessee is not attempting any job that is more important than this. Some of its undertakings are, possibly, not as important." With the gender presumptions characteristic of the time, he indicated the "urgent needs" of education, including four new professors. The first was for "one extension man. He should be a thoroughly trained Education man." His requests were as gender explicit for professors of school administration, educational psychology, and elementary and rural education. His request for an elementary and rural education professor to train elementary school "leaders" raised the issue of the university's role in training elementary teachers, a topic of intense and often hostile debate during the 1920s and 1930s. He also recommended that the faculty of a proposed demonstration school should consist of one male principal, two men teachers, and three women teachers. He suggested that the men teachers be paid "around $2,500" each and that the women teachers who "should have the same qualification as the men teachers, and would have the same type of work to do" be paid "around $2,000" each.[12]

Education got the education professors, but not the demonstration school that had been a perpetual issue at Tennessee, beginning with the Department of Education's establishment in 1902. Thackston advanced the timeworn arguments of his predecessors: "It is just as ridiculous to attempt to train teachers without a demonstration school, as it is to train chemists or botanists or agriculturists, or engineers without their laboratories and the great expensive equipment they now have, every man who has had any training in teaching . . . knows this is a fact."[13]

On February 23, 1926, President Morgan presented a plan to the board of trustees' executive committee to establish a College of Education "on the same basis as the other colleges of the University." The board accepted the plan unanimously. Great fanfare had accompanied the establishment of the Teachers' Department in 1891 and the Department of Education in 1902. University recognition of the new college was more subdued, and Morgan downplayed the significance of its creation:

> Because of the misinterpretation of the educational public relation of the members of the faculty of the colleges of the University to the *School of Education*, it has been decided to clarify this by the organization of a *College of Education* within the University. While we have always had this in practice, no definite announcement of it has been made.[14]

In a short news item, the alumni magazine indicated that the college was established primarily because of increased demand resulting from the rural education program. (I discuss the rural-life project in chapter 6.) In a statement reminiscent of the announcement of the Teachers Department in 1890, readers were assured that "standards" would be "the same as those of the other colleges of the University." A somewhat longer story in the university monthly "News Letter" agreed that the new college's "outstanding feature" was the rural education program, but national claims by educationists of the time for a science of education was echoed by Thackston in his comments on the purposes of the new college: "Teaching is becoming so scientific and exact that much special training must be had if teachers and educational administrators are to render the type of service demanded of them."[15]

John Thackston, an education professor since 1916, was appointed dean of the new College of Education. A native of Spartanburg, South Carolina, and a Furman University graduate, his Ph.D. was from New York University. After serving as state high school inspector for Florida, he was dean of the College of Education at the University of Florida for seven years. A health education specialist, he wrote a number of public school health textbooks.[16]

A political and religious liberal and educational progressive, he and the university's chief academic officer, James Hoskins, a political and educational conservative, were often at loggerheads. Part of their differences was due to personality. Hoskins often appeared stern, forbidding, and self-righteous. Thackston was perceived as warm, friendly, and humorous. A favorite of students, they often asked him and his wife to chaperone their dances. The student newspaper reported that the consensus of the secretaries was that he was "the finest person on the campus." Considered "very broadminded and modern" in his educational ideas, he embraced progressive education, a position that would eventually lead to serious trouble with Hoskins.[17]

He, like Hoskins, was a visible member of the Christian community of Knoxville, chairing a committee to take the census of Sunday schools in the community, chairing the university YMCA, and, for many years, teaching a "co-ed" Sunday school class at the First Baptist Church. He was much given to speechmaking to parent and teacher groups, high school commencements, and Bible and Sunday school classes. He was also given to making provocative statements that were quoted by the press, such as his declaration (heresy in fundamentalist Tennessee at the time) that "I think Jesus came to teach us, rather than to save us. I think He came to teach us how to live." On another occasion, he outlined for the local newspaper an elaborate plan for countries to pay their World War I debts by exchanging students between debtor and creditor nations. Hoskins found him a continuing source of irritation and, after years of squabbling, forced him to resign in 1943.[18]

The university catalog listed forty-four professors as the faculty of the new college, including President Morgan and Dean Hoskins. But only eight professors, including Thackston, were teacher educators, and three of those were in agricultural education. Professors in departments throughout the university who worked with education students were included, and much was made of the total university commitment to training teachers. Thackston explained how the system would work: "A specialist in Botany will teach classes in Botany and will teach the methods of teaching Botany. He will especially interpret to those who are going into school work, the Botany, both content and method, taught in the public school system from kindergarten through college."[19]

Thackston insisted in his budget requests to Hoskins that the size of the teacher education faculty in pedagogy was inadequate for Morgan's plans for the college. "Our classes are so large that it is impossible to do justice by the individual students," Thackston wrote, as he made university administrators' perpetual plea that they need more money for the good of the students. Not only did he need more *men*, he needed good men, "men well-trained and thoroughly experienced. I repeat we cannot put over this program with men who are not as well-trained as the best men in the University faculty. . . . Weak men trying to do big pieces of work are certain to put us in worse light than if the work were never attempted at all." In particular, he asked for an associate professor and critic teachers for practice teaching. Student teaching was supported, and, in June 1926, the trustees approved plans to place student teachers in the Knoxville public schools.[20]

Education as Social Panacea

Educationists have a tradition of promising more than they have been able to deliver, particularly of presenting schooling as a social panacea. They have not appreciated sufficiently the virtues of making modest claims, and the education faculty did not suffer from modesty in articulating the mission of the new college. They were going to save the society as well as the school system. President Morgan encouraged such hyperbolic promises. In 1923, a local newspaper quoted from his grand scheme to bring the university to all citizens of the state: "It is possible for the University of Tennessee to lead the way in every home and every hillside in Tennessee. . . . The problem is to get the university to become an effective force in those homes and communities, and the next problem is to get the people receptive to the efforts of the university, and in effectual cooperation with it."[21]

In 1927, the faculty submitted to Morgan the college objectives. Dean Thackston set the tone. The college was to make the lives of citizens "fuller, happier and better" by "entering into every phase of the work and life of the State wherever or however men, women or children of the State live and work and play. . . . Wherever a problem of the education of the people of the State exists," he announced, "there exists a College of Education problem." Joseph E. Avent, professor of educational psychology, agreed. Tennessee citizens "ranging from idiocy to genius" were to be "possessed with capabilities" for improving the state. Although the mission of the college was primarily to uplift rural life, Avent also pointed to urban problems from poverty to "the choice of playgrounds" that cried for solutions. And to be sure that no obstacles to the good life were left that the College of Education might tackle, Avent outlined problems that were neither peculiarly urban or rural but were simply "characteristic" human problems:

A. Problems already solved, to keep them solved;
B. Problems of the present, either conscious or not yet conscious;
C. Problems likely to be persisting through the years to come;
D. Problems pending;
E. Problems solved.

Of course, mere academic or intellectual skills were inadequate weapons for attacks on problems so formidable. Avent insisted that the function of education was to change "people for the better physically, intellectually, morally, vocationally, economically, recreationally, civically, and religiously."[22]

Professor Harry C. Humphreys had obviously learned his Seven Cardinal Principles of Secondary Education. In his report for Morgan, he restated them in his own words and added a liberal eighth. High school boys and girls were to be taught the science, laws, and art of living, which were to include:

1. Knowledge of health and health habits
2. Enjoyment and use of leisure
3. Worthy home membership, home builders, home makers, etc.
4. Vocational knowledge, knowledge and skills
5. Ethical character, morals, religion
6. Information and knowledge of the business and political world, business
7 Knowledge of, participation in community life, community leadership
8. Knowledge of, broad and liberal sympathies with different classes and races, through history, economics, sociology, simplified or written down.[23]

The education faculty recognized, regardless of their extravagant mission to improve the overall quality of life, that their primary responsibility was to work with public schools. They did not perceive this to be a limited task. Thackston stated that the immediate objectives of the college were "the study of the problems of childhood in Tennessee," including problems with their "social and moral life"; the reorganization of the public schools, including their curriculum methods of instruction, physical facilities, and "more suitable administration"; to train teachers (including "special demonstration" elementary teachers, since the university had an agreement, which the educational faculty despised, with the normal schools not to train elementary teachers), administrators, normal school teachers, and even "future and present" boards of education members; and, finally, publicity efforts among the general public on behalf of better public schools, a function of the education faculty since the Department of Education was established in 1902. Professor R. B. Parsons didn't mince words; he listed the first objective of the College as "propaganda."[24]

As chapter 6 indicates, rural education was the mainstay of the work of the education faculty during the 1920s. Despite more grandiose aspirations, they recognized that, in the immediate future, rural education would continue to be their major responsibility. Immediately after the establishment of the college, Thackston told the student newspaper that the college was created as a result of the university's rural mission and that its purpose was "special" training for rural teachers. The faculty justified "special" methods for rural teachers because urban methods would simply not work in the rural South: "Might as well try to put the country in town." The spring session for teachers in 1926 offered the following courses: "The One, Two and Three Teacher Schools and Their Problems," "Curriculum for Rural and Small Town Schools," "Teaching Rural Life," "The Correlation of Elementary Science and Agriculture with Rural Schools," and "Physical Education for Rural Schools." The university was on a quarter calendar, but most classes for teachers were offered in a separate six-week spring term for teachers, beginning late in April when the short public school term was over.[25]

The Struggle to Retain the College

With the establishment of a College of Education in 1926, a secure place for teacher education in the university seemed at long last assured. However, as had happened again and again since the creation of the "art of school-teaching" course in 1844, it was not to be. Almost immediately, doubts were raised about the wisdom of establishing the college, and plans for elimination or reorganization were proposed. Attacks came from several directions. From outside the university, private institutions and the state teachers colleges complained that, by offering education courses in the freshman and sophomore years, the college duplicated one of their missions—training elementary teachers. Critics within the university were also unhappy with the lower-division education courses, insisting that students should be in general education courses in the freshman and sophomore years and that professional courses should be upper division or graduate. Besides, they argued, the college was requiring too many education courses, leaving insufficient time for high school teachers to gain mastery over the disciplines they would teach. Less openly, some liberal arts professors questioned the academic quality of the education courses.

In the summer of 1928, Morgan and Hoskins proposed making education a graduate college only, offering upper division hours in education through the College of Liberal Arts and eliminating all lower division hours in education. B. O. Duggan led the resistance from the education faculty with the acquiescence of Thackston. (In a cover letter for his objections to Morgan's proposals, Duggan wrote: "It has been read by Dr. Thackston, who makes no objection to my submitting it to you.") Duggan, the most outspoken member of the education faculty, was an activist rather than a scholar. He delighted in choosing sides and doing battle. Weighing in at about 110 pounds, he was always in a fight; "I used to wear out secretaries dictating resignations." Later, when he was state superintendent, his nickname with the press was "Scrappy." He did not write for publication, but he sent a continuing stream of letters and memorandums to university and state officials campaigning for his views and discrediting his adversaries. Duggan told Morgan that the proposed changes for the college "disturbed and distressed" him, but that his interest was in the needs of "public school men of the state," not his own selfish interests or prejudice.[26]

In his campaign, Duggan marshaled a number of arguments. First, the college had not been given sufficient time to prove itself: "Organized only two years ago with a heavy and wide-ranging program placed upon it and with only meager financial support, the College has *not* had a 'fair chance.'" To eliminate the undergraduate college so soon would be an embarrassment to the university; the leaders would appear not to know what they were doing. Reorganization and readjustment rather than elimination of the college would "save the face" of the university, he argued. And, in a favorite tactic, the combative Duggan appealed to a recognition of common enemies, other colleges in Tennessee, arguing that the changes would give "sardonic pleasure that will stir the enemies of the University."[27]

More important was the argument that the education faculty could best accomplish its important mission for the citizens of Tennessee in a comprehensive College of Education. "While the University had only a *Department* of Education," Duggan wrote, "its influence upon the educational policy of the state was small." But, he argued, the lesson seemed to be lost on the university administration: "Further, and undoubtedly, the emasculation of the College of Education will destroy the prestige of the University in the public school field." In their defense of a strong (and large) teacher education program, the education faculty polished off an old argument that had been used since the public school system was created: the University of Tennessee was "the legal Head of the Public School System of the State," and, as a result, had responsibilities they could not evade. The university had fulfilled these responsibilities in the past, and the citizens had a right to expect that it would continue to do so.[28]

Immediately after the proposal to eliminate the undergraduate program, the High School Association, a group composed primarily of high school principals, began to lobby Morgan to preserve the undergraduate college. The role of the education faculty in organizing this lobbying is unknown, but Duggan served on the executive committee of the association. In an echo of the education faculty's message to Morgan, Robert N. Chenault, secretary of the High School Association, pointed to the different functions of the teachers colleges and the university. The teachers colleges were helping to solve the problems of the elementary schools; "but we feel that the field of secondary education is properly that of our State University, through its College of Education." Chenault ended his letter by suggesting that Morgan call a conference of high school principals so that they could further inform them of their needs. Morgan reassured Chenault that he was "very much interested" in the welfare of the high schools but declined to call a conference.[29]

The High School Association continued to press its case on behalf of the College of Education to Morgan. In June of 1929, Chenault wrote of "definite plans" that the teachers colleges had for creating high school departments. He admonished Morgan: "Frankly, I do not understand how the State University can afford to hold back in view of the situation. Are the high school people of the State to understand that our University is completely abandoning this field?" Chenault warned of political consequences if the university did not serve the interests of schools in the way it serves agriculture, engineering, and others: "The influence of the high school people constitutes a force." Morgan "hastened" to reassure Chenault that the College of Education was being organized rapidly to do for public schools what the College of Agriculture did for farms. Morgan indicated that he felt that educators of all levels would not be disappointed with the college of education's ability to address "all of the economic, educational and social problems of the State." And he suggested that it would be a "fine thing" for the officers of the High School Association to meet with him "some time."[30]

Plans for the reorganization of the college stalled for a time, but, during the Great Depression in April of 1932, Morgan returned to a plan similar to the 1928 proposal. The College of Liberal Arts would take responsibility for the undergraduate program in teacher education and the number of hours in education courses would be reduced to twenty-seven. The College of Education would be retained for graduate work only. Duggan led the counterattack again. Some arguments were familiar: The constant changes in teacher education would cause public school "leaders and thinkers" to "lose faith in the fitness of the University." Some were bitter: "The most severe and unfair criticisms that I have heard, *or heard of,* anywhere in the state against professional education in the University of Tennessee has been made on the campus and in the classrooms of the University by members of the University faculty."[31]

The administration was adamant, and, after token protests, the education faculty accepted the inevitable and attempted to salvage as much as they could. In addition to the twenty-seven hours required for certification, the educationists proposed that nine hours of education be placed on the liberal arts elective list and that juniors and seniors who wanted to take additional hours in education, with the permission of their department heads, be allowed to take three graduate courses. Duggan made the most bizarre, and least likely to be accepted, suggestion—that Education Dean Thackston be appointed dean of liberal arts.[32]

President Morgan made it clear to correspondents outside the university that the College of Education was a college in name only: "The University of Tennessee has an organization which, in lieu of a better name, we speak of as the College of Education, but it is in no sense the type of College of Education that predominates in the higher institutions of this country." The faculty of the college comprised all the professors in the university; a plan that, Morgan argued, reconciled subject matter and pedagogy and interested all professors in public school needs. He told a correspondent that the arrangement helped "to overcome the prejudice that some Liberal Arts Professors have had against pedagogy." This organization led to the phrase that would be used for a number of years: the College of Education was the "clearing house" for teacher education in the University.[33]

Hoskins, who became president of the university in 1934, remained dissatisfied with the College of Education. His correspondence with potential education deans and professors throughout the 1930s indicates a desire for further restructuring. At a trustees meeting in 1937, Hoskins made his continuing dissatisfaction known. He told the board that one of the most important issues that they faced was "whether or not the College of Education should take its place in the educational system of the State, in keeping with the position of the University, or whether it should assume a status of mediocrity." In 1943, he initiated another controversy over reorganization of the college, an issue examined in chapter seven.[34]

Elementary Education in the University of Tennessee

The education professors chafed at the agreement with the teachers colleges that prohibited the university from preparing elementary school teachers. They never liked it, and they were ever eager to subvert it. During the 1920s and 1930s, they campaigned unceasingly to abrogate it, basing their campaign on two major arguments: The elementary schools of Tennessee were in miserable condition and the university was obligated to improve them, and other teacher-training institutions in the state were expanding their missions and curricula and thus not respecting the accord.[35]

Using almost any criteria, the first case was not hard to make. Tennessee elementary schools in the 1920s and 1930s were simply terrible. The state commissioner of education reported in 1930 that over 40 percent of the teachers had only a high school education or less; only about 7 percent had graduated from college; and only 20 percent had professional certificates. Duggan, in his continuing campaign to show that teachers colleges were insufficient in training elementary teachers, prepared a chart to display the dismal statistics:

	Number	Percent of Total
College graduates	740	.07
Three years in college	481	.05
Two years in college	1,494	.15
One year in college	4,006	.40
High School graduates	2,336	.24
Three years in high school	289	.03
Two years in high school	278	.03
One year in high school	91	.01
Elementary school only	217	.02

These statistics were for white teachers. Racial segregation so pervaded the society, including the university, that educationists rarely noted the existence of African-American elementary schools, much less their condition.[36]

Even in Knox County, the home of the university, a year of college or normal school was not required until 1927 for newly hired elementary teachers; before that high school graduation and one summer session of teacher training was sufficient. Even this low new standard was quite controversial, and it passed only after "warm discussion." Outside of cities, more than half of the white elementary schools were one-room schools, and only about 20 percent had three or more teachers. The average school building was estimated to be worth $3,300 and the equipment in it less than $400. Elementary teachers' salaries averaged $606, almost exactly half of high school teachers' average of $1,213. In a report to Thackston and Morgan, Duggan described what the statistics meant for children:

> It is obvious that the average county elementary school child is taught by a poorly-trained, under-paid teacher who is hampered by a poor building and little or no equipment. . . . The student responds to this environment by dropping out of school at an early age, or, if he continues in school, he shows his lack of interest by a poor daily attendance record and by the fact that he is over-age.

In the view of the educationists, the university had a legal and moral responsibility to respond to these dismal conditions. The shopworn slogan (which often seemed to be used as a mantra by the education faculty) was chanted again: The university is "the legal Head of the Public School System of the State." And the elementary school "presents the outstanding problem of the system."[37]

As usual, Duggan led the campaign, marshaled arguments in support of the university's responsibility toward elementary schools. He decried the creation of "artificial barriers" among the levels of public schools. Instead of integration, he lectured, "disintegration has taken place until it is not unusual to find those who believe that the interests of elementary, secondary, and higher training are inimical." Using a drug metaphor, he wrote that research and extension were the responsibility of the university, and the elementary school was the obvious place to "inject" programs for social and economic uplift "into the veins of the state and so quicken the pulse of its people." The elementary schools, Duggan proclaimed, are the centers "of the social, moral and intellectual life of the commonwealth. . . . They are the one common meeting place of all people. They represent the stronghold from which every movement for a better civilization must sally forth." Obvi-

ously then, elementary schools were not only worthy objects of research but were the chief dissemination point for university researchers to the people. Furthermore, he warned, the university could not
ignore the quality of elementary schools and still expect students to be
prepared for the university classroom. Trading the drug metaphor for
an electrical one, he argued that as a "current is worthless if the circuit
is broken, so the loss of transforming power if the university and elementary schools are not in the proper relationship to each other."[38]

Duggan also appealed to his liberal arts colleagues. The university
was the best place to train teachers of all levels, he wrote, because
"the fundamental prerequisite of any teacher should be a liberal education." Only a university has offerings "rich enough" to produce a truly
educated teacher. Alas, lesser institutions had been given that responsibility, but, at least, the university was responsible for training elementary principals and supervisors. And that function, Duggan argued, could go far in solving a major problem of elementary schools.
Because even teachers who had been well trained, he reported, too
often failed to teach as well as they knew how; they followed "the line
of least resistance." He told Morgan that he had asked many young
teachers why they were not teaching the way they were trained. Their
usual answer, he complained, was "'It's too much trouble. The people
don't like new ways,' or some such answer." The real problems, he
argued, were poor administration and improper supervision, problems that the college could do something about.[39]

President Morgan was sympathetic to the arguments that the university should educate elementary teachers, and he rejected the popular notion that scholarship was not essential in elementary teachers.
As early as 1922, Morgan had endorsed university elementary teacher
education in a sentimental talk at the Tennessee State Teachers' Association meeting:

> The little child, the child in the grades, is most impressionable. The earliest
> impressions are the most lasting and have most to do in character forming in
> life. This little child, therefore, should be in the hands, or under the direction,
> of our most efficiently trained people. The four-year college training above
> the high school is not too good for his teacher and less training would be
> unsatisfactory for the supervisors of his teacher.[40]

But Morgan was unable to change the policy. As late as 1932, he
was clarifying the limited and ambiguous role of the university in elementary education: preparation of supervisors, elementary princi-

pals, and the "investigation of the relation of the elementary community and elementary education to the whole program of state education." Despite school principals' entreaties about the needs of teachers, he could not foresee the university creating courses "designed specifically for elementary teachers."[41]

Traditionally, southerner educators attempted to maintain at least a facade of cordiality in the face of conflict. And much of the conflict between educationists at the university and in other Tennessee institutions over the training of elementary teachers was civil, at least publicly. In arguing for university training of elementary teachers, Duggan wrote that he would make "no reference . . . to the service of the splendid group of teachers' colleges and other higher institutions" that had for years provided the elementary teachers for Tennessee. Privately, educational politics was much rougher, although university administrators attempted to keep peace between their educationists and the state teachers colleges. In 1928, President Morgan prefaced a letter of concerns about the College of Education with the recognition that "for years there has been an imaginary or otherwise jealousy existing between the Teacher Training Institutions" and the university education faculty.[42]

But the university administration itself was often in contention with these institutions. The administration and trustees often considered and treated the state normal schools and their successors, the state teachers colleges, as inferior institutions. In 1932 when the creation of a statewide board of trustees for the normal schools was under discussion, university trustee Paul J. Kruesi wrote that he was "just wondering whether, if we dignified this string of schools by the creation of a new Board of Trustees" the result would not be "bigger and better Normals," the result of "logrolling and pap."[43]

Conflict over transfer credit exemplified the attitude of superiority by the university. Although President Brown Ayres in 1914 had agreed to allow two years of credit toward bachelor's degrees, presidents of the normal schools throughout the 1920s accused the university of reneging. For example, in November of 1920, President Sidney G. Gilbreath of East Tennessee State Normal School wrote Dean Hoskins, attempting to clarify the university's position on transfer credit with normal schools and adding, perhaps as an oblique warning, that "Peabody College accepts our students, giving credit in the College of credits worked out here, Quarter for Quarter." Over a month passed before Gilbreath received a response. President Morgan explained that

Hoskins had been too ill to respond and suggested, somewhat ominously, that he thought that it would be "better to have a committee visit the Normal and go over the whole situation with you." Gilbreath was not at all pleased and fired back a letter the same day: "Please do not think I am impatient or impertinent." But he insisted that the issue had been discussed before in person and in correspondence and he wanted an answer. "I know how busy you are, of course," he concluded, "but may I not urge that we have your decision on this matter which is of importance to a number of prospective students at the University, including my own son." Only limited underdivision credit for liberal arts courses was granted to the normal school students.[44]

The university administration was thin-lipped when they perceived the normal schools as going beyond their proper mission of training elementary teachers, and differentiation of mission became more of an issue when they were designated state teachers colleges in 1925. (In the 1920s, normal schools across the country were being converted into state teachers colleges.) A staff writer for the *Knoxville Journal* complained that the teachers colleges were acting as "local universities," directly competing with the University of Tennessee. An East Tennessee state senator, W. P. Monroe, was more explicit. He complained that the teachers colleges "under the function of training teachers" were training Tennesseans, and "persons from other states, for many vocations, professions, and callings" in direct opposition to the legal functions of the colleges.[45]

The administrations and faculties of the new teachers colleges were not content educating only elementary teachers, and Hoskins, among others, sensed a conspiracy by them and their supporters in the legislature to expand their mission. In July 1934 Hoskins wrote to Trustee Kruesi, asking if the law renaming the normal schools did not explicitly state that their function was to train elementary school teachers. Kruesi questioned Walter D. Cocking, chairman of the Tennessee Educational Commission, who confirmed that the original law had placed such a limitation on the teachers colleges; but, in a revision of the law, "the word 'elementary' was dropped out." The ever-suspicious Hoskins had the change in the law confirmed by the dean of the Law School. Hoskins glumly (and correctly) concluded that the university had been outmaneuvered and that the teachers colleges could not be put back into the normal-school box.[46]

Kruesi immediately wrote to Hoskins, indicating that he should not be so pessimistic, that it was an ideal time to reach an agreement between the teachers colleges and the university. A week later Kruesi was less optimistic and considerably more testy:

> Personally, I have long believed and as long urged on your predecessor that to stop the bickering and suspicion as between the state's own institutions of high learning, they ought to get together or have their heads bumped together. I believe that if you and the Presidents of the other institutions were locked up for even a day, not necessarily in jail, although that could be considered, but somehow shut up with no outside interference, a modus vivendi would be arranged.

Any pretense of differentiation of mission in undergraduate teacher education was about over. In June 1938, the university's curriculum committee approved a course of study for educating elementary teachers at UT.[47]

Teacher Training in High Schools

A major argument against teacher training in the normal schools and teachers colleges was that they lacked the rich academic resources of the university. Ironically, most of the teachers in the rural schools of Tennessee, to the degree that they received any formal training at all, were not trained in normal schools—but in high schools. In 1922, according to an advocate of teacher training in high school, Mabel Hardin, there were only 22 graduates of normal schools teaching in the 3,500 one-room schools of Tennessee. In contrast, about 300 graduates of the one-year training program in 40 teacher-training high schools were teaching in such rural schools. And a total of 1,162 high school graduates were "entitled to elementary school teaching certificates."[48]

In 1917 the Tennessee legislature authorized the granting of elementary-school-teachers' certificates to graduates of teacher-training courses in high schools; and in 1921 it provided funds (a minimum of $500 per high school) to help support such courses in "one high school for white pupils and one for colored in each county." Much of the opposition to these high school teacher-training programs came from the educationists in the university. As usual, Duggan's strident voice was heard:

> Beginning in 1917, when a "joker" in an educational bill authorized the certification of high school graduates to teach in the county rural schools, the state has been rioting in an orgy of certification of boys and girls—chiefly

girls—to teach in the county schools. Now there are literally thousands of incompetents in the state holding teachers certificates.

Hoskins, who rarely agreed with educationists on anything, was of a like mind on the high school program, calling it "a great mistake." In 1935, he wrote Claxton and complained that teacher training in high schools had "done untold damage to the cause of education and set back the movement started by the General Education Act of 1909 more than anything else that has been done in the State."[49]

The high school teacher-training programs had advocates. In her 1923 master's thesis, Hardin defended the high school teacher-training programs vigorously. Her chief argument was that normal school graduates were *too* cosmopolitan and well educated to teach in the rural elementary schools. Normal schools (much less universities) tended to train teachers "away from country life instead of for it." She maintained that teacher training in county high schools would lead to "loyalty to the county and to the County Superintendent."[50]

Teacher Education in Hard Times

The stock market crash enormously exacerbated economic suffering, but most Tennesseans had been living in hard times for years. During the early 1930s, over 100 banks failed in the state, including East Tennessee's oldest and largest, East Tennessee National Bank. And, worse for the university, which had over $400,000 deposited there, Holston National Bank also collapsed. The crash hit university students hard. The university loaned money to students who had lost their college funds in local banks that crashed in order to help them survive the 1930 Fall term. Five times the number of students made application for part-time work by the fall of 1930 compared to the year before. Many male students took baby-sitting jobs ("hired out as 'nurses'"), and a number of students sold their blood for transfusions. In a bit of hyperbole, the Dean of Men, Colonel F. M. Massy, compared the newly poor UT students who were working part-time, doing their own laundry, and living in basements to Civil War soldiers "reared in the lap of luxury who gladly did without food and proper clothing in an effort to lead the armies to victory. . . . There are just as many examples of supreme sacrifice during financial depression as there are during a military crisis."[51]

Enrollment fell by 25 percent from 1931 to 1932; especially hard hit were women students. In a surprising straw poll before the 1932 election, the normally conservative and Republican students gave Roosevelt a two-to-one margin over Hoover; Norman Thomas, the Socialist candidate, received almost 5 percent of the vote.[52]

In their study of education and the Great Depression, David Tyack and his colleagues remind us that the impact of the depression on education was uneven, and, with devalued dollars, some institutions prospered. However, the depression was a terrible time for the University of Tennessee. In 1933, with the depression worsening and state warrants of $5,000,000 unpaid, legislators proposed bills to abolish all normal schools and teachers colleges and to sell their property. Some rural legislators argued that the state university should go as well; and there was a strong move to abolish its state appropriation entirely. That didn't happen, but in 1933 the university appropriation was slashed by 50 percent; some faculty members were released, and the rest took pay cuts. President Morgan's salary, which had once been $12,000, was cut to $3,000. The budget of the college shrank from almost $41,000 to $26,445 in one year.[53]

Still popularly called the Summer School of the South by many teachers, the summer session offerings were soon reduced. A relic of the Summer School of the South was classes in elementary education, one way that they were bootlegged into the university. In 1932, much to the chagrin of local teachers, the university dropped elementary education courses from the curriculum. Teachers in Knox and surrounding counties unsuccessfully but "most earnestly" petitioned university officials to rescind their decision. The tradition of importing summer school faculty from across the nation, also surviving from the Summer School of the South, was discontinued in 1933. Jobs were reserved for local professors.[54]

During this time of retrenchment in the university, the College of Education went on the offensive. The college faculty conducted a vigorous campaign to prove their worth to the university and to the state. Numerous new programs were started by the college during the 1930s, including:

1. An elaborate, statewide program in health education established in 1933 with support from the Commonwealth Fund of New York.
2. An extracurricular curriculum: to prepare prospective teachers to train extracurricular leaders. The curriculum was to train Boy Scout, Girl Scout, and HI-Y leaders, among others. It

began with great fanfare in the student newspaper, and ninety students had enrolled by Fall quarter 1933. It was just the sort of thing to cause professorial eyebrows in other colleges to rise.

3. An exceptional children curriculum in special education, offering both a bachelor's and a master's degree.

4. A curriculum in business education with undergraduate and graduate degrees.

5. An audiovisual education program, "because of the rapidly increasing use of sensory aids (moving pictures, and so forth) to learning."

6. A curriculum laboratory, open year-around for teachers and school administrators to assist "in their own particular problems and situations." It was designed to function somewhat like teacher centers of a later time.

7. A Child Study Center that offered "clinical services" to public schools and other agencies anywhere in reading and behavior problems.

8. A Psychological Clinic, under the auspices of the college, for UT students.

9. A statewide testing program in academic subjects for high school students.

10. A Weekly Youth Radio Hour broadcast by station WSM in Nashville.[55]

Inaugurated in 1938, the radio program was surprisingly popular. It was designed to "deal with youth's problems" and to meet their needs whether they were in school or out. Thackston said that its aim was to help youth "understand the significance of what he learns in school, sees in the movies, hears over the radio, reads in books and periodicals, and what his friends and associations may tell him." With an ear to Franklin Roosevelt's popular radio "fireside chats," Thackston told his radio audience that we want to "sit down with you for a friendly chat about the things which interest and stimulate you. We should like you to feel that we are not simply a voice coming over the radio—but rather, that we are a group of companions who very genuinely share in your everyday life and thought."[56]

The College of Education could expand during a period of economic retrenchment because of the skills of the faculty as promoters of themselves and their programs. Always on the defensive in the university, professors of education courted allies among public school teachers and administrators, politicians, foundation officials, and the press. For generations, educationists in the university had spent more time than other professors (with the possible exception of agriculturists) lobbying the powerful; they were good at it. As an example, Duggan spent most of his time off-campus, campaigning on behalf of the college and sending a "continuing stream of letters and memoranda" to public officials. The interests of the college were enhanced when he became state Commissioner of Education in 1935.[57]

New Deal agencies with federal dollars represented new possibilities for UT educationists to pursue. Tyack and his colleagues discussed animosity of school people toward the New Deal, quoting the executive secretary of the NEA in 1935: "The New Deal was a Raw Deal for Public Schools." The conservative administrators of the university and its College of Education were ideologically opposed to the New Deal. President Hoskins was a longtime foe of liberalism of all stripes, and Dean Thackston had some criticisms of the kinds of programs that would make up the New Deal. In a 1931 speech to the Tennessee Teachers Association, he argued that "the solution of today's economic and social problems lay in education, not in loans to farmers, doles to bread lines, farm boards and presidential special committee reports." Their positions were politically popular with East Tennesseans, who were overwhelmingly Republican.[58]

But, as the depression worsened, ideological considerations were overwhelmed by the need for help in a struggle for survival. In 1933, people lined up for miles to see Roosevelt when he visited Knoxville, the city's greatest celebration since armistice. And in 1937 the student New Deal Party swept all student offices; the student newspaper announced that the New Dealers had "the largest majority ever enjoyed by a political party on the campus."[59]

The popularity of the New Deal was not lost on the administration; besides, the federal government was the source of desperately needed funds. The College of Education incorporated the New Deal into the summer school curriculum. In 1935, the college offered courses on "social and economic problems of today [including] the work of the New Deal, the TVA, and other developments." Following a long tradition of the summer school for teachers, entertainment and excursions were promised: "Trips will be made to the Smoky Mountains National Park, Norris Dam, and other points of interest in East Tennessee. There will also be parties, tea dances, watermelon cuts, and the like."[60]

Dean Thackston requested that students and their parents lobby their senators and congressmen to pass the "Federal Aid to Education

Act of 1939." In a front-page story in the *Orange and White*, Thackston marshaled support for the bill with a number of arguments that included tugging at heartstrings: "It will be the death knell of the little one-room shacks with their ruddy, tin stoves and makeshift desks. Nor will the pupils have to try to study with dirty dog-eared books under the supervision of a teacher hardly out of high school." The bill was defeated, and federal aid to elementary and high schools had to wait a quarter of a century.[61]

The College of Education had successes and failures in attempts to get funds from existing New Deal programs. The letter below from Hoskins to the United States Commissioner of Education suggests the inauspicious beginning of a training school for unemployed teachers supported by the Federal Emergency Relief Administration:

> A few days since, a lady came into my office representing the Federal Government, and stated that she had been advised that the University of Tennessee would be selected as a training school for unemployed teachers with a view to placing them throughout the state to conduct the work of adult teaching. I have misplaced her name. Since she left, I have had no definite instructions about what to do in making preparations for this training school.

The Federal Emergency Relief Administration reestablished contact, and twenty-eight out-of-work teachers from four southern states enrolled in the program in 1934. They received $18 a week while in training to be adult educators. They enrolled in what could be called a depression curriculum: courses in the organization and methods of adult education, labor problems, economic history, and "The New Deal."[62]

The most notable failure of the college was with the Works Progress Administration (WPA). As indicated before, the college administration and faculty wanted a demonstration or laboratory school. They had been campaigning for it relentlessly since establishment of the Department of Education in 1902. The WPA provided for two buildings on the main campus and a good deal of construction on the agricultural campus. But, despite an elaborate campaign, the College of Education was unable to get funding for a combination college building and laboratory school.[63]

The college finally got a demonstration school in a joint venture with the New Deal agency that it had its closest and longest relationship with, the Tennessee Valley Authority. The TVA provided funds and personnel for support of both conservation education courses and the statewide health education program. The most sustained collaboration was the establishment of "a model progressive school" jointly sponsored by TVA and the College of Education at the new town of Norris, the site of the first TVA dam. The demonstration school was "used for observation and experimentation by faculty and students of a program extending from the nursery school through adult education." "As supervisor of the Norris School," the *Knoxville News-Sentinel* gushed, "the College of Education has its hands on another fine laboratory. The college has made some of its neatest discoveries at Norris in new methods of handling pupils." Some of the reforms at Norris School anticipated current education reform movements. Instead of student teaching, an internship program was established, using only post-baccalaureate students. And serious attempts were made to give teachers more influence in administering the school "rather than leaving all that responsibility and initiative to the principal." The local newspaper called such "progressive" administration one of "Dean Thackston's pet aspirations."[64]

In the various reports, position papers, and assorted defenses of the College of Education in the 1920s and 1930s, little attention was given to research and publication. But, as the authors of the standard history of the university point out, research and writing were "not highly prized" in the university generally at the time. Among a handful of scholars known for their research and publications by the end of the 1930s, they list education professor Rhea Boyd Parsons. In the biennial report from 1932 to 1934, Thackston uncharacteristically devoted considerable attention to research, perhaps because Hoskins had required an accounting of the faculty research activities. In addition to numerous school surveys, Thackston reported (without specifics) that several professors had written books and many had published periodical articles. He strongly endorsed scholarship by the faculty, proposing that every professor should be required to take one quarter off without pay every two years for research and writing. "To do this," he wrote, "better salaries will have to be provided so that the man will be financially able to take the quarter off."[65]

Part of the problem was that teaching loads were heavy at Tennessee in the 1920s and 1930s. Even Dean Thackston taught twelve hours per week in 1925. Frank C. Smith, academic dean in 1938, inquired into the teaching load of the college's most activist professor, Duggan. Thackston reported that Duggan had been scheduled for twelve three-hour courses over the past three quarters, including Saturday courses in the fall and spring. In addition, he was directing two school surveys, eight or ten building surveys at the request of the state Department of Education, and supervising graduate students who were conducting eight additional surveys of elementary school buildings. He was also lobbying the legislature for the Tennessee Education Association, including direct "responsibility for the state educational campaign in the Third Congressional District." "I believe you will find this to be a complete outline of Mr. Duggan's work," Thackston concluded, "and that you will understand fully just how he is spending his time for the university." Conspicuously absent from the report was mention of research or writing. The only pieces in the "Faculty Publications File" of the university for Duggan are two three-page mimeographed pieces, "Suggestions for Developing a Curriculum Program for the State of Tennessee," January 14, 1931, and "A Program of Action for Tennessee," October 24, 1935.[66]

There were other education professors at the university during the period who were well known for their research and publications. In addition to Parsons, the best known outside of Tennessee was probably educational psychology professor Joseph E. Avent, who came to the university in 1923 and served on the faculty for twenty-five years. Among other books, his multivolume "The Teacher Education Series" went through eight editions and was used as textbooks in over 250 colleges. The indefatigable Avent organized and managed the state testing program for all students in Tennessee in 1936, testing hundreds of thousands of students annually.[67]

Chapter 6

Outreach: The State Is Our Campus

The social reform thrust of the education faculty was congruent with President Harcourt Morgan's vision of the university. In 1925, the "Prosperity and Progress" edition of the *Knoxville Sentinel* included a lengthy column by Morgan with the headline, "University of Tennessee Today Has Whole State of Tennessee as Campus." "The State Is Our Campus" became the motto of the university and was reprinted on publications and signs for decades. According to Morgan, the only limit on the role of the university was the needs of people, and it was sometimes necessary to help people understand their needs: The university "must be a prophet to its people." In his view, the university, through teaching, research, and service, should touch every aspect of people's lives in the state, not just the intellectual but the economic, social, and political as well. Morgan expounded his position in his 1930 commencement address, "The State University In Public Relations." He seemed to give carte blanche to educationists as he indicated the responsibility of public educators. Their job was not just teaching students, it was influencing communities.[1]

The education faculty, who had long devoted much of their time to off-campus activities, were delighted with the mandate. Knoxville newspapers in the 1920s and 1930s included numerous articles about presentations of the education professors to teachers workshops, PTA meetings, service clubs, school commencements, and other audiences. But, more important, there was no end of things that the education faculty needed to do to directly influence the quality of schooling. In their plan for 1930, "Immediate Projects to be Undertaken by the College of Education," the faculty indicated that it was imperative that they make one-week surveys of high schools in every county, getting "suggestions, solutions, and remedies back to the counties as soon as possible." They needed to prepare a syllabus for each course taught in high schools with suggestions of teaching methods for them. And, as if this were not enough, they also needed to help the state department of education supervise high schools and call group conferences of high school principals and teachers in each county.[2]

The educationists seemed tireless. In November 1932, the *Orange and White* wrote of "another very busy season" of the education faculty who exemplified the campus motto: "The State is our campus":

> Last Saturday Dean Thackston spoke before a large group of Sevier County teachers. On the same date Dr. A. D. Mueller delivered an address to the Maury County Teachers' Association in Dandridge while Dr. Phillips is in Memphis throughout this week teaching classes in extension work and attending a meeting of the West Tennessee Educational Association. Prof. Duggan is at present instructing extension classes three days per week in Cleveland and Chattanooga. . . . Miss Zella Hines . . . has just returned from a parent-teacher meeting in the mountains of Sevier County.[3]

The School of Education faculty regularly brought public school officials to the campus for instruction and indoctrination. For two weeks in 1922, as an example, it sponsored "the largest gathering of school superintendents ever held in this state" (87 superintendents and 50 boards of education members). U.S. Commissioner of Education John Tigret, who addressed the superintendents several times, was one of a number of distinguished speakers. The superintendents' conference was held at the university annually for a number of years.[4]

Every fall for seventy-five years, the East Tennessee Education Association held its convention on the UT campus. Thousands of teachers attended annually, largely because membership in the association and attendance at the conference were required by school officials. Thackston required the college faculty to join and to attend meetings of the association, although a few slipped through the net. The university dismissed classes during the conference, and classrooms and auditoriums were used for addresses and workshops by UT and imported faculty. Some of the best-known educationists in the country addressed the conference, including Charles H. Judd of the University of Chicago and William Heard Kilpatrick and William C. Bagley of Teachers College, Columbia. "Co-eds" and later Boy Scouts acted as ushers and took attendance by punching the tickets of teachers who often preferred using their trip to Knoxville for shopping and visiting beauty parlors than listening to the speakers, however distinguished. The *Knoxville Sentinel* reported that the stores were overcrowded since many teachers waited until the convention to shop, and the beauty parlors, swamped with demands "for waves, marcel and permanents," had to hire extra operators. On the other hand, even in the Depression when many were suffering pay cuts and sometimes received no pay at all, they came in large numbers. Six thousand teachers, many "wearing old clothes and old coats," attended in 1931.[5]

College of Education professors were also active in the Tennessee State Teachers Association (later Tennessee Education Association), making up a sizable part of the program and sometimes serving as presidents. Here again, membership was required. President Morgan assured state educators that "we have insisted that all of the folks associated with the College of Education should become active members of the State Teachers' Association."[6]

The Country-Life Project

During the 1920s and 1930s, the major outreach of the college was the country-life project, a vigorous statewide movement to uplift country life and improve rural schools. President Morgan was the father of the movement in Tennessee. He conceived it; he persuaded the university trustees to finance it; he selected the education faculty to organize it and do the day-to-day work; and he campaigned for it throughout the state. Part of the agricultural establishment that competed for almost a century with the liberal arts faculty for control of the university, he was Dean of Agriculture when the trustees selected him as president in 1919. Although popular with farmers and other rural interests, he was considered too much of a hayseed in the university. Some of the trustees agreed that they would have to "dress him up" to make him presidential.[7]

Morgan shared the premise of the national country-life movement: Every generation of Americans needs to fetch virtue from the countryside in the form of farm boys and girls, and the isolation and hardships of farming should be relieved by modern technology. Active in the American Country Life Association's Committee on Rural Social Organizations, he cautioned that the committee was not approaching its study of the relationship of social and economic factors to rural progress "quite the right way." He argued for a regional approach, pointing out that the "social, economic, and educational life" of southerners, including those not in but on the periphery of the cotton belt, was "molded very largely by the backbone production of cotton." He helped organize regional conferences on rural life and was the standard-bearer for the movement in Tennessee, regularly preaching the "gospel of rural education" to meetings of the state Country Life Conference and the Rural Education Association.[8]

The national leaders advocated better roads and mail service; Morgan understood the difficulties of constructing roads in the isolated valleys and hollows of the Cumberlands and Appalachia. His answer was rural electrification: "copper wires can be extended into every nook and corner." This was good thinking from the man who was to become a member of the first board of directors of the Tennessee Valley Authority. Morgan spoke the language of the country-life movement in the style of a southern evangelist. In 1927, he concluded an address before the Southern Division of the National Electric Association with this appeal:

> All over the land the cry is going up: "Save the rural population!" . . . Save the rural population! Nothing will save the rural population unless we make accessible to the country people the conveniences and the means for the more abundant life now enjoyed by the urban dweller. No cry of "back to the land," no exhortation from press or pulpit will avail. But I say again, the salvation of country life lies in the magic of the strands of copper wire. . . . God speed the day when into every village and hamlet this broad southland over, your lines and your service shall penetrate![9]

In Tennessee, as in the national movement, there was a kinship between university reformers and progressive-minded churchmen who despaired of the rural church that "still clung to a narrow emphasis on doctrine and on outworn orthodoxy." Morgan supported the efforts of the reform-minded mainline churches. He corresponded with John McDowell, secretary of the Board of National Missions of the Presbyterian Church U.S.A., on country life; but he was most active with the Rural Life Commission of the Holston Conference of the Methodist Church, his own church. He spoke at the annual conference several times on the work of their Rural Life Commission and was addressed by their superintendent of rural work in formal correspondence as Brother Morgan. In 1928 he helped organize an interdenominational short course on rural life for rural ministers, "not to solve the farmers' problems but to sympathize and confer with him." But he usually demanded direct action, not sympathy. The general secretary of the General Sunday School Board of the Methodist Episcopal Church, South, after hearing a presentation by Morgan, looked to a union of Jesus and the University of Tennessee to lead a social gospel crusade to regenerate country life and the country church:

> To the extent that religion and religious teaching has been thin, unsocial,
> purely individualistic, overlooking all of those matters that go to make up the
> complete life of the people has it lacked the social-mindedness of Jesus and
> has it failed to join hands with other forces such as the work of the State
> University of Tennessee in helping to solve the problem of our rural life.[10]

But the institution in which the university would place most of its
faith, or at least its money, to uplift rural life was the public elementary school rather than the church. Morgan wrote Howard Odum of
the University of North Carolina that UT was going to work on "the
rehabilitation of the rural community through the rural elementary
school" or, he added, perhaps the rural school will be rehabilitated by
"a more prosperous rural community."[11]

Despite the crucial leadership of Morgan and token involvement of
the entire faculty, the rural life project in the university was an activity
of the School, later College of Education. The trustees organized the
Department of Rural Education in February 1922. Morgan appointed
Benjamin O. Duggan, long-time State High School Inspector in Tennessee, to head it. Surprisingly, Duggan lacked a college degree. "The
future of your position," Morgan wrote in his letter of appointment,
"will be based upon your getting your Bachelor's degree next summer
and following with a Master's degree as early as possible." He did as
requested, taking a master's degree with his own dean while department head. Duggan (known throughout the state as B.O.) was an excellent choice. Appointed because of his close relationships with school
administrators and teachers, he also had extraordinary energy, organizing ability, and barely concealed ambition. He ended his career as
Tennessee Superintendent of Public Instruction.[12]

The Department of Rural Education was to revive teacher education. The School of Education had fallen on hard times. The glory
days when teacher education at Tennessee considered itself a rival of
the University of Chicago and Teachers College, Columbia, were over.
Rockefeller money from the General Education Board, which had paid
for the department in the early years of the century, was going to less-
worthy causes elsewhere; and the Summer School of the South was a
casualty of World War I.

The objective of Duggan's new department was research, study,
and experimentation to "promote more satisfactory conditions in the
rural counties of Tennessee with special attention to the improvement
of educational, social, and economic conditions"—no mean task. The
means as well as the objective were typically administrative progres-

sive: efficiency in school administration, curriculum "readjusted" to meet the needs of the rural populace, and the establishment of the rural elementary school as a "community center." The original proposals said nothing about the training of teachers for rural schools. As discussed in the previous chapter, in an attempt to reduce conflict with the state normal schools, the university agreed not to train elementary school teachers—a major reason for the puny size of the School of Education. The rural education program not only gave the education faculty work to do in surveying, curriculum development, and community organization, it provided a backdoor for elementary teachers into the university. The normal school faculties were immediately suspicious. Morgan assured the elderly but active P. P. Claxton, soon to be president of Austin Peay Normal School, that he did not "assume" that the university should prepare rural elementary teachers but that it should design a rural life curriculum to recommend to institutions that did train them.[13]

Morgan was, however, already considering a proposal that he had received a month before from N. E. Fitzgerald, head of the Department of Agricultural Education, to create a two-year course to train teachers for "rural elementary one-room and consolidated schools." An elaborate proposal called for a demonstration school and the need for "a man and a woman" to train elementary teachers in "elementary science, agriculture, and homemaking." In October 1925, Morgan proposed that all who wished to prepare to teach in rural schools should enroll in the Agricultural Education Department of the College of Agriculture. Duggan responded with a stern letter to the president, giving his "deliberate" conclusions: "FIRST all the teacher-training should be done in the School of Education." He supported the contention in four closely argued pages that helped carry the day. As discussed in chapter 5, the education faculty parlayed its increased responsibility and growing activity into college status in 1926: "The establishment of the college was brought about by the demands made on the university in carrying out an extensive program for the improvement of all the rural schools, and especially elementary schools throughout the state."[14]

Morgan, an effective politician among farm people, campaigned actively for the rural education program. Duggan urged upon him a particularly strong propaganda effort among the county superintendents of schools, explaining that even though practically all supported the program, a good many of them were "only negatively sympathetic."

Morgan wrote to superintendents and principals throughout the state, recommending the rural education program as a defense against the "quackery in the world" that the ignorant "fall prey to politically, socially, economically, and sometimes religiously." In the fall of 1924, he wrote to a number of superintendents asking them to come to Knoxville in February to work for a master's degree in rural education. He assured them that if they attended spring and summer, they could take a degree in just one additional term. "We are prepared to give you the best work in rural education . . . of any institution in America," he promised. If the superintendents couldn't come, they were urged to send some of their "mature" elementary teachers.[15]

Morgan gave Superintendent Sue Powers of far-off Shelby County in West Tennessee an especially hard sell. In male-specific language, he urged this woman superintendent to support UT courses for solving the "biggest educational problem" in Tennessee and in the nation:

> In order to give emphasis to this problem we are making an effort this year to put 1,000 men in the Short Course during January. We are asking the County Superintendents to call the Principals of the rural schools together and assist in encouraging all your men not in school and others who may be available for the short course to attend during January. We are asking the banks to loan any young man sufficient money from $60.00 to $75.00—in order to insure his taking the course.

As an inducement to enter the rural education program, Morgan in 1924 began to offer loans up to $300 per year to qualified students who agreed to teach in rural elementary schools. A number of superintendents praised the university's efforts to train teachers for rural schools and upgrade rural life. The Robertson County superintendent endorsed the rural education program, complaining that most teacher-training schools ignored "the rural situation" that "really broadened the unspanned chasm between the urban mind and the rural mind." In closing his letter to Morgan, he wrote "that the University is doing more for the rural folk than has been done at any former time."[16]

Changes in the curriculum in rural education through the 1920s exemplified the transformation of the program from a reformist thrust directed at uplifting rural life to an elementary teacher education program indistinguishable from others across the country. From 1922 to 1925, the courses in rural education stressed the unique social institutions of rural communities and "the school as the central agency in the unifying of social forces." Duggan wanted teachers to understand that the problem of the rural school was "administrative rather than curriculum," because the solution was *complete consolidation.*" In the spirit of southern progressives, he warned that practical arts must be specially emphasized in rural schools. "It would be ideal if all our citizens could be able to appreciate the beautiful in all things," he observed, "but if they cannot have both the practical and the aesthetic in equal measure, then their major must be the practical." By 1926, the "Teaching Rural Life" courses had lost their social-foundations base and had become methods of teaching courses for the elementary science project described below, although the course titles were not changed until the 1928–29 catalog when they became a three-course sequence in "A Science Program For Elementary Schools." Periodic efforts were also made "to relieve the courses of the criticism that they are too easy."[17]

Rural Surveys

The progressive impulse was an impulse to survey, and the new Department of Rural Education joined enthusiastically in an orgy of surveying. President Morgan's proposal to the university trustees for the establishment of the department listed as its first function—"to study intensively rural school conditions in the State." The department quickly expanded its information-gathering beyond schools. The surveys were to make detailed examinations of all aspects of rural life so that programs leading to "improvement and readjustment" could begin. In typical, if unwarranted optimism, Duggan reported that the next step would be to use accumulated accurate and detailed information to prepare programs directed "toward the relief of unsatisfactory conditions."[18]

The reformers were unencumbered by doubts about how country folk ought to live—what their values and their behavior ought to be. The university administration and education professors had a long tradition of leadership in mainline Protestant churches in Knoxville (every large Presbyterian and Methodist Church in town seemed to boast of an education professor as an adult Sunday school teacher). The small, rural fundamentalist churches in which lay leaders shouted vivid images of hellfire and damned the leaders of the congregation in the next holler for misinterpreting the scriptures were not a good fit with the reformers' idea of the role of the country church in uplifting rural life. One of the organizational questionnaires used to conduct county educational surveys asked more questions about churches than about anything else:

1. What is the attitude of the ministers toward education?
2. Do they take an active interest in the school?
3. What recreations are provided by the churches?
4. What salary is paid each minister?
5. Do the churches take an active part in public school affairs? How?
6. Is there a spirit of co-operation among the churches of the community? How shown?

Another questionnaire asked if "the needs of the people" were being "met in religious leadership, vision and spiritual power," and if "fundamental policies of economic, social and religious living" were being "achieved and taught in the schools and from the pulpit."[19]

There was no discussion of the criteria by which researchers were to make judgments about the quality of religious leadership and life. Duggan's 1922 survey of Union County is instructive. Along with statistical information on the sixty churches in the county, he reported that six ministers "were said to advise the people as to economic, social and religious living." He concluded, however, that religious leadership in the county was generally "inadequate." In ten communities in Union County, the major difficulties in uplifting school and social life, he reported, were factors that had resulted from "church jealousies and consentious" [sic]. He feared that it would take at least a generation to unite the factions and that the only hope appeared "to be a more liberal and broadening education of the children."[20]

The surveyors were not hesitant in contrasting moral conditions in different communities, although, again, the criteria for making moral judgments were not explicit. They may not have been able to define it, but they knew immorality when they saw it. Duggan thought that, despite a good deal of moonshining, the "moral tone" of Union County was good except for two communities where dissatisfied leading citizens were working with the sheriff to eliminate the nefarious activities of local ne'er-do-wells. The research methodology of the surveys was tainted by selecting a "committee of citizens who are familiar with the conditions of the community" rather than a cross section of the populace. There is little reason to believe that poorer farmers in the hollers were heard from. Virtually all of the correspondence covering the surveys was with businessmen, attorneys, and school administrators— distinct minorities in rural Tennessee in the 1920s. Duggan assured President Morgan that these leading citizens could give accurate information or, at least, "approximate pretty closely."[21]

Duggan reported that the local populace was "glad to see us" and that, in a variant on boarding around, they were rarely charged for lodging and food, reducing expenses considerably. (Years later, in an interview with a Knoxville newspaper, Duggan told a different and better tale: he was shunned because of a rumor in the "hollows and ridges" that he was a revenue agent in disguise.) Letters in the archives indicate that communities throughout the state were eager to be surveyed. In a typical letter, the school superintendent of Monroe County requested a survey, reminding Morgan that the local board of education had passed two resolutions for a survey and that the Chamber of Commerce had endorsed the request, "in behalf of the business interests of the county." Some communities couldn't seem to get enough. The commissioner of education in the West Tennessee town of Jackson, which had previously been surveyed by Dean Thackston, wrote President Morgan that the citizens would have more confidence in a survey and recommendations for their schools (which they wanted "to be equal to any and second to none") if he, the president, would come to Jackson and spend "as long as necessary" to make recommendations. Morgan graciously responded that, unlike Thackston, he was not an expert in education, and that they needed a real scientific survey by a "competent expert."[22]

The surveys not only gave professors of education worthwhile work to do, it justified a sizable graduate program. Master's degree students, usually secondary school teachers, were granted a stipend and a degree for twelve months' work: the thesis was a county survey. The faculty did not pretend that it expected creative or original research. All followed the same formula, using the same instruments. In May 1926, Pikeville teacher Samuel Hixson wrote that he didn't have a summer job and would like an M.A. from the university. He offered to survey Meigs, Sequatchie, or Rhea County and wanted to know what Duggan thought of the "proposition." Duggan responded that his preference was for Meigs. "The report of this survey would be your thesis," Duggan assured him.[23]

It is difficult to convey the range and depth of the information sought in the surveys. Consider, as examples, questions about two quite different inhabitants—hogs and dentists:[24]

Number of Hogs in County:
(a) Relation of hogs to corn acreage
(b) Relation of hogs to mast range (Mountain Co.)
(c) Compare hog population 1910 with 1920
(d) Age and weight of marketing hogs
(e) Age and weight of killing hogs for home use

(f) Breeds of hogs in County—
     (Bacon
     (Lard
(g) Pure bred herds of County
(h) Study of methods of hog management as to
     1. Sanitation
     2. Pastures
     3. Self-feeders
     4. Home raising
     5. Purchase of feeder
(i) Method and recipe for home curing of meats

Number of Dentists in County:
(a) Their location as to population
(b) Ages and time of graduation
(c) Number per 5,000 population
(d) Number of commercial dentists
(e) Number of itinerant dentists
(f) Prevailing diseases
(g) Does health officer consider dentist
(h) Do dentists take part in medical society meetings
(i) School Dental Clinics
     (Elementary
     (Secondary

Educational statistics from the surveys gave a dismal picture of school conditions. In the first county surveyed, only one of the sixty-seven teachers was a college graduate, and forty-three had two years of high school or less; eighteen had attended only elementary school. When the questionnaire asked if the teachers were native born, it didn't mean in the United States but in Union County. Fifty-seven of the sixty-seven teachers were born in the County, most of them in the school district where they were teaching. Even more striking was the short tenure of the teachers; the average time that teachers had held their position was less than six months.[25]

The southern progressives had a particular concern with school toilets. The first county survey noted that thirty-one of the thirty-nine one-room schools had no toilets at all, eight had toilets for girls and only three for boys. Toilets that did exist appalled Duggan:

> The toilets which are provided are in almost every case poorly located and unsanitary in the highest degree. They are usually unprotected—even by a screen in front of the door. Apparently they are never cleaned out and no attempt is made so far as we could see to prevent the spread of disease from these sources of infection.[26]

Surveys were only the first step in the campaign to remake rural life; the education faculty consisted of would-be change agents. In 1923, after the first two county surveys, Union and Crockett, had been completed (there were eventually twenty-six), Thackston recommended to Morgan that the rural education faculty should go into each county and:

Meet representative citizens in every section of the county and explain the findings and the recommendations of the survey.

Ask for the appointment of the committees as suggested in the recommendations.

Call a meeting of these committees to discuss the problems arising from the survey.

Cooperate with the County Superintendent and Board of Education in putting on a county-wide campaign in the interest of the recommendations made.

Go before the County Board of Education and County Court in behalf of the recommendations.

Do everything possible in the county that will aid in advancing the county educationally and otherwise.

Have the findings of the survey thoroughly analyzed and published in bulletin form.[27]

"It would be manifestly unfair for the University of Tennessee to take credit for all the educational progress that has been made in Crockett County during the past three years," Duggan wrote modestly to Morgan in 1928, but he was willing to allow that the survey and recommendations of his department "materially contributed." And there had been remarkable successes. Four new consolidated schools had been built. One-teacher African-American schools had been reduced from twelve to two, and two new black schools had been built with Rosenwald Fund money. Two new white high schools had been built and another enlarged. The high school enrollment had grown by a third, and the number of high school teachers with college degrees had increased from three to fourteen. Five of the degreed teachers were from the University of Tennessee, Duggan proudly announced.[28]

In a *Knoxville Sentinel* interview on the results of the Union County survey, Duggan exhibited the same modesty that he had about Crockett County: "While it was my idea, I don't want any credit for what has been done." He said that the power of good examples was the main tactic for community uplift in Union County. They sent a first-class teacher from Knoxville to teach in the Plainview Community with the charge to "teach the best school she ever did and go into every home." Soon people were coming to her asking how they could improve their lives, according to Duggan. Before long they had built a new school and had remodeled the church so it would compare favorably with the school. Rural education instructor Zella Hines was sent into the community to talk to girls about home economics and making clothes, and soon their mothers came to learn as well. Clubs were organized with "trips to Knoxville to see how things are done." The ripple effect of "social gains," according to Duggan, went on and on. Houses, livestock, and crops were improved. Fairs, clubs, and other organizations resulted in "new social meeting ground"; and, as a result, many of the old factions were "wiped out."[29]

President Morgan received a steady flow of letters from Tennessee's "best people" lauding Duggan and the Department of Rural Education. A campaign of support for Duggan may be suspected. In December 1928, as an example, there was a flood of resolutions, letters, and other testimonials to Morgan from county officials, lawyers, businessmen, and school administrators extolling "the worthiness" of Duggan's work. If he had not "taken a hand in affairs in this county the past few years," the high school principal wrote, "Union county with its bitter political faction would have regraded educationally rather than made some remarkable progress as is the case." Without a campaign to solicit support for Duggan, the motivation of the Maynardville lawyer who wrote the following is obscure: "I am not familiar with all the work that has been done in this (Union) County by Professor Duggan, but I know that he has spent considerable time in the county, and the work done by him, of which I am familiar, appears to have been well worth while." Morgan's polite but unenthusiastic replies to the testimonials may indicate that he was aware of a campaign of support.[30]

In time the rural education professors ran out of communities to survey. But there were always new possibilities in worlds already conquered. Professor R. B. Parsons in 1928 proposed that some graduate students under his supervision survey adult education in "typical Tennessee communities." With a broad definition of education that would please cultural revisionist educational historians, he would have included, in addition to "formal systematic schooling," such activities as "informal reading, club work, attendance at lectures, travel and experimental projects." Although Parson's proposal was not accepted, the educationists found that they had not exhausted the possibilities for surveying; in the early 1930s county "administrative surveys" were conducted. The explanation for yet more surveys was that the educational surveys of the 1920s "gave little consideration to the administrative program."[31]

Rural Elementary School Science Project

In a 1933 memorandum, Duggan reflected on a decade's experience with the Department of Rural Education. He restated its ultimate objective, which was nothing short of educational, social, and economic transformation of the rural counties. If the faculty's faith that this could be accomplished ever wavered, they never acknowledged their doubts. In characteristic progressive fashion, Duggan wrote of the changes that were necessary in the schools to accomplish such a transformation: educational efficiency, including more effective administration of schools, and curriculum reorganization to meet more of "the needs of the people." The curriculum adjustment most needed, he announced, was a science program for the elementary schools in order to develop "an understanding appreciation of the application of science to everyday life" and to help the children understand how science could make "happier and more abundant" lives.[32]

Duggan indicated that the need for an elementary science curriculum became apparent when the survey results demonstrated the "utter ignorance" of the rural dwellers toward science. He was attempting to demonstrate the relationship between the surveys and educational policy. Actually, the science project and the surveys were planned from the time of the creation of the department. Romantic country-life advocates embraced science in schools in the hope of creating "an ideal rural civilization by allowing country folk to enjoy the comforts of modern technology." A science curriculum was, then, fundamental to the goal of maintaining "the social and political virtues of the agrarian past" while enjoying the material benefits of industrialization.[33]

Tennessee rural education leaders talked about "modernizing" their curriculum with the addition of an elementary science curriculum, but there is little evidence from extant documents that they had nostalgia or romantic notions about the virtues of rural living. As was true of the national leadership, they had rural backgrounds; but, unlike many of their counterparts elsewhere, they had remained close to the countryside and its people and did not blink when viewing the ugliness and despair in the lives of many in the Tennessee hills. Poverty, isolation, and ignorance of the outside world were, of course, more extreme there than in most other places. Too, there was little fear of rural depopulation. They produced children in abundance. Youth of the hills and valleys remained even when the economy couldn't support them, and, when they left, the mountain subculture often called them and their own children home later.

The dilemma of the country-life movement, according to William Bowers in *The Country Life Movement in America*, was "looking backward to a largely mythical Arcadia of simple rusticism and forward to a twentieth-century society in which farmers would need to rely on scientific efficiency and business practices to succeed." If Duggan and his colleagues recognized such a dilemma, they seemed untroubled by it. They were not only intent on bringing better technology and more efficient methods to families, but better values as well.[34]

For the first decade of the science project, reports and syllabi stressed that the objective was an "appreciation of the application of science to everyday life," not to teach the content of the various science disciplines. To help the rural teacher, who often lacked any science training at all, education professors Adams Phillips and Zella Hines, with help from President Morgan and members of the science faculty, prepared a 135-page mimeographed curriculum guide. It could be used independently from other training, but (and better from the viewpoint of the Department of Rural Education) it also brought teachers to campus to take "Teaching Rural Life," which used the curriculum guide as the basis of the course. It was also taught as an extension course to over 2,000 students, mainly teachers. President Morgan prepared an elementary-school children's lesson for the curriculum guide on "The Alphabet of Agriculture" that included suggestions to teachers such as: "The farm boy knows the pig and knows the corn; he can begin now to comprehend their relations."[35]

The department began supervising field testing of the program in 1926, giving Hines a full-time job in the field for most of the year. In 1930, a peak year, the field testing involved thirteen East Tennessee counties, 130 teachers, and 4,000 students. "All were enthusiastic in their approval," Duggan bragged to the state superintendent. In 1931, in order to introduce the program to schools in West Tennessee, the administration at the Junior College at Martin and the State Teachers College at Memphis agreed "heartily" to help introduce it into nearby counties. This expansion of the program into more urban counties, including Shelby County (Memphis), which had teachers using it in every school by the early 1930s, Knox (Knoxville), and Hamilton (Chattanooga) indicated that it had lost its special goal of uplifting rural life. By 1932, Duggan could report that the plan from the beginning was to start with "typically rural counties," which were most in need of help, and move progressively into "higher types" of urban counties. By the middle 1930s, the elementary science curriculum had become a more general "introductory study of the earth, sky, plants, and animals," and had lost much of its rural emphasis.[36]

Expansion of the program was curtailed by the depression. In October 1931, Morgan wrote to the superintendent of schools in Shelby County that university funds to help with the science project would have to be limited as "we are all in the same boat these days with reference to public funds . . . under a very great strain."[37] As a modernizing influence on rural East Tennessee, the effects of the science project were significant although unmeasurable. Eventually its impact, great or small, would be dwarfed by the imposition of the outside world through New Deal programs, particularly the TVA.

Rural Community Organization

The rural reformers seemed to have no fear of imposition. Accomplishment of their objectives, according to Duggan, required an "intimate" interrelation of the individual, the school, and the "collective homes" of the community. Professor A. W. Hobt added that "the work of making a community healthy, wholesome, and happy is not the responsibility of an individual. It is a state problem." The basic premise of the department work in the community was "the assumption that every human being, regardless of his condition, will try to help himself, provided he can be convinced that the thing proposed to him will promote either his own happiness or the happiness of those in whom he is personally interested or both."[38]

The method that the department proposed was characteristically progressive: small group meetings for "frank discussion" of school, home, and community problems; only in this way "can they learn their needs." Community workers had to convince rural people "to adopt a common interest for which all will work, thus forgetting their jealousies, their differences." Finally, the professors had to present a definite, joint goal to them. Duggan emphasized that the faculty alone could not uplift rural communities; active involvement of other organizations, particularly the Federation of Women's Clubs and the Parent-Teachers Association, was required. And both gave that kind of support to the program. Indeed, much of the community organizing activity was done under the auspices of the Parent-Teachers Association. The college courted and supported the state PTA by providing the leaders an office as well as courses to prepare them for the campaign to uplift rural life. The Knoxville newspapers reported that the agricultural dean gave the PTA leaders one of the most illuminating talks in these short courses on the topic: "What Country Women Would Have Their Boys Do."[39]

College faculty solicited cooperation with outside groups, encouraged local teachers to become "active leaders," and tried to convince rural folk that they were responsible for their own progress; but the work, Duggan insisted firmly, was to be "directed from the university." But, acquainted with progressive theories of social change, Duggan thought it best for requests for aid to come from citizens in the community rather than to be initiated by university faculty. And, Hines assured him that in her community work, she "made suggestions only when absolutely necessary."[40]

Professor Hines, who directed the "community organization" activities of the department, worked to improve child-rearing practices with the goal of helping parents and teachers "*cooperate intelligently*" so that each child could "grow physically, mentally, morally, and spiritually." In 1932, Hines gave the Tennessee Conference on Child Health the benefit of her long experience in working with parents. If they "only could and would make necessary adjustments," she explained, many faults of the home would be corrected and "public agencies would not have to correct the errors of parents" in child rearing. She was particularly firm in her denunciation of overindulgent parents who produced selfish children.[41]

Hines, who was also "chairman at large" of the state PTA Congress for Parental Education, worked at a frenzied pace. She organized more than 5,000 persons into a thousand study groups. Most were concerned with model child-rearing practices, but anything practical or ornamental was fair game for a lesson—better uses of leisure time, beautifying the home, storing winter vegetables, preparing "the poultry houses and flocks for winter," and redoing last winter's coat so that it would look new for another winter. In one year she visited fifty-seven communities, wrote 500 letters, and gave speeches to over 5,000 "hearers." Among her more popular talks were: "The Four-Square Child," "Guide Posts for Parents," "Memories," and "Finding One's Place."[42]

Health Education and the Commonwealth Fund

A state-wide health education program was another ambitious project directed at improving the lives of the poor rural people of Tennessee.

The program was originally funded by the Commonwealth Fund, endowed in 1919 to improve public health in America. The program in Tennessee was envisioned as a comprehensive program of rural uplift and involved the UT College of Education, teachers colleges, public schools, the state departments of education and health, medical societies, and Parent-Teachers Associations. With the coming of the New Deal, the Tennessee Valley Authority also became a major sponsor.

As was true of most of the philanthropic funds of the time, the Commonwealth Fund worked primarily through local elites to communicate with "ignorant locals." White women, particularly leaders in newly formed PTAs, were recruited as agents. The Fund worked closely with the public schools to teach nutrition, sanitation, and other good-health practices. At first, there was much resistance from the populace with rumors that children would be taken from their parents if they were brought to clinics and that people were to be "forcibly bathed." Despite more cooperation, even enthusiasm, from the African-American community for the project, much more attention was paid to whites, perhaps out of fear that failure to do more for white schools "would upset local racial sensibilities."[43]

William J. French, director of the Division of Public Health of the Commonwealth Fund, wrote to President Morgan in February 1930, announcing that Tennessee was the first state to receive support from the Fund for a comprehensive plan in public health and asking if the university would be interested in assisting Tennessee normal schools and other institutions in training teachers "in the purposes and methods of health education." Morgan responded to the "challenge." He pointed to the elementary science project as a parallel to what might be done in public health and explained that the College of Education could undertake effectively such a project since it included professors from all university departments (including the sciences). However, Morgan warned that the university would not undertake such a formidable task unless the Commonwealth Fund would support it for a "number of years." The proposal seemed to have been stillborn when French responded that the Fund would support the project for only three years and with more limited funds for an additional five. Morgan replied that, although he was enthusiastic about doing such good work, he was convinced that the time was insufficient for developing political support for government funding. "I should regard it a waste of your money and our energies to be forced to drop the work."[44]

Tennessee Department of Public Health Commissioner Bishop helped engineer a compromise in which the then significant sum of $32,000 was to be distributed on a sliding scale over eight years. "No university in the country, it is believed," the *Knoxville Sentinel* reported proudly, "has ever attempted a project of such wide scope. . . . While not 'socialization' of medicine, its intent is to raise the health welfare of the masses just as the New Deal is working to better them economically and socially."[45]

The College of Education was responsible for developing a public health education curriculum. "After these courses have been proven by experiment," the UT College of Education and every state teachers college was to require them for prospective elementary and secondary teachers. In 1931, the Commonwealth Fund authorized additional money to support four $300 graduate fellowships for teachers to assist in developing the curriculum. By the fall of 1932, the director of the Fund, Clarence Scamman, appeared to be a bit anxious about what was being accomplished. He wrote that he was impressed with Morgan's personal interest in the program but noted that the curriculum should have been developed and arrangements for incorporating it into teacher-education programs made. "I should be glad," he wrote, if "within the next ten days or two weeks" you would indicate the status of the program. In July 1933, a college representative took the three-volume curriculum project to the Commonwealth Fund office in New York.[46]

The aims of the curriculum were all-encompassing: "the introduction of a sound and efficient health education program into our educational system from top to bottom, one which will continue to increase health knowledge from the kindergarten through to the end of life." The content of the curriculum was also comprehensive, from prevention of infectious diseases and accidents (at home, at school, on the highway) to hot-lunch facilities to clean milk supply to "safe excreta disposal." The courses were tried in selected schools. Junior- and senior-level courses were established in the teacher-education curriculum. After some curriculum skirmishes in the university, including a debate about whether the health courses should be taught as "science" or physical education, the curriculum was finally approved. In Fall 1935, eighteen students enrolled in the first regular class of the college's Public Health Education course with the goal of training "teachers to teach health." Among the many lecturers in the original class were the state commissioner of health, the state commissioner of education, and the director of health of the Tennessee Valley Authority. TVA had agreed to jointly sponsor the project in 1935.[47]

In the end, not much came of the project. In 1941, only about a dozen students enrolled in university health-education classes. The state coordinator of health education, Robert White, wrote to Hoskins. He commented on the "pitiful enrollment" and indicated that the university had reached a crisis with the disappointed supporting agencies. "Permit me to say that my discouragement over the situation at the University does not obscure a ray of light. I have been up against an even more sombre sky 'on the hill,' and when I laid the situation before you the 'thin' but obstructing clouds passed away." Enrollment in the state teachers colleges was better—700 or 800 in 1941.[48]

Bowers asked a number of research questions about the assumptions, proposals, and methods of the country-life reformers. His answers for the national movement and the Tennessee experience are congruent. The reformers in Tennessee shared with those elsewhere an exalted faith in the power of schooling to transform rural life, in the survey as the major instrument to effect change, and in consolidation as the solution to the fundamental problems of rural schools. They shared progressive beliefs in the power of science and technology to uplift the quality of life for country folk and the need to replace what they viewed as a narrow fundamentalism in rural churches with a social-gospel theology.[49]

There were also some differences, at least in emphasis. The Tennessee reformers did not seem to be devoted to an agrarian myth; perhaps they had less to romanticize. There was less fear of urbanization and fewer concerns about depopulation. And there seemed less condescension by reformers toward farmers than Bowers found. The Tennessee reformers appeared to have remained closer to their rural roots and could talk of modernization as a native rather than as an outsider. In part, the more genial voices of the Tennessee reformers may be more a function of southern style, of the chivalrous manners still common in the 1920s, than of a distinct difference in attitude. Those most likely opposed to the "reforms" were isolated, clannish, and often illiterate. They didn't belong to the Grange, write letters to the editor, or send resolutions to Nashville. Alienated from the outside world, their best defense was to ignore it as much as possible, a kind of passive resistance often practiced by the powerless. The voices that are heard on the project tend to come from the county seats and market towns, from the Chambers of Commerce, the attorneys, the school administrators—"progressive" voices which favored modernization.

Viewed from its effects on the university, the rural education project was a success. It revitalized an ailing school of education. It gave the university, dismissed as a school for rich men's sons throughout its history, an opportunity to meet the criticism that it was "some foreign institution set apart for the benefit of the few . . . a drain upon the state . . . giving nothing in return." From the viewpoint of the progressive agenda of the reformers, allowing for exaggeration in their reports, there were significant successes: an elementary science curriculum was put in place across the state; some schools were consolidated in almost every county; rural schools, churches, and some homes were renovated. And, perhaps most important if more nebulous, public support was created for improving at least the most deplorable schooling conditions.[50]

The Depression helped to bring to an end the country life movement in Tennessee and to obscure its effects on the lives of people. By the early 1930s, financial difficulties were already curtailing the community work of the college. And the modernizing influences of the program were soon overwhelmed by the impact of New Deal agencies, the Civilian Conservation Corps, the Works Progress Administration, and, most important, the Tennessee Valley Authority.

Chapter 7

War and Postwar

World War II came to a campus that was southern, conservative, and relatively isolated. The enrollment for Fall 1940 was less than 3,500 students; only a handful were from the North. The social disruptions created by the war, particularly the stationing of soldiers from all over the country, changing roles for women, and, eventually, the coming of veterans of fights on battlefields and in bars around the world would irrevocably change the university. At the beginning of the decade, the university was still acting as a straight-laced parent to the students. At a social night (calling it a dance would have created an uproar in local fundamentalist churches) in 1940, Dean of Students Massey "brought the roof down" by announcing that "girls" living in dormitories could stay out until 10 P.M. instead of the normally required 9 P.M.[1]

The university felt the gathering storm before Pearl Harbor. On October 16, 1940, it dismissed classes so that male students could register for the draft in Memorial Gymnasium. "Come early to avoid a rush," the *Orange and White* urged. By Fall 1941, the campus was feeling the effects of the draft; the enrollment was down to 1,200, most of whom were women. A headline in the student newspaper reported that "DRAFT TAKES MANY OF U-T'S LEADING STU-DENTS," among them three fraternity presidents and the president of the Non-Fraternity Association. The paper reported that some students were taking "defense jobs to keep from the draft." President Hoskins reported that professors joining the military or also leaving for war industry jobs mitigated the effects of the enrollment drop.[2]

The women students (still commonly called girls in the press and elsewhere) on this small, southern campus were tightly constrained by "proper" gender roles as "men build the ships and fire the guns in the defense of America." They collected waste paper, sold defense stamps, knitted for the Red Cross, studied first aid, and planned a "backward dance" with proceeds going to "some war fund." But some women students were studying "motor mechanics," a suggestion of changes to come in gender roles. They also took on unfamiliar roles in the university, serving as editors of the *Orange and White* and the *Volunteer*, the student yearbook.[3]

In May 1942, over two hundred persons registered for a two-day industrial plant protection school at the university. They were to learn from builders, architects, and FBI agents how to protect factories from sabotage.[4] War had come to the University of Tennessee. "War is a serious business, and the university means business," President Hoskins lectured the student body at the beginning of the 1942 Fall term. Hoskins, always thin-lipped about frivolous attitudes among the young, used the war to press his theme: "There are a few who look upon college life as a lark . . . a special adventure replete with daydreams. I want to tell these students to return to school this fall prepared for serious study or stay at home and go to work—or, better still, enlist in the armed forces immediately." He also told them to leave their cars at home—"a waste of tires and gasoline."[5]

In good Calvinist fashion, the Presbyterian lay leader saw sin as the cause of WWII: "Sin is the perversion of man's capacity to do righteously; wars are the perversion of man's capacity to enjoy peace." The mission of the university was to teach war. Hoskins insisted that the war justified his hard-line views. "For years," he said, "we have piddled with the idea of universal peace, educating our own group to a point where many of them at this time feel that the fiendish lawlessness of war is a thing that we can abolish." No, the war confirmed the truth of the Bible, "There shall be wars and rumors of wars!" The lesson for education from elementary schools to the university was "to indoctrinate" youth in Americanism not only during the war but for all time; it should be "a fundamental in our educational ideas."[6]

By 1943 hundreds of soldiers were on campus for military training, taxing the facilities of the campus. The programs of A. W. Hobt, professor of physical education, were particularly affected. He insisted in letters to the university administration that he was cooperating completely but that the gymnasium facilities were inadequate for both the regular physical education students and the army physical activity program. He also complained that the administration did not allow him to participate in making decisions about the use of the facilities, and it disturbed him that the Army Air Corps Cadets were less inclined than regular university students to respect the Sunday blue rules. "I have been told," he wrote to Hoskins, "that several Army Air students were found playing on the tennis courts last Sunday before noon." He assured Hoskins that he had prepared a notice that was to be read to all sections of the Army Air Corps students: "University regulations prohibit the playing of tennis on Sunday until noon. Please observe this regulation."[7]

The tennis courts serve as a symbol of the attitudes that were threatened by the world that was coming. Walking across the campus in the late spring of 1940, Robert Lindsay Mason (an artist who "painted nudes extensively") was shocked and offended to see male students playing tennis without even "a small covering over their torsos." He could not imagine how any person of either sex could be thrilled to see "navels and hairy chests." He reported to Hoskins that he had "just as soon scan their privates." Hoskins assured him that the university had rules "against the very things that you mentioned in your letter, and I am going to have these rules enforced."[8]

Sunday movies created the hottest debate in the student newspaper over blue laws. Reporters for the *Orange and White* informally polled students in October 1942 and found overwhelming support for Sunday picture shows. Several hundred students petitioned the city council to allow the movies. Mary Pryor ventured that "It's better to go to the movies than to go dancing on Sunday," but added that "There's not really much difference, however." Bob Eskew was more provocative, claiming that it would "cut out those long Sunday afternoon poker games." The city council feared fundamentalists more than students, and picture shows remained closed on Sunday. But the returning WWII veterans merited special dispensation from a grateful people. In 1947, the *Orange and White* editorialized that an "overwhelming majority" of the staff of the paper endorsed Sunday movies and supported their position by an appeal to the needs of the veteran, who "used to Sunday movies throughout his service career, finds it particularly hard to understand." The most powerful endorsement came, however, when "the entire U-T football squad" announced it favored abolition of Sunday blue laws.[9]

War Comes to the College of Education

Miss Rosalie McDaniel of the Southern Teachers Agency set up a booth at the Fall 1940 meeting of the East Tennessee Education Association and forecast a teacher shortage and higher pay as a result of the draft of teachers. At Spring commencement in 1941, the director of the university Bureau of Personnel Service called the job prospects in teaching "wonderful." Dean Thackston explained: "The government program of training defense workers and the vacancies created by selective service duties of teachers have caused an abnormal demand." Tennessee experienced a teacher shortage within months after the United States went to war. Education professor William M. Alexander provided alarming statistics: 27 percent of the state's high school teachers had resigned in one year and 40 percent of the teachers were expected to leave during the 1942–43 academic year. He reported that many communities could not find qualified teachers and were resorting to emergency certificates, and "retired teachers are being asked to return to their desks. Positions are being left vacant."[10]

Alexander admitted that only a "negligible percentage" of teachers were entering the armed forces, but they were leaving for better paying jobs, particularly in defense industries. He saw little hope for sufficient teacher salary increases to offset higher pay in the booming outside economy created by the war. The College of Education responded with special programs in teacher training to compensate for the growing shortage of qualified teachers. In Spring 1942, the college offered seven special teacher-training "refresher courses," particularly for former teachers. The following summer session was the largest on record as many retired teachers returned for the special classes. By 1944, the college had replaced the special workshops with a regular six-week Spring term, "as a special wartime service" to new and to former teachers who were returning to classrooms during the crisis.[11]

In 1944, Education Dean N. E. Fitzgerald wrote to an alumnus in the South Pacific: "We still get shorter and shorter of students so I suppose we will have less and less to do so far as teaching goes." The education faculty, always eager to get off campus and into "the field," also tried to meet the teacher shortage by training teachers in special six-week programs in the counties where they would teach. In rural Appalachian Campbell County, Professor Mildred Dawson taught new teachers "each morning in a local school building." Those who completed the course received nine hours of academic credit toward their certificate and their degree.[12]

The dean and faculty of the College of Education accepted the conventional institutional wisdom that survival required expansion. In a report to the administration soliciting additional resources for the 1941–42 academic year, the college administration reflected the values and anxieties of educationists of the period. They justified expansion of their program because of the needs of a democratic society and, at the same time, they seemed oblivious to class and gender biases in their proposals. According to their report, democratic education required an expansion of public schooling not only to serve school-aged children, but everyone in communities, since public schools in a democracy must provide needed education for all its citizens. This goal for schools, of course, required more teachers and other specialists trained by the college. World War II made democratic education more crucial: "Our ability as a nation to stem the tide which threatens democracy as a way of life depends more upon trained intelligence than upon anything else." The report matter-of-factly proposed a differentiated education for "followers" and "leaders" so that each person could "be educated to his fullest capacity for the nation's protection."[13]

"Minimum Additions" required by the college included seven new faculty positions. In all but one case, the language of the proposal required men. The proposal justified four new assistant professors (in language-education, mathematics-science education, social science-education, and physical education and recreation) by listing "field" responsibilities for "these men." The modified preamble of the job description for a professor of arts and crafts read: "this man (or woman)."[14]

The college presented itself as the university's Cinderella. The report pointed to all of the grave responsibilities of education professors and then bitterly complained about their lack of resources, describing their "dire poverty" in staff and facilities. They were not just poor; they were mistreated: "The College of Education is by far the most poorly equipped and staffed of any college or school in the University. We have no building whatever and very little material equipment for teaching, and our personnel is not half what it should be."[15]

The educationists often justified their existence by arguing the importance of their field work in the schools. This report was no exception. Travel funds in order to work with the public schools were crucial: Dr. Alexander was getting requests to evaluate high schools from throughout Tennessee; Miss Essery desperately needed to continue working with the state PTA to survey the education needs of exceptional children; Miss Dawson was receiving more requests than she could accept as a consultant in elementary education and spending her own money to travel across the state; and Dr. Fuller and Dr. Lund were in demand to help high schools throughout Tennessee. The report argued that the university administration was treating education unfairly because other colleges were getting more resources for similar activities. The College of Education deserved the same opportunity as the School of Home Economics, the College of Agriculture, and the College of Engineering to bring the university to the people of the state. Unlike the College of Education, "They have ample funds for travel, several automobiles, and staff members who have plenty of time for state work."[16]

Despite complaints about their mistreatment, the college found resources to make the 1940s another decade of expansion. Aviation education exemplifies the education faculty's attachment to new technology as well as their instinct for finding funded, politically attractive programs. Not only was air power needed to win the war, but in the new technological age to follow, the family car would be replaced by the family plane: "A new day has come for the school teacher! Science has taken a new place in the everyday activities of this and the coming generation. Where trains and automobiles were once the means of speed and distance, the airplane now ushers in a new day of space-annihilation." Best of all, after state approval, the federal government funded aviation education. Citing an "urgent need," Thackston lobbied Tennessee Commissioner of Education B. O. Duggan to approve the program: "As you know, the best army men come from the South, and Tennessee has always been a leader in the South. We cannot afford to let our boys and girls be handicapped by not getting this training so gravely needed now for national defense." As further justification, Thackston indicated that such a course would be powerful motivation for high school students in mathematics and science. He suggested that the aviation course be developed by "18 or 20 outstanding high school science teachers." He advised Duggan to call a meeting of the state board of education immediately to gain their approval. Duggan did as requested; the board accepted the proposals, and forty scholarships were awarded to high school teachers for the summer of 1942.[17]

Progressivism

Educationists in the university had long supported progressive reforms. As early as 1927, Professor Harry Clark visited Gary, Indiana, to observe the famous Gary Plan for platoon schools. Clark was an advocate of another basic progressive reform, the junior high school. He advocated one for Knoxville that would include a "swimming pool, gymnasium, cafeteria and motion pictures." As the decade of the 1940s began, the faculty affirmed progressivism in the schools and in teacher education. They declared themselves dissatisfied with traditional teacher education and "ready to embark on a long-time experimental approach."[18]

Although the South was often considered behind in support of pedagogical progressivism, the educationists in the university, with the enthusiastic support of Dean Thackston, portrayed themselves as leading a regionwide progressive reform movement. Under the sponsorship of the Southern Association of Secondary Schools, the South claimed to be "leading the entire nation" in progressive curricular reform. Replete with the jargon of progressivism—problem solving, self-initiated activity, and learning by doing—southern progressives declared old methods of teaching isolated subjects "gone with the wind." Professor S. E. Torsten Lund was particularly active in the "Southern Study," working in several of the thirty-three schools involved and often seeing changes in high school teaching methods firsthand: "I have experienced the thrill which is due a professor of education who has theorized about what ought to be done in our schools but as a doubting Thomas never quite expected to see it in broad daylight." In May 1940, the university hosted eighty-nine delegates from southern states to discuss reforms in high school curriculum and instruction. The University of Tennessee was chosen as the meeting place because it provided leadership in the struggle to replace the "lecture-recitation" with the new "problem method."[19]

University educationists equated progressivism and democracy. In April 1940, Professor Mildred Dawson lectured to a thousand women who attended a three-day meeting of the Tennessee Congress of Parents and Teachers. She called for more democratic relationships between students and teachers and teachers and principals, and, much in the fashion of John Dewey, avowed that education of the whole child includes participation in the political life of the community. Thackston agreed, insisting that the university "must train teachers democratically, they must be democrats and they must teach democratically." A few weeks later, Thackston spoke on the topic at the University of Missouri. In vintage progressivism, he argued that autocratic school systems could not train good citizens:

> Children and teachers must freely share in setting up school conditions and
> regulations, otherwise they cannot identify themselves with the purpose and
> value of these regulations. . . . School administrators must provide the facili-
> ties for children to grow into democracy by a democratic school government.[20]

Administrative progressivism was enhanced in 1943 when Commissioner B. O. Duggan established a statewide committee to improve
teacher education, particularly for high school teachers, in postwar
Tennessee. Committee recommendations endorsed the practical, technical, and vocational, including guidance and courses for students not
bound for college. Teacher education should also "be more practical
with more time set aside for practice teaching while the trainees are
still in college. Perhaps a year's 'internship' for young teachers while
in training—similar to that required of young doctors—would be desirable."[21]

It would be nearly half a century before the college established full-
year internships, but practice teaching was lengthened and enriched
immediately following the war. Until 1946, practice teachers taught
only in four local schools and only for part of a day while they continued to take classes on campus. Beginning in Fall 1946 with "girls" in
home economics, practice teaching became full-time (even if only for
a month at the beginning) and was placed in towns some distance
from Knoxville. Dean Fitzgerald explained the change was to allow
student teachers to get "a real experience by seeing schools in the
total situation." The practice teachers were to live in "private homes"
to see the school in its total community setting and to take "part in
local civic and social life."[22]

The first off-campus teaching center was at Norris, a new town
established by the Tennessee Valley Authority. Sue Downs wrote of
her and her cohorts' experiences in student teaching at Norris. The
five women lived together in an "unfurnished house," sleeping on steel
cots. The lone male student teacher lived in a local inn "since one man
living in the house with five women is frowned upon by the University
and by Norris citizens. They agreed, however, that it would be permis-
sible for him to eat dinner with us."[23]

Downs remembered that they descended upon Norris "wrapped in
pink clouds of 'progressive education.'" Sitting in a circle, the first day
they talked of textbook theory and discussed the child-centered curriculum and other principles of progressive education. In experiences
typical of generations of student teachers, and despite regular faculty
warnings about the need for teacher-directed order and discipline, they

experimented with child centeredness. They were "befuddled," "haggard," and disappointed when things didn't work out at all as they were supposed to. E. S. Christenbury, the Director of Student Teaching, "listened sympathetically" to their "tales of woe" and made suggestions that didn't sound very progressive to them.[24]

Much of Downs's story is about mutual support and the sharing of experiences among the student teachers, of helping each other look less like college students and more like schoolteachers, of learning to balance housework and cooking (on their last night in Norris, they accidentally set the house on fire), and of learning to balance the reality of their own experience with educational theory. "Believe it or not," Downs wrote of their experiences, "we still believe in 'progressive education,' but now we realize that it is quite a different thing to carry it on and to read about it."[25]

Hoskins's Antiprogressive Offensive

In the 1940s, President Hoskins went on the offensive with widely publicized attacks on progressive pedagogy. His 1942 commencement address compared essentialists in education with "the so-called progressives." While the essentialists emphasized learning subject matter, he argued that progressive educationists minimized mathematics, science, history, and the other basic academic disciplines. He did not let the opportunity pass without indicting educationists for their preoccupation with teaching methods or "tricks of the trade."[26]

Extensive press coverage and favorable letters from a cross section of Tennessee citizens resulted in a more vigorous attack the next year in a commencement address at East Tennessee State Teachers College at Johnson City. He was particularly contemptuous of child-centered education, calling it a "perversion," and illustrating it with the "true story" that every critic of progressive education of the period seemed to know: "Now, children, just what would you like to do today, if anything? What shall our project be?" He urged stronger discipline in the home and school to curb juvenile delinquency and blamed a lack of traditional values for the problems of youth: "Let us remember that these are the children and grandchildren of the last war whose parents passed through the 'jazz age' following World War I." He accused progressive education of hindering the war effort. It had failed to teach self-discipline (we were morally unprepared), it had failed to prepare the youth academically (as exemplified by the university having to teach air cadets secondary school subjects), and it had failed to teach loyalty to American principles.[27]

He drew his audience's attention to "an immense mass of information" on subversion gathered by the Dies Committee and criticized the progressives' "fetish of tolerance." "It may be," he wrote doubtfully, "that a critical attitude in certain respects does make a good citizen, but in the formative stages of youth's development, it is much more important to develop judgment on and loyalty to the sources from which spring our freedom." Criticism of American institutions and tolerance of other ways of living, he continued, are "luxury commodities" that are possible "only if we put unity and loyalty first."[28]

Nothing else that Hoskins said or did in his long career brought anything like the applause from this speech. His files in the archives are bulging with letters of appreciation, and newspapers gave the speech wide distribution, often printing much of it verbatim. Editorial support often followed, and the religious right of the period was highly appreciative. In a letter to Hoskins, Bob Jones, founder of the fundamentalist Bob Jones University, agreed that the moral collapse of the young over the last generation was a result of "neglect of the fundamental principles" of the right kind of education. He found, particularly, that "moral looseness" was a result of the elective system that resulted from "the satanic philosophy." In private letters, Hoskins warned Tennessee educational leaders of the dangers of progressive education and educationists (the two were always related in Hoskins' mind). He admonished Andrew Holt (secretary-treasurer of the Tennessee Education Association and later president of the university) that college enrollments in Tennessee would be low as long as high schools stressed preparation for life instead of academic subjects.[29]

After the speech and the publicity that followed, many citizens considered Hoskins an authority on pedagogy. Mrs. James Clark, Chair of the Athens Board of Education, wrote him in January 1943 concerned that the local teachers were doing a poor job of teaching reading because they were using a word recognition method rather than phonics. Hoskins responded by blaming the problem on progressive education and indicating that he had solved the problem in teacher training at UT: "I instructed the Dean to throw out the progressive education method and proceed to get some method by which the fundamental tools of an education can be taught more successfully and with satisfactory results." Hoskins urged Clark and the board of education to use the same method of ridding themselves of "so-called progressive education." Call the superintendent and any principals who insist on using "word recognition" in for a conference and "frankly tell" them that it doesn't work.[30]

He also dispatched Professor Florence Essery to Athens to examine the reading problem. The diplomatic Essery sent a detailed report on her trip to Hoskins. She summarized her visit and cordial reception and concluded that, although the schools were not problem-free, the children of Athens were doing quite well compared to national norms in reading. She also observed that it appeared "we had misinterpreted Mrs. Clark's letter," that she was primarily concerned with her own son, a second grader: "an average child with average second grade reading ability, and an only child." She also observed that "the mother is not well," Hoskins replied with a short "acknowledge receipt," commenting that he was "glad" that conditions were better than he had been told. He did not mention progressive education.[31]

In an earlier letter to Clark, he had conceded that "a certain amount of the study of pedagogy" was a good thing but cautioned that it had "been carried too far." He advised the school board member on the criteria for selecting good teachers: "First, a person of excellent character. . . ; second, one who has respect for church affiliations and the sacred things of life; third, one who is well qualified to teach that subject." He did not mention a study of pedagogy.[32]

In 1943, Hoskins replaced John Thackston, dean of the College of Education since it was created in 1926. As indicated before, Hoskins disliked Thackston and had been threatening to fire him for years. Thackston agreed to resign, expressing hope to Hoskins that it would "help to remove some of the prejudice toward the professional education of teachers which now exists on the campus." But Thackston tried to bargain. He would resign when the college was reorganized with direct control of all programs for teacher education (business education, physical education, industrial education, etc.): "I want it to be clearly understood that any change in my own status is to take effect *only* if the recommendation with regard to the new reorganization of teacher-education is followed out completely." He also requested that Hoskins appoint him dean of the summer school without a reduction in salary.[33]

At a board of trustees meeting on April 29, 1943, Hoskins "regretted" to tell the trustees that the performance of the College of Education had been unsatisfactory and that there had been "much criticism" of it within and without the university, in particular the college had failed to provide expected leadership for public schooling in Tennessee. Hoskins informed the trustees that he and Vice President Fred

Smith had been looking for "a suitable man" to be dean for two years and, after a national search, had chosen N. E. Fitzgerald, head of the Department of Agricultural Education. The Fitzgerald appointment was not without opposition. The feisty state Commissioner of Education (and former UT education professor) B. O. Duggan protested Fitzgerald's selection because he "was not considered a Public Education man." Hoskins reminded the trustees that he had been searching for two years and had found no one better qualified; they accepted Hoskins's candidate. In triumph, Hoskins wrote to his old mentor, former UT President Charles Dabney, that he had reorganized the College of Education and "have placed a new dean over that organization."[34]

On May 11 in a terse letter without any customary expression of appreciation for past contributions, Hoskins informed Thackston that his "resignation" had been accepted and that Fitzgerald had been appointed dean; "all requisitions and bills are to go through Dean Fitzgerald's hands." Thackston responded with a request that as dean of the summer school he be paid throughout the year as the other deans were. Hoskins responded with a terse note, commanding Thackston to resign without making any requests: "Please write me a statement as to whether or not you accept my offer as stated in my letters that I wrote to you setting forth the offer. In this answer do not include anything else but a statement as to whether or not you accept my offer."[35]

Thackston remained on the faculty, teaching history and philosophy of education, among other things, and serving as dean of the university Summer Quarter. A local paper published an extensive tribute to Thackston, calling him a "genial, elderly faculty liberal."[36]

The Postwar Campus

By the Spring of 1944, the effects of World War II on the campus were being reduced. The coffee shop and dining room facilities used by soldiers reverted to student use. Dormitories that had housed army trainees were returned to women students who had lived in private homes during the height of the war. "We feel that we have been rendering excellent service to the nation at war," Fred Smith told the student newspaper, "and with the return of all facilities to civilian use we expect to adapt curricula, facilities, and services to the needs of the state."[37]

In 1945, a slashing of university funds thwarted university plans to meet the needs of the veterans and postwar Tennessee. Hoskins as usual used patriotism in defending the budget. He spoke of 100 new courses designed for veterans, calling them "new courses for new needs in a new world." "Shall this program be scrapped," he complained, "and the veterans be told that Alabama, Georgia, Kentucky, perhaps, may offer such courses but not Tennessee?" He appealed to public opinion through the state's newspapers: "I can only plead with the state legislature to act with the justice and patriotism worthy of the youth now fighting for democracy abroad. I can only plead with the public to uphold the hands and the hearts of the legislators who must face this issue." Hoskins was an able propagandist; thousands of telegrams and telephone calls protesting the cut in the university's budget "poured into Nashville," and most of the budget was restored.[38]

Leadership of the postwar university soon passed to others. Hoskins was seventy-five in 1946, and faculty and trustees were anxious that he retire. When approached by distinguished faculty and told that it was time, Hoskins unexpectedly accepted their advice and submitted his request for retirement in June 1946. The trustees appointed an acting president, Cloide Everett Brehm, who was dean of Agriculture. After a national search lasting two years (with a great deal of conflict, antagonism, and intrigue among trustees), Brehm was appointed president. He was genial in personal relations, awkward on public occasions, and a supporter of teacher education.[39]

The finances of the university were so bad when Brehm was acting president that he wrote for political support to the infamous Boss Crump of Memphis. A friend of Brehm suggested that, since Crump was an avid football fan, it might be a good idea to play two games in Memphis each year instead of the customary one. The suggestion was not acted on; to Tennessee football fans, some things are more important than friendly politicos. However, Brehm was surprisingly effective with the legislators, and in 1947 they voted a two percent sales tax to support most of the appropriation that the university had requested.[40]

As a consequence of the G.I. Bill, veterans came by the thousands, swamping the university facilities. In 1946, for the first time in its history, the university closed enrollment—in this case, to nonveteran new freshmen, sophomores, and out-of-state students. Students were housed in the gymnasium; and as on campuses across the country, temporary structures symbolized the democratization of American higher education:

Squatty Army barracks—tarpaper tops and weather-boarded sides—are spring-
ing up among the collegiate Gothic brick buildings. . . . Also nearing completion are some 172 new temporary dwelling units constructed of barracks
acquired from the former Prisoner of War Camp at Crossville, to be rented to
married veteran students and to faculty members.[41]

By the early 1950s, the effects of the war were less visible; and the
older, more serious veterans were less of a presence on campus. Undergraduate silliness reappeared, and the panty raid phenomenon
spread across the country, including Tennessee. In an ironic beginning of concerns about student unrest, Chancellor Clark Kerr of the
University of California corresponded with President Brehm about
the national problem. Brehm refused to take harsh measures, fearing
confrontations between students and police. In July 1952, the general
secretary of the campus Christian Associations sent Brehm a sensa-
tional article from a London newspaper. The article said that two
hundred police with riot guns and tear gas had to fire over the head of
a thousand Tennessee men students who were storming the women's
dormitories. "Shrieking girls with brooms and butcher knives helped
the police to beat them off," the report continued. In a frightful response to the panty raids the state director of Selective Service wrote
Brehm, instructing him:

As soon as you have ascertained which students, if any, are *definitely guilty*
of these acts, please furnish this Headquarters their names and selective service numbers, each in a separate statement and signed. We will forward this
information to their respective local boards for appropriate action at the next
board meeting.

In a courteous reply, Brehm, with his characteristic calmness, indicated that the disorders had been exaggerated in the press and that
the university would be able to discipline the guilty if serious infrac-
tions could be proven. Perhaps the most thoughtful public reaction to
the raids was a long letter to the *Orange and White* by a graduate
student, Dan Hale, who observed that panty raids were symbolic rape.[42]

African Americans Enter the University

Following the war, a more cosmopolitan student body was the result
not only of veterans but also because the university was finally forced
to enroll African Americans. The legal battle to integrate higher education began to experience success in the 1930s. On January 31,

1936, the dean of the UT College of Law alerted Hoskins that Lloyd L. Gaines, an African American, had brought suit against the University of Missouri Law School. A few days later H. C. Byrd, president of the University of Maryland, wrote Hoskins about the court decision upholding a mandamus to admit Gaines to the law school and warned him that it was going to happen all over the South. After the 1938 Supreme Court decision that citizens must be provided education within their states, Byrd wrote Hoskins again and asked what he thought Tennessee could do to "to meet the exigencies created by the Missouri decision." Dean Fred C. Smith answered in Hoskins absence but missed the significance of the Court decision, assuring Byrd that "We have been taking care of the problem of Negro education in Tennessee" through the appropriation for out-of-state-tuition.[43]

The Supreme Court decision finding that out-of-state tuition provisions for equal facilities were unconstitutional led to attempts by African Americans to enroll on the Knoxville campus. In September 1939, six young black men in two taxis drove through the university gates, parked in front of the administration building, and went to Dean Smith's office, passing Hoskins on their way. A local newspaper reporter reported that "President Hoskins spoke to the Negroes as they passed him on their way to the Dean's office, and, then realizing what was up, he turned and watched them go up the stairs with a look of mild surprise on his face." They asked to enroll in the university based on the lack of "equal facilities" for African Americans. Smith asked the reporters, who had been told of the meeting ahead of time, not to cover the event for their papers: "No, sir! Not a word!" Hoskins, quoting provisions of Tennessee law, declared that it was illegal to enroll black persons and that he would be subject to a jail term of up to six months. Besides, he insisted, Tennessee had been "very generous" in providing for black education.[44]

Hoskins, who refused to endorse (even privately) abolishing the poll tax, was suspicious of the ability of African Americans to pursue advanced academic work. In resisting changes in the distribution of federal funds for collegiate agricultural education, he pondered differences in the "scholastic" abilities the races: "I think we should take into consideration not only the question of illiteracy among the Negroes but the question of their being prepared to use this fund as the law intended it to be used."[45]

Hoskins's good friend at UT, Victor Davis, director of the Bureau of Personnel Service, tried to assure him that everything would be all right:

Squire Turner came by yesterday to see you in regard to the race situation. He says there is nothing to worry about in Tennessee. The facilities not offered by A& I in Nashville can be purchased from Fisk and Meharry. He feels that everything can be cleared up in the next legislature and up until then it is a matter of stalling in the Courts. I spent a long time with him and got every bit of information possible as I thought it might take a bit of worry off of your mind and make it possible for you to relax.

After having started it before, I am now back at "Gone With the Wind" and so have been shedding a few tears over the plight of the South—and withal am becoming a more passionate Southerner.[46]

With the provision for out-of-state tuition declared unconstitutional, segregationists were forced to create or upgrade professional and graduate education in Tennessee. The Tennessee legislature in 1941 voted to provide equal education between the university and the all-black Agricultural and Industrial State College in Nashville. In February 1941, the state board of education requested that the president of UT create a committee to help develop graduate programs at A&I. Since much of the demand was for graduate work in education by African American teachers and administrators, Hoskins appointed Deans Thackston and Smith to supervise its development. In December 1942, Commissioner Duggan forwarded to A&I President W. J. Hale the committee's report for an education program "equivalent" to that of the university's College of Education. The report was quite explicit and included courses to be offered, faculty to be hired and their salaries, who should be the department head in Education, and library resources that should be purchased. As late as 1950, Andrew Holt, assistant to Brehm, warned that real comparable education in quality must be achieved at A&I "if a wholesale influx of Negroes into the University is to be avoided."[47]

Legal appeals were finally exhausted, and the university admitted students to the graduate and law colleges in January 1952. The first African-American student in the university was a Knoxville hotel bellhop, Gene Mitchell Gray. In April a special committee appointed by Brehm reported to the trustees on the experiences of the university's two black students. The committee informed the board that there was no trouble "or incident of any kind." The committee summarized the experience of Gray:

[He] had inquired about the location of the cafeteria, that he had received this information and had taken one or more meals at the cafeteria, passing through the line as other students did; also that he had inquired of his professors where he should sit in class and had been informed that he might sit any-

where in the room; in addition, he had asked if he was eligible to buy a basketball ticket, and bought a ticket and had used this ticket in attending basketball
games.[48]

Students were not activists in the desegregation struggle. "It's just
one of those things. Like the atomic bomb, it was bound to happen,"
one student responded when Attorney General Beeler ruled that African Americans must be admitted. In the late 1940s, ALE (Andrew Lea
Eastman), a columnist for the *Orange and White*, wrote a series of
editorials supporting integration on grounds of democracy and Christianity. His columns, but not others, were often followed by a disclaimer indicating that his views did "not necessarily reflect" those of
the rest of the staff. But polls indicated that students approved the
1954 *Brown v. Board of Education* decision overwhelmingly; after
giving enthusiastic support in an *Orange and White* interview, however, one student had to admit that he was a Yankee.[49]

Not surprisingly, the administration restricted severely civil rights
activities on campus. The university refused to allow Dr. J. Herman
Daves, Tennessee Valley Authority director of Negro Personnel, to
discuss President Truman's civil rights program with the students' World
Affairs Discussion Group. Smith denied use of a university space, explaining that there was "a policy prohibiting interracial discussion groups
dealing with these delicate problems." Two years after the *Brown v.
Board of Education* decision, the university administration refused to
sanction (because it was a political action group) a campus chapter of
the NAACP.[50]

Since the Agricultural and Industrial State College did not have a
graduate program in special education, students in the College of Education were prominent in the desegregation struggle. Lilly Jenkins
was the first black student to be awarded a degree from the university,
receiving a M.S. in special education in 1954. Five black teachers
enrolled in the special education program in June 1953.[51]

By January 1955, forty-six African Americans had been admitted
to the Graduate School and College of Law, but the university resisted
undergraduate admissions throughout the 1950s. Andy Holt, assistant to President Brehm, in April 1953 still ventured that "Negroes
prefer to attend school with people of their own race." And Brehm,
even after the Brown decision, warned that allowing one black admission would "let the camel get his nose in the door" to the satisfaction
of the National Association for the Advancement of Colored People.

Farther-right, rabid segregationists saw desegregation of the university as a Communist plot by those who "enjoy seeing Negro boys embracing white girls." In November 1960, threatened by a lawsuit demanding admission to the undergraduate program, the trustees finally surrendered and passed the long overdue resolution: "That it is the policy of the Board that there shall be no racial discrimination in the admission of qualified students to the University of Tennessee."[52]

Postwar Teacher Education

At the end of the war, public schools of Tennessee were in terrible shape. In 1946 state Commissioner of Education Burgin E. Dossett reported that half of the county school buildings were "badly in need of repair." The teachers were undereducated and inexperienced; nearly one half of teachers and principals had been in their jobs for less than three years. Accelerating school enrollments soon exacerbated the problem. In 1948, Andrew Holt, Executive Secretary of the Tennessee Education Association, told the School Board Association that school enrollments had increased more than 43,000 students in the previous two years and the state needed at least 1,000 teachers.[53]

The public schools received strong support from Brehm. Even in a time of crucial financial needs in the university, he insisted that increased funds could not be at the expense of elementary, high schools, and teacher educators: "A chain is no stronger than its weakest link. If the barefoot boy in the rural elementary school gets a good education, he must have teachers with adequate knowledge to teach. Where do teachers get their training and knowledge? At the universities and colleges!"[54]

Since the time of Karns and Claxton, the College of Education administration and faculty campaigned actively for increased funding for public schools. A tradition in their propaganda efforts was to use statistics, without regard for the finer points of cause and effect, to prove a strong relationship between school expenditures and community prosperity. Dean Fitzgerald continued the traditions in campaigning for increased appropriations to solve the postwar school crisis. During American Education Week in 1947, he argued for "an outstanding system" of public schools because it was a good investment:

1. Where schools are best, average incomes are greatest.
2. Where schools are best, retail sales are greatest.

3. Where schools are best, more telephones are used.
4. Where schools are best, more magazines are read.

The college used the needs of public schools as justification for expansion. With an acute teacher shortage and thousands of first-generation college students (a population more likely than others to choose teaching) among the veterans, enrollment in the college soared to 1,151 students, about one-third of the university students, in 1947. (College enrollment had been 301 in 1939 and had dropped to 121 in the war year 1943.) In 1947, the university appointed fifty-seven new professors, including five in education. But the next year, five professors left the college for administrative positions elsewhere, three as deans and two in state departments of education.[56]

The dean and faculty took a good deal of pride in the publicity created by their teacher education program, particularly the off-campus student teaching centers: "One of the few experiments of its type in the world." Educators from throughout the United States and from several other nations made visits to the centers. Professor Edward S. Christenbury, director of student teaching, received much of the credit for the idea that was modeled after the original center in the new Tennessee Valley Authority town of Norris. Christenbury came to the college after six years as education officer for the TVA: "Dr. Chris felt that off-campus student teaching would force college seniors to break their campus ties (with sororities, fraternities, athletics, social friends, etc.)" and become a part of the community where they were student teaching. A preteaching seminar to analyze social and economic data on the community where the student was placed preceded the twelve-week student teaching quarter. During student teaching, students had to live in the community where their schools were located, participating "in community dramatics, scouting activities, local-talent concerts, church work and other community activities." In 1953, the American Association of Colleges for Teacher Education cited student teaching in the college as "one of the nation's most highly regarded teacher training programs."[57]

The Field Service Corps

The *Orange and White* suggested a new theme for the College of Education in 1947: "Teach the teachers while they teach." After the war, the education faculty went on the road, holding workshops for teachers and administrators throughout Tennessee. In part, the faculty was responding to the postwar teacher shortage that allowed many inexperienced, nondegreed persons without any training in pedagogy to "keep" school. In part, it was a response to a new law that required "permit" teachers, those without a degree from an approved college or university, to take eight quarter hours of college work each year. In either case, many teachers were in need of training. Florence V. Essery, long-time professor of special education, described the least prepared and most isolated of the mountain Tennessee teachers:

> Lean, lanky, starved from hidden hungers of physical and mental wants, shyly striving to qualify for the meager wages paid the three to six months teacher-janitor eager to supplement his meager living from the hillside tobacco crop. Forced into institutes, short courses, summer school terms as special students, struggling to learn the what, why, and how of the teacher's art and skill.[58]

The special education faculty was in the forefront of the postwar workshop movement. At first, the teacher workshops were often just one- or two-day inspirational conferences but were gradually lengthened to several-weeks. Special-education workshops in the early years always included instructors, consultants, and coordinators from a variety of institutions and agencies. For a number of years, 100 Tennessee teachers, chosen by local superintendents of schools or by the Tennessee Department of Education, were given scholarships to attend these workshops. Many participants drove as far as 100 miles "to home and farm chores—daily." And a number came from other southern states. There was a dearth of usable teaching materials for disabled children, and the workshop participants served other teachers by preparing bulletins for them, including such titles as "Teaching a Partially Sighted Homebound Child," "A Unit on School Lighting," and "Slow Learning Children."[59]

By Fall semester 1946, Dean Fitzgerald had organized a "Field Service Corps" to send teachers throughout the state to improve methods of teaching. In Fall 1947, more than 500 teachers enrolled in workshops. During the regular academic year many of the workshops were conducted in one afternoon each week with two-week workshops during the summer. All education professors were required to participate in the off-campus program. "The faculty works in shifts," the Orange and White explained. "Those who are working in Trimble this week will be replaced by five others for Brownsville next week."

The college faculty traveled across the state, even to far West Tennessee, 400 miles away. As soon as the West Tennessee kids were dismissed for cotton picking, the professors from Knoxville, in groups of five to seven, descended on their teachers, offering the latest teaching methods in "'field workshops." The faculty, sometimes calling themselves circuit riders, spent much of their time on the road. At first they often traveled by night Pullman. Later, in the 1950s, the college sent them out in a fleet of Ford cars. Retired professor Lawrence Haaby said that Dean Fitzgerald didn't seem happy unless most of the professors were off in a Ford someplace.[60]

Special Education

Special education grew rapidly in the postwar period. Teacher educators in the university had long been concerned with disabled children. As an example, Harry Clark addressed the University Education Club in 1911 on the schooling needs of "defective" children, telling "pathetic stories" of their lack of care. However, the college did not develop a sequence of courses in special education until 1937. At first, volunteers from the state department of education and other agencies (often unpaid by the university) taught the classes in the summer. The courses were assigned graduate-level numbers in 1938–39, making special education an official graduate program. As indicated earlier, since special-education certification was unavailable at Tennessee A&I, African Americans enrolled in this program in large numbers, helping to racially desegregate the university. The first master's thesis by an African-American student in the university was Lillian Jenkins's "A Survey of Vocational Training in Cosmetology for Deaf Girls in the United States."[61]

Much to the delight of the educationists, a 1949 U.S. Office of Education publication reported that the University of Tennessee was the only southern university with a comprehensive curriculum for training teachers in special education. The Office of Education seemed excessively explicit in describing the status of the UT special education curriculum in the South: "the most complete of its kind south of Illinois and east of California." The special education program had a great deal of support from teachers, public school administrators, and from the rest of the university.[62]

The college and university administrations used the popularity and status of the program in efforts to increased funding. In 1947, Brehm responded to the plea of the state Commissioner of Education for more emphasis on training teachers for the disabled with the explanation that the College of Education was too "handicapped financially" to provide these needed services. Fitzgerald sent an annual complaint to Brehm that money was too short to hire faculty for the popular program: "Once or twice when money was available we were unable to secure a suitable person at the salary range on this campus. Persons are available now, as they have been many times before, but we do not have the necessary funds."[63]

Looking for a head of the Department of Special Education, Fitzgerald made a strange, if wonderfully successful choice, Dr. Leonard Xavier Magnifico, a Latino from Corpus Christi, Texas. Fitzgerald worried needlessly about how Magnifico would be accepted in Appalachian Tennessee. He called himself Dr. Mag, the Magnificent, and he must have been a curiosity if not a shock to rural Tennesseans, but he seemed to create an atmosphere of humor and lightheartedness wherever he went. With the strong support of the dean, Magnifico spent much of his time visiting schools in East Tennessee, convincing school officials on the need for special services for disabled children, and recruiting able teachers for the special education program in the college. He was also a capable scholar, publishing one of the first special education survey textbooks.[64]

The success of the special education program allowed Fitzgerald to make the "best in the South" claim again. In 1957 he was bragging that the Southern Regional Education Board had approved the college training program as one of the few certified to train teachers for the deaf "for the whole South."[65]

Educational Administration and Service

Educational administration was another strong program with a powerful leader in the postwar college. With a new doctorate from Ohio State University, Orin B. Graff was appointed associate professor of education and principal of the Norris School in 1943. Two years later, he was named head of the new department of Educational Administration and Service (EA&S), although he was the only faculty member. He quickly became one of the most influential education professors in the college, often acting as a countervailing force to deans. The department grew quickly under his leadership.

Graff was particularly effective in getting funds and publicity for EA&S through foundation grants. In 1952 the W. W. Kellogg Foundation awarded the department the then-sizable grant of $43,000 for a three-year project to improve the training of school administrators. A later Kellogg grant provided funds to study the personality traits that made effective school administrators. The General Education Board, which had been such a crucial source of funds early in the history of the college, provided money to hold a series of conferences to train school board members in Tennessee. EA&S professors held conferences in eleven cities with 252 board members and 112 school superintendents from 77 counties. In 1961, a Ford Foundation grant funded the School Planning Laboratory that for many years provided building consultants to school systems across the country.[66]

Graduate Programs in Education

The College of Education developed comprehensive graduate-level programs in the 1940s and 1950s. The university approved a Master of Education degree in 1940 and a Doctor of Education degree in 1949. (The first university Ph.D. degree was awarded in 1947.) The Doctor of Education was authorized in curriculum and instruction, educational administration and supervision, and home economics education; it was first awarded in 1950. In 1951, the university awarded its first doctorates to women, including one in education to Dora Roberts Tyler. The advanced graduate program in education grew rapidly. By the Summer of 1952, sixty-three students were enrolled in postmaster's degree programs.[67]

Graduate programs in education provided further opportunities for conflicts between the College of Education and the College of Liberal Arts. In 1947, Fitzgerald complained to Brehm that the university's graduate study committee was "loaded" with five representatives from Liberal Arts while the other colleges had only one person. Emphasizing the unique needs of professional schools, Fitzgerald wrote that he did not want a "lowering of standards" but different standards to meet the needs of persons working in schools who were not well served by "language hurdles" and other features of traditional graduate programs.[68]

The college dean and faculty used the growing graduate enrollments in their continuing campaign for more funds. Support for graduate assistantships for future public school leaders in Tennessee was, they insisted, particularly crucial: "We should provide five times as much money for this phase of our program, and even then we would be short." As had happened so often in the past, the faculty viewed the educational successes of their arch rival, Peabody College, with horror. In 1951, Fitzgerald reminded Vice President Smith that Peabody had hired two of America's best-known educationists for their graduate programs, Harold Benjamin and Willard Goslin. In addition they had received a large grant from the General Education Board for hiring faculty and for scholarships in educational administration. The dean complained that the college could not continue educational leadership for the state "without a greater contribution to the development of graduate training for leaders in the public schools of Tennessee."[69]

Curricular Reform—Competency-Based Teacher Education Before Its Time

A major theme of this book is that teacher education was always on the defensive, always trying to redefine and often attempting to reinvent itself. Such was the case in the 1950s when a major university-wide "revision" of the teacher education curriculum was instituted. The report of the revisions was released in 1956. It is imposing—five volumes and over eleven hundred pages. The report includes a syllabus for every required course for any major in teacher education. And all of the courses are competency based, even those in liberal arts. (The national movement for competency-based teacher education did not take place until the 1970s.) The report was the culmination of years of reform activity.[70]

In addition to a national clamor for teacher education reform, the impetus for change in the University of Tennessee was a result of the state Certification Act of 1951. The law came after powerful education officials had roundly criticized the sorry condition of Tennessee's schools, particularly what they perceived to be excesses of progressivism. In 1950, Education Commissioner Jack Smith urged elementary principals to stress the "old educational fundamentals—sugar-coating them if necessary." He warned that he would "hate" to see children leaving school who "can't read, can't spell, and can't figure ordinary business transactions."[71]

Not for the first time (or the last) in Tennessee, widespread public school curricular reform was followed by mandates for teacher education reform. As a consequence of the law, the state department of education requested President Brehm to conduct a university-wide teacher education review. Brehm called the deans and selected education professors together to plan the review. An eleven-page, single-spaced transcript of Brehm's notes of the meeting is extant. In the meeting, Education Professor Dale Wantling indicated to the university deans that, although the act was ostensibly aimed at certification standards, teacher education reform was the real goal.[72]

The institutional status-consciousness that infuriated faculties in other Tennessee colleges was blatant in the meeting. Education professor Earl Ramer opined that the university could "largely write the state curricula and state certification [requirements] for teachers." Brehm agreed that the state department of education wanted to take the university's recommendations to the other public and the private colleges with the message that: "This is the way the University wants it." After all he reminded them with the familiar mantra, the university is "the chief educational system in the State and head of the educational system."[73]

Professor Wantling argued that reform could not be achieved by changing the number of required hours in a particular discipline. He called such tinkering superficial and said that it "would not get at the evils of teacher improvement." Rather, the study was to identify the characteristics and competencies of effective teachers in general education, subject matter preparation, and professional programs. Jessie Harris, dean of home economics, responded apparently with some alarm that there was a rumor that certification would not be based on college credits but on competency tests. "It would require a 'battery' of research people," she complained. The group of professors and deans worried with questions of control and autonomy. The specter of the National Education Association accepting only "certain institutional programs" was raised. Wantling indicated that there was a move afoot among education groups to organize a "national accrediting association." This outside interference could limit flexibility in training teachers to meet local needs. After all, agricultural teachers had a responsibility to help raise cotton production in West Tennessee, and home economics teachers needed to teach girls to can tomatoes in Appalachia. (The National Council for Accreditation of Teacher Education soon reported that the UT College of Education had an exemplary program, and the college administration has strongly supported NCATE accreditation for all teacher training institutions since.) In typical university committee fashion, after stating reservations and suspicions, the group accepted their mandate.[74]

Andrew Holt, administrative assistant to the president, moved that a university-wide committee (with representatives from all departments) be appointed to make recommendations. The report was to be submitted to the president who would decide "how to release it and place whatever restrictions the administration deems proper to place on it (lest we might get into controversy with other educational groups in the State)."[75]

Smith sent Brehm a "Progress Report" in August 1953. Smith did not make extravagant claims for the report. He called it incomplete, unspecific, sometimes unclear, and without the support or understanding from many professors but "the best we have achieved to now." He confessed particular difficulty with securing faculty support for the "competency approach." Even though he reported that no faculty group had developed a comprehensive and defensible competency pattern, competencies in ten areas were included in the progress report. The final five-volume report submitted to the Tennessee Board of Education in 1956 included similar competencies.[76]

The fury of activity by scores of professors to produce the five volumes of competencies seems much ado about almost nothing. The competencies often seem a restatement of the obvious and the traditional in an attempt to make the familiar seem new and different. Professors were (or seemed to be) engaging in the time-honored and often sensible strategy of going-through-the-motions to give the administration what they wanted with faith that it would not affect their lives very much.

To emphasize that they were building the teacher education program on competencies rather than on the traditional disciplines, the curriculum makers listed competencies under major headings such as "Man's Relation with the Physical World" and "Man's Relationship with Man." (Gender-specific language was yet to receive effective challenge.) Lest there be misunderstanding, they identified the more recognizable field of study in parentheses. A few examples will give the flavor of the competencies. Under "Man's Relation with the Physical World" is found "comprehends the basic physical laws of the universe and how these affect man's pattern of living." Only a little less modest is competency six under "Communicating with Others:" "Uses habitually and intelligently the mass modes of communication such as newspapers, periodicals, books, pamphlets, radio, motion pictures, the public platform, forums and pamphlets and panel discussions." Liberal arts professors did not surpass their education colleagues in the breadth of knowledge to be apprehended. Competency twelve under "Materials, Methods, and Curriculum" reads: "Employs a general grasp of the accumulated knowledge in all of the great fields of learning."

The educationists also proposed more modest and attainable competencies; under "Evaluation," competency two was to develop "some skill in designing procedures for collecting data to be used for evaluation purposes."[77]

Detailed class syllabi from the final 1956 report suggest the effect on the reforms on curriculum. The required undergraduate history sequence serves as an example as its syllabus was typical of the general education volume. Competency four was "to acquaint students with some of the most insistent, socially significant problems of the present day while at the same time developing social perception and sensitivity, and the appreciation of the need for scientific and democratic discussions and decision-making." But the topics were every history department's 101 course:

1. Introduction: The Threshold of Modern Times.
2. Renaissance and Reformation.
3. Expansion of Europe and American Beginnings.
4. Development of European National States in the 17th and 18th Centuries.
5. The Age of Revolution in Europe and America.

The learning activities were class attendance, daily reading assignments, participation in class discussions, and "occasional papers and reports." The administration and the state department of education accepted the illusion of teacher education reform.[78]

The catalogs for 1952, before the reforms were underway, and for 1962, which allowed time for changes to work their way through the institutional labyrinth, show almost no change. The curricula were almost exactly the same; normal tinkering would have been expected to produce more curriculum change in a decade. For the elementary teacher, the major difference was the addition of a three-hour requirement in speech and a reduction of the history requirement from fifteen to nine hours. All other general education requirements remained the same as did the fifty-four hour requirement in education. The two major changes in the secondary curriculum were the addition of a three-hour requirement in geography and a *decrease* of four hours in the teaching area. It is difficult to know how much difference the "competency-based" curriculum made in the way that courses were taught. Two retired professors commented on this possibility; one said that it had a "considerable influence," and the other said "some."[79]

Despite much noisy activity, little came from the undergraduate teacher education reforms. The reforms were imposed from above, and the commitment of the faculty to them was limited. The education faculty was loath to share power over teacher training, and they had long experience in passive resistance.

Struggle for Reorganization in the 1950s

Lawrence Cremin once wrote that the faculty of Teachers College, Columbia, was just one big unhappy family; the difference at Tennessee was only in the size of the family. The college entered the 1950s with a plan for reorganization into departments but, because of incessant quarreling among the faculty, had been unable to put it into effect. And control over teacher education in the university remained an issue. In 1949, Fitzgerald complained to newly installed President Brehm that the university was "pulling apart" in teacher education rather than coordinating. Fitzgerald wanted control of all teacher education programs in the university.[80]

Fitzgerald also wanted control of all activities within the College of Education. In the Spring of 1952, the twenty-eight members of the faculty had an all-day retreat at the Whittle Springs Hotel to settle the issue. After interminable votes, the faculty agreed to departmentalize. But, even after departments were established, the dean refused to relinquish any power. Fitzgerald could be close-minded and high-handed, and he was even more frustrating to the university administration than Thackston had been. Brehm and Smith grew weary of the constant bickering between the dean and the faculty. Smith had responsibility for what he called the "whole mess." In a confidential, handwritten memo to the Brehm, he blamed Fitzgerald for most of the problems of the college:

1. Dean writes all minutes of all meetings.
2. Refuses to bring in *whole* Ed. Col. faculty to discuss administration problems.
3. Seems to insist on remaining head of C&I Dept. and budget.
4. Resists suggestions that the President and Vice President sit in on College of Ed. faculty with the Dean and put cards on table in open discussion.[81]

As the controversy continued, educational administration department head Orin Graff kept up a behind-the-lines warfare with the dean, sending a stream of criticisms to Smith. Smith directed Fitzgerald to appoint a department head for each department, to "divorce himself from departmental administration" (including allowing the departments to prepare their own budgets), to use the department heads as an advisory committee, and to elect a faculty secretary to keep minutes and records of actions taken in faculty meetings. Over a year later, Brehm complained that, although Fitzgerald received these requests in writing and they were discussed with him in person several times, results of the conversations just "faded away."[82]

Finally, after further prodding from the administration, Fitzgerald agreed to complete reorganization by appointing a head of the Department of Curriculum and Instruction. In May 1954, Earl Ramer, a native Tennessean with a doctorate from Teachers College, Columbia, was placed in charge of C&I. Speaking with a drawl, courtly, and mild mannered, Ramer was much the southern gentleman. He eschewed controversy and was effective in achieving compromise and consensus. He served as head for sixteen years. At first, the omnibus department included elementary and secondary education, social foundations, educational psychology, and special education.[83]

Part of the conventional wisdom of the national reform movement of the 1950s was that teacher education was too important to leave to schools of education. Articles on the state of teacher education and proposals for reform in *School and Society* and in the new *The Journal of Teacher Education* (first published in 1950) indicate the nature of the debate among educationists. The essentialist *School and Society* advocated more study of the disciplines for prospective teachers, whereas *The Journal of Teacher Education* found greater virtue in the study of pedagogy. Education literature criticized the animosity between liberal arts and education in training teachers. In the March 1951 issue of *The Journal of Teacher Education*, well-known progressive Harold Rugg lamented a lack of cooperation and argued that former state teachers colleges were doing better than universities and liberal arts colleges, where professors did not accept education as a "respectable university discipline." Theodore C. Blegen, Dean of the Graduate School at Minnesota, wrote of "rancor, if not open war" between education and liberal arts professors. He placed much of the blame for the distrust on the quality and relevance of educationists' research.[84]

The panacea for this ill will between education and liberal arts professors, prescribed in numerous articles during the 1950s, was to make teacher education an "all institutional activity" by creating teacher education councils with representatives from all faculties. University-wide responsibility for teacher education was central to the reform effort at Tennessee. The wider university faculty needed to be involved not only to improve teacher education, but also to foster a commitment to training teachers. Brehm began the May 1952 meeting that initiated the reforms in Tennessee with the challenge to colleges to reconcile differences among their own faculties. Wantling agreed, warning of "alarming and disturbing differences among us in the University" that the faculty had to "thresh out." After the submission of the 1953 "Progress Report," state Superintendent Quill E. Cope noted that membership on the committee that developed the report was voluntary and informal, and he requested the creation of a formal structure with members from across the university professoriate to provide leadership in teacher education program development.[85]

In the Spring of 1957, Fitzgerald announced that all teacher education programs were finally located in the College of Education, except business education and physical education. He explained the change:

> Some of the subject matter especially in science had been taught in the College of Education for teachers and practically every department in Liberal Arts had its own ideas on how to teach its own particular subject matter. All these special methods courses for teaching in the several subject matter departments were discontinued in Liberal Arts and the subject matter that was taught in the College of Education was discontinued.[86]

The same year the university administration accepted an elaborate "Revised Suggestions on Organizational Procedures." Each college had a representative on the advisory committee that was to make policy recommendations on teacher education and develop procedures for teacher selection and certification. A College of Education subcommittee was to make recommendations for certification to the state. Fitzgerald, always striving for control, immediately wrote to Brehm requesting him to advise the state department of education that the College of Education had the responsibility for recommending graduates for certification and that all "comments and questions . . . should be directed to the Dean of the College of Education." Fitzgerald did not get his way with the president. Brehm's letter to the department of education did not grant authority to the dean and the college in the language that Fitzgerald requested. Brehm reiterated that a university-wide committee had responsibility for screening and recommending students for teacher certification and that the College of Education was the "agency" within the university through which the committee would "channel" recommendations. Brehm may have sensed the eventual fate of the university-wide committee, however. Less than a month after his letter to the department of education, he commented in a deans' meeting that the various colleges could have had direct contact with the state for teacher certification, but with all of the paper work involved "Business and Liberal Arts were very happy to 'unload on Education.'"[87]

The university-wide committee on teacher education led a mystery existence. I could not find a record of its activities. Yet, according to the 1962 NCATE report, "The organization of the University for teacher education includes an important University-wide advisory and coordinating committee." On the organization chart included in the report, the committee is prominently displayed between the vice president and the various colleges. Retired faculty (including English professor Bain Stewart, co-author of the document that created the committee) who worked on the reforms do not remember that the committee functioned. William Coffield, who became associate dean of the college in 1972 and dean in 1977, reported that he was unaware that such a committee ever existed. Such was the illusion of university-wide participation in teacher education policy at UT. James D. Koerner, the most vociferous of the educationist bashers of the period, commented that "too often the so-called 'institution-wide' approach to teacher education [became] mere window dressing." As it pertains to Tennessee, Koerner, for once, engaged in understatement.[88]

A Home of Their Own

To almost everyone's surprise the state legislature appropriated a million dollars for a College of Education building in 1955. In collegiate Gothic style, the ugly but serviceable building was named for P. P. Claxton. As indicated before, teacher education had long struggled for adequate housing. Because of the endowment of Peabody College in Nashville, UT failed to receive the grant from the Peabody Fund that other southern states used for education buildings. As early as 1920, President Morgan urged the Board of Trustees to support the construction of a "Teacher Training Building." But building needs were critical across the campus, and the state legislature did not appropriate funds for any major university buildings between 1925 and 1945.

The college tried but failed to gain support for a building from outside sources, notably the Public Works Administration and the General Education Board. In 1939, despairing of ever getting a new facility, Thackston requested that an old building, Humes Hall, be remodeled and assigned to the college. Even this attempt to get a hand-me-down was unsuccessful. The best the college was able to do was to gain office space in an army surplus pre-fabricated building that had been in a prisoner-of-war camp in Crossville, Tennessee. The wooden structure quickly became known to the students as Splinter Hall.[89]

In 1950, in addition to the barracks, College of Education departments were scattered across campus in liberal arts, agricultural, home economics, biology, and engineering buildings. The *Orange and White* reported that the units of the college had been "flung like scattered orphans on the Hill." "Nomadic tribes making their way from building to building" was another metaphor used for education students and faculty in the same issue. The student newspaper editorialized that having their own home might be a psychological boost to timid education students and to their faculty who had "been subjected to some pretty irritating criticism from their cousins in other parts of the University." A case for a new facility was strengthened when an accreditation committee of the American Association of Colleges for Teacher Education ranked the college faculty "extremely high" and the physical facilities "strikingly inadequate."[90]

Not surprisingly, the building was named for Philander P. Claxton, "the Horace Mann of the South," and founder of the original UT Department of Education. Mrs. Philander P. Claxton (the only name she publicly used) mounted a campaign to have the building named for her husband. Retired President Hoskins and Brehm reacted favorably. Hoskins wrote her that he was "determined" to have the education building named for Claxton, but that she should keep it quiet. Hoskins kept his word and supported strongly naming the building for Claxton: "It is the only recommendation that I have made with regard to the naming of buildings." Brehm concurred, and the tribute to Claxton was popular with the press. The building was dedicated on November 15, 1957, shortly after Claxton's death.[91]

Local newspapers praised the Claxton Education Building for reflecting the "latest trends in schoolhouse construction." The "refreshing ventilation" offered by the air-conditioning system was highly praised. "It's air conditioned—every room of it," gushed a local newspaper commenting on how much it would make "the sweltering summer" comfortable for teachers who came from throughout the state. The contemporary blond furniture, the 300-seat assembly room, an education library, and the "play therapy room" with two-way mirrors ("covered with wire grills to protect them from flying blocks and picture books thrown by irate children at play") also received much favorable comment.[92]

Chapter 8

From a Southern to a National College

The 1960s was a time of fundamental change for the college as well as for the nation. N. E. Fitzgerald, dean since 1943 and faculty member since 1919, retired in 1961. Fitzgerald, who argued that teacher education should be practical rather than theoretical, was replaced by E. C. "Pete" Merrill. (Merrill, born just over the mountains in Asheville, North Carolina, received his master's degree from UT and his doctorate from George Peabody College for Teachers.) He urged the faculty to be more philosophical and to devote "more time to the discussion of educational issues, concepts, and ideas." During a time of national preoccupation with education, Merrill argued for more "growing-edge" thinking in the college.[1]

In the 1960s, Merrill and the college had a strong friend in the university president's office. Andrew D. Holt, "Andy" to everyone, was president of the university from 1959 to 1970. His doctorate in education administration was from Teachers College, Columbia University. He was a former public school teacher, professor of education at West Tennessee State Teachers College, long-time executive secretary of the Tennessee Education Association, president of the National Education Association, and one of the most powerful and popular political figures in Tennessee. During his tenure, the number of university students tripled, faculty doubled, and the budget quadrupled. He was a cheerleader for the university, using "wit, folksiness, glib charm" to affirm everyone and ameliorate conflict.[2]

Holt wrote numerous, hyperbolic letters of appreciation and support to Merrill: "Every letter of yours I read, every speech of yours I hear, and every decision of yours which I hear about strengthen my determination to hold you at UT until time for your retirement." And when Merrill announced his resignation, Holt assured him that "never in my life have I been associated with a more dedicated, capable, and

genial person than you, and I will treasure your friendship always."
After Merrill left, Holt gave the new dean, James McComas, "a wonderful guy," the same support and good will.[3]

Growth in Teacher Education

Enrollment in the university at Knoxville grew from about 4,000 students in 1946 (when 40 percent of the students were veterans) to
almost 10,000 in 1960 and to nearly 30,000 in 1980. Baby boomers
were going to school, there was a chronic teacher shortage, and nearly
anyone who was certified could get a job. The National Defense Education Act (N.D.E.A.) helped poorer students, always the mainstay for
schools of education, by providing loans for students that could be
forgiven for teaching. Education students received an unexpected source
of funding when an eccentric, retired mail carrier in a rusty black suit
appeared at UT in 1965 with an initial gift of $100,000 to support
students who wanted to teach in public schools. Clayton Arnold had
originally approached Peabody College with the idea of a gift, but
they didn't seem particularly interested, and a disgruntled Peabody
professor told him that he might have a better reception in Knoxville.
By the time of his death in 1987, the self-described miser who had
made some "fortunate investments" gave gifts to the college that were
worth more than $1.5 million. He had worked out a formula that
within a century his gift would have provided scholarships for 6,000
Arnold Teachers who would "eventually influence 24 million lives."[4]

Students packed education classes, and the college was on the move.
Enrollment in the college increased from about 12 percent to over 20
percent of the university's undergraduates during the decade of the
1960s. In 1961, nearly 1,000 full-time undergraduate students enrolled in the college, and a decade later the number had reached over
3,800. The number of student teachers increased at a dizzying pace,
from 263 in 1961–62, to 584 in 1966–67, and to 946 in 1970–71.
In 1977, the college newsletter bragged that the Student National
Education Association chapter was the largest in the nation.[5]

Education graduate enrollments kept pace. In 1960, 330 full- and
part-time graduate students enrolled in education. By 1970, 1,314 of
the 4,362 graduate students in the university were in education. And
by Spring 1972, the college enrolled over 34 percent of the graduate
students at UT. From 1975 to 1979, the graduate school awarded
2,360 master's degrees and 352 doctoral degrees in education. And
there were jobs for the new Ed.Ds as well as for new teachers: A 1973

survey of recent doctoral graduates found that only one was not employed in education. Despite the growing size of the graduate population, the college remained a regional rather than a national institution. In a 1970 survey, more than 80 percent of the graduate-degree recipients had received their undergraduate degree from a southeast college and over 60 percent from a Tennessee school.[6]

Even during the heady time of growth and with the college "just beginning to catch up" with enrollment increases, administrators started worrying about an apparent national teacher surplus. A new mission statement for the 1970s proposed more emphasis on graduate education, in part because "a teacher surplus forecasted for the 1970's makes this policy appear prudent." In Fall 1972, university enrollment dropped for the first time in decades, although College of Education enrollment continued to increase through the mid-1970s.[7]

Changing Nature of the Faculty

Even with the G.I. Bill and the looming teacher shortage, at the end of the 1949 academic year the College of Education had only 19 faculty members. With the support of the benevolent Holt, the size of the education faculty grew rapidly, from 46 members in 1960, to 88 in 1969, and to 157 in 1969. But new hires could not keep pace, and the faculty complained that there were "formidable needs" for new faculty in most departments. The advising loads were particularly heavy; 100 advisees was not uncommon and some professors "advised" 150 students: "Unless a faculty member is extremely conscientious . . . the extent of his advising can easily become that of signing registration and drop and add forms."[8]

Through the middle-1970s, many new faces appeared at Fall faculty meetings; 23 were hired in 1974 and 19 in 1975. And the faces were usually young, as most of the hires in the 1960s and 1970s were at the assistant-professor level. In 1970, there were 74 assistant professors in the college, more than associate and full professors combined. With declining enrollments, by 1980 the size of the teaching staff leveled off with 155 faculty members; and with easy (compared to later generations) promotions and fewer hires, the faculty was already top heavy with 42 percent professors, 35 percent associate professors, and 15 percent assistant professors.[9]

With the large increase in size, one might expect a more cosmopolitan faculty. The college mission statement for the 1970s included a commitment to faculty diversity in "philosophy, interests, and back-

ground." College of Education professors at Tennessee had traditionally been southerners, and the college's regional culture was challenged
during the period. The college administration and faculty supported
employing faculty from "throughout the country." On a survey questionnaire, the faculty agreed 85 to 3 that "Faculty should be hired
from different regions of the country." Goals for diversity had only
some success. The 1980 faculty had received their highest degrees
from 56 graduate schools. Thirty members had earned their advanced
degrees in Tennessee, 25 at UT and 4 at George Peabody College.
Other states in which faculty earned their terminal degrees in order of
frequency were Ohio (17), Illinois (10), Florida (9), and Michigan (9).
With 46 faculty members, Curriculum and Instruction was the largest
department. In 1979–80, 30 faculty including most of those at the
assistant professor level had received their doctorates from southern
institutions.[10]

Issues of Mission and Quality

After Merrill left the college to become president of Gallaudet University, James McComas was appointed dean in 1969. From West Virginia with an Ohio State doctorate, he represented a break with his
southern predecessors. The new, ambitious dean insisted on a particularly intense study of the college's mission in preparation for Southern Association and National Council for the Accreditation of Teacher
Education (NCATE) reviews. In his inaugural address to the faculty,
McComas asked them to reconsider the mission of the college: "What
should be the philosophy of a college of education in a land-grant
university which is also *the* state university?" After much faculty debate, there was more continuity than change in the "Program Mission" statement that the faculty produced. The question of moving
more to a graduate school of education was raised. Since the creation
of the Department of Education in 1902, the college liked to compare
itself with Teachers College, Columbia, and the University of Chicago, and they did not resist doing so again: "Pressure often is applied in a major university to reduce undergraduate programs and to
expand graduate programs. This pressure is especially felt in teacher
education since many prestigious institutions such as Teachers College, Columbia, The University of California, Berkeley, and The University of Chicago have moved in this direction." After much discussion, the college decided to keep undergraduate and graduate programs
"balanced." The college faculty also decided not to try to expand their

sphere of influence beyond Tennessee and the region; only "to some extent" did they want to pursue the goal of national educational leadership. Rather they wished to create a "TVA for Education" to improve schooling opportunities for children and the many illiterate adults in "Tennessee generally and in the Appalachian region specifically."[11]

Throughout its history, teacher education in the university had been criticized for the academic quality of its students. In 1961, Aaron Montgomery Johnston, an elementary education professor who made a nuisance of himself with some of his colleagues by pushing for higher academic standards, published a seventy-page report on the academic quality of UT education students. The report was obviously considered sensitive and was marked "confidential" on the cover. Johnston compared 166 student teachers with norms on the Graduate Record Examinations (GRE)—including the social science, the humanities, and the natural science tests as well as the "advanced test" in education. He found that the college of education students were significantly below the GRE norms and were "equally poor on both verbal and quantitative aptitude."[12]

On the basis of the data, Johnston constructed a profile of the typical 1961 student teacher in the college. She was twenty-eight-years old, unmarried, with a rural or small town lower middle-class background. Her parents were high-school graduates who lived together, and her mother was a "housewife." She came from conservatives' model American family. This typical student teacher was not an exemplary scholar. She ranked below the mean on the subject-matter tests, and at the 35th percentile on both the GRE verbal and quantitative aptitude tests, although she ranked in the 64th percentile on the advanced education tests.[13]

Over three-fourths of the student teachers were women; because a number of experienced teachers who were holders of provisional certificates were require to earn degrees, their average age was higher than might be expected. (Tennessee passed legislation in 1956 that required the bachelor's degree for certification.) Although many nondegreed teachers had taught for years, they had to student teach to earn standard certification. On the education subtests, the student teachers scored lowest on sociological foundations. Johnston, who for many years was highly critical of the way social foundations of education were taught, recommended revising the social foundations curriculum to assure that it included the proper, specific understandings that were tested.[14]

Academic requirements for entering teacher-education programs were low. Students normally applied for admission to the Teacher Education Program in the second quarter of their sophomore year. The requirements were easy to satisfy:

(1) A 2.0 overall grade point average
(2) An expressed interest in teaching
(3) Satisfactory physical and mental health
(4) Favorable ratings from instructors in core professional courses and from advisers.

Only a 2.0 grade-point average on a 4.0 system was required for student teaching, graduation, certification, and for endorsement in a "teaching area."[15]

The quality of the academic program became a major issue for the college when NCATE accreditation was deferred in April 1962 because of concerns that the machinery for making teacher education a university-wide concern seemed ineffective to the review committee, the admission standards to teacher education "were relatively low," and the programs in general education were inconsistent across the college. Dean Merrill answered for the college. He agreed that the University Advisory Committee on Teacher Education did not "appear to be adequate or functioning properly" and that there were problems with academic standards and the rigor with which they were enforced. He assured W. Earl Armstrong, Director of NCATE, that he had sent an "open letter" to the faculty preparing them "to face up to the problems cited" and to make the necessary corrections.[16]

Merrill and the university administration developed a series of programs "to give the faculty some new perspectives on teacher education":

Vice President [later president] Edward J. Boling addressed the faculty on State-wide needs in teacher education. Vice President Herman E. Spivey spoke about the role of a professional school in the University setting. State Commissioner of Education Joe Morgan discussed the legal and financial aspects of the forthcoming biennium. Dean Walter K. Beggs of the University of Nebraska gave a major address to the faculty on "The Teacher of Tomorrow."

Discussion of missions, characteristics, role, resources, objectives, structure, programs, and the future of the college took place. The college proposed that the 1957 University Advisory Committee on Teacher Education and Certification Recommendation be replaced with a University Committee on Teacher Education to "make proposals concerning any phase of teacher education." This was an idea supported by the best-known critic of teacher education in the period, James Conant. Holt endorsed the change: I "congratulate you and your colleagues on the fact that our [University Committee on Teacher Education] rather well meets the standards set up by Conant."[17]

The college recommendations to raise academic requirements for admission to teacher education were slight and gradual, from a 2.1 GPA in 1962–63, to a 2.2 in 1963–64, to a 2.25 in 1964–65. Nevertheless, full accreditation was granted to the college in May 1963. Speaking for NCATE, Armstrong expressed hope that the college would direct "attention to the quality of students being admitted to the program and allowed to complete it at the undergraduate and graduate levels." President Holt told Merrill that he "let out a war hoop like a Comanche Indian when I read Earl Armstrong's letter. . . . Please send copies of it not only to the members of your faculty but also to every person in the United States."[18]

A few years later, when the faculty was conducting self-studies for the 1971 NCATE and Southern Association reviews, they were no more enthusiastic about increasing academic requirements. Standards for admission required a 2.2 grade-point average (not the 2.25 agreed to in 1963); the GPA could still drop to 2.0 and allow admission to student teaching and certification. And A. Montgomery "Gummy" Johnston was still complaining about academic standards: "Currently we exercise very little quality control on admission, retention, or recommendation." From 1967 through 1970, the college admitted 4,214 of the 4,704 students who applied. Most of those not admitted were refused for failure to achieve the 2.2 GPA; only four were refused admission for lack of an advisor's recommendation. In response to a questionnaire on college goals, the faculty agreed overwhelmingly that undergraduate and graduate students' "ability to work with students and professors" was more important than academic achievement. When asked if a minimum American College Test (ACT) score of 20 should be required for college admission, 10 faculty strongly agreed, 22 moderately agreed, 20 moderately disagreed, and 23 strongly disagreed.[19]

The report of NCATE evaluation in 1971 contained some bad news. Faculty overloads, inadequate facilities, lack of sabbatical or leave policies (the need for a sabbatical was the only item that the faculty agreed to unanimously on the goals questionnaire), and "the need for systematic evaluation of undergraduates and graduates" concerned the visiting team. NCATE classified the college as "adequate." The Southern Association evaluation observed that the college was "somewhat passive" in recruiting outstanding students.[20]

McComas was disappointed with the reviews and disturbed with the growing national attacks on schools and teacher education from the right and the left. He urged the faculty to take critics seriously. He quoted liberally from Charles E. Silberman's popular *Crisis in the Classroom* to the college faculty and concluded that one could "perhaps take issue with points of view here and there which are expressed, but the issues he presents are not easily dismissed." He was particularly upset by a local, powerful critic of teacher education, Hugh McDade, a member of the Tennessee Board of Education and an executive with ALCOA whose headquarters was a few miles down the road from the university. In the press and public speeches, McDade denounced education colleges. In 1973, he reported that even Dean McComas "admitted that there were some Poor programs at U.T.!" McComas insisted that McDade had used an incorrect and untrue quotation" from him, but he warned the faculty that McDade and other critics were not going away, and that the best response was to improve the quality of the college.[21]

By the time of the 1981 NCATE reaccreditation visit, the faculty had made several additions to the familiar requirements for admission to teacher education: a "social-emotional" evaluation based on the 16PF Personality Inventory to "ensure against admitting students with abnormal moral and emotional characteristics"; a clean record with the Office of Student Conduct; a "field experience"; and satisfactory scores in basic language and mathematics achievement as measured by the California Achievement Test, Level 19. But almost everyone who applied to the college continued to be admitted. In 1976, a typical year, the college admitted 378 of the 443 students who applied "on initial application." Thirty-nine of the sixty-five students refused initially were admitted on reapplication.[22]

Research and Service

Faculty as well as student quality has long been an issue in colleges of education, particularly in research and publications. But, as indicated before, teaching and advising loads were heavy in the 1960s and early 1970s, and professors had difficulty finding "time for intensive, formal research." The normal teaching load was twelve hours a week with full professors teaching less because they were more likely to direct doctoral research. By 1970, a common, if often unfair, practice in the college was for assistant professors to teach twelve hours, associate professors nine, and professors six. Young faculty really did, as was commonly said at the time, have to take research time "out of their hides." Perhaps the most surprising response to the 1970 "goals" questionnaire was that three faculty members disagreed that faculty should not be assigned "more than four (4) three-hour courses per quarter."[23]

In addition to the heavy teaching loads, there had not been an ethos of research and scholarship in the college. Fitzgerald with his Fords carrying professors to schools throughout the state had emphasized the service function of the college. In the five years from 1956 to 1961, the college faculty reported to NCATE that they had conducted more than 100 "consultant services" with schools, agencies, and educational organizations, including survey teams, and had given more than "200 speeches." Over the five years, they also reported that more than fifty articles were published, including stories in newspapers. Four "books" were also listed as publications by education professors during the period: *Gregg Transcriptions for Colleges, The Education of the Exceptional Child, Home Gardening*, and *Reflective Thinking*.[24]

Dean Merrill pushed the faculty to greater "professional" efforts but did not demand research or publications specifically: We would like for every person on our faculty to identify one specific objective for himself which he is very determined to do this year." McComas was much more directive. In "The UT College of Education—An Immovable Object or An Irresistible Force?" his first address to the college faculty, he challenged them to demonstrate the kind of scholarship that they asked of their students.

> I would submit that any professor who has anything worthwhile to say to his students, has something worthwhile to share with students and his peers on other campuses and that an efficient way of communicating it is through selected publications. If there is any among us who does not have any unique or adapted personal philosophical or creative ideas of his own to communicate *which may make a difference*, then we can program his class, assign readings and spend the money which we would have paid him on salary for learning materials and equipment!

McComas's emphasis on publications was resisted by a number of faculty and department heads who argued that professors could not be expected to be equally adept at teaching, research, and service.

Faculty argued that they should help decide their "assignments and duties" within a clear "work-load formula."[25]

Throughout the 1970s, the service function of the college remained paramount, in part, because school systems and other agencies were paying "big bucks" for consulting services. In 1965, the college created the Bureau of Educational Research and Service that, in its early years, was much more devoted to service than to research. One of its responsibilities was to "relay requests for professional services to departments and faculty members in order to determine their interests and availability." Many faculty criticized it for playing favorites and directing consulting activities to privileged professors and administrators. An ad hoc committee created to study the activities of the Bureau decided the problems that had "plagued" it were a result of a lack of faculty involvement in its policies and activities.[26]

The School Planning Laboratory was a major funded service project that reemphasized the southern focus of the college. It was established in 1961 under a Ford Foundation grant, and the next year it was designated the Southeastern Regional Center for Education Facilities Laboratories, Inc. It provided assistantships for a large number of graduate students and consulting funds for privileged faculty. By 1970 it had collaborated with over twenty-five school systems to build or renovate more than 500 schools, primarily in the South; but, with its rural high-school planning project, it helped design and construct schools as far away as Alaska. The work of the laboratory ended tragically in 1978 when four consultants, including a graduate student and Charles Trotter, the director, were killed in the crash of a UT plane after a consulting trip to Maryland.[27]

With a grant from the U.S. Office of Education, the college in 1966 established the Educational Opportunities Planning Center to advise and give technical assistance and training to local school officials and school patrons during and after racial desegregation. It was the second university desegregation consulting center funded by the Office of Education. The university administration worried about the political fallout from a "Desegregation Center." President Holt asked his assistant, [later president] Joe Johnson, to review the proposal. Johnson assured Holt that the center would "not promote integration" but would "help teachers and administrators meet the administrative and instructional problems" that were exacerbated by desegregation. Johnson expressed concern to Holt about the appointment of the director and advisory committee for the center: "If the employees of the Center are crusaders, we could encounter problems, but Dean Merrill and Dr. Spivey can prevent this situation by their evaluation of candidates for employment." He also warned that the proposal read that "the Center will both speed and smooth the mechanical process of desegregation." In a period when the Supreme Court mandate that schools be desegregated "with all deliberate speed" still rankled many southerners, he worried that using the "word 'speed' may raise a few questions." But overall he though the proposal "generally sound." That the administration's decision was sagacious was confirmed a few weeks later when Governor Frank Clement, unaware that a proposal had already been sent to the U.S. Office, wrote Holt praising the College of Education for conducting desegregation training institutes for school personnel and suggesting that the college apply for a federal grant to finance such a center.[28]

Soon renamed the Mid-Atlantic/Appalachian Race Desegregation Assistance Center (MAARDAC), it served Tennessee, Kentucky, and the Carolinas. After 1976, with U.S. Office of Education grants awarded from the Women's Educational Equity Act Program, it was joined by the Southeast Sex Desegregation Assistance Center. The related centers produced "bias free" curriculum materials, including games. The Anti-Defamation League of B'nai B'rith distributed MAARDAC materials nationally. Funding lasted until 1987, and *intercom*, the monthly college newsletter, contained numerous reports of training sessions, workshops, and other services to school systems in the South. As an example, in December 1982 in Orange County, North Carolina, training on race relations was given "to 126 people, including central office personnel, principals, teachers, instructional aides, parents, and school board members." Five teachers received much more "intensive and extended training" and were certified as trainers for the school system. Business, government, and citizen groups were also participants in workshops.[29]

A striking feature of the faculty activities during the 1960s and 1970s was the workshops, sometimes lasting for days or weeks, away from campus. The workshops included the "hot" topics of the period: use of behavioral objectives, nonverbal communications, and multimedia. The amount of consulting was controversial. Some faculty (particularly those who did little paid consulting) complained that colleagues were not teaching their classes and were receiving double awards: consulting fees as well as credit for service activities on their faculty evaluations. McComas warned the faculty about the excesses: "A very *few faculty may be abusing* the right to consult by excessive absences from the campus. It is hoped that everyone will exercise restraint and good judgment. Won't you please help by keeping such activities at or below the level which the University had indicated and also have such activities recognized in the regular way. *Thanks.*"[30]

By the 1980s, service activities decreased as consulting grants became more scarce and the university began to demand and reward publications. In lists of faculty activities in *intercom*, workshops and consultations with teachers, principals, supervisors, and other school-based educators began to give way to more presentations at meetings of scholarly and professional associations. In January 1970, *intercom* began a section listing faculty publications for the previous month. The number of publications was often impressive, but the same relatively few professors were doing most of the writing; the May 1970 issue listed fifteen publications by eight professors and the June issue twenty-six publications by twelve professors. The lack of a research ethos was revealed by one of the "goals" questions for the 1970 self-study. Fifteen faculty agreed and seventy disagreed (twenty-nine "strongly") to the proposition that the college should hire only new faculty with "identified research interests," a position that within a few years would be much at odds with college goals as the university began to identify itself as a research institution. As research and publications became important for merit pay and required for promotions, faculty hired in the early 1970s and before began to complain that the "rules had changed" for faculty rewards, a complaint that became more bitter in the 1980s and 1990s.[31]

The lack of faculty research expertise and productivity was an issue for the growing graduate programs. As the university graduate council became more rigorous in its standards for approving professors to direct dissertations, suggestions were made that, to encourage the development of research competency and to foster "creativity and innovation," the college should stop hiring its own graduates. In 1971, McComas, after "a perusal" of recent dissertation titles in the college, expressed his own concern about the quality of graduate research: "Do the titles suggest the level of sophistication one would expect for doctoral dissertations?" . . . "Do dissertations within departments show a wide disparity in quality?"[32]

At a time before research had become central to graduate study in the college, many students were critical of their research experience. They were "turned-off to research," they complained, because often there was "no help from faculty." Students argued for a new image of research; they criticized the standardized quantitative doctoral dissertations required and voiced support for new types of studies, including "participant observations." Some argued for alternatives to "written" dissertations, including published articles, presentations at national conventions, and films and other "creative work." Other graduate students, reflecting the antiresearch attitude of some of their professors went further, suggesting that it was unrealistic to expect them to all become competent researchers and that it was enough to require all graduate students "to be able to sufficiently interpret research findings."[33]

Protesters and Hippies

Large numbers of hippies and war protesters appeared on the UT campus long after they were commonplace at Berkeley and elsewhere. But in the 1969–70 academic year, after the killings at Kent State University and the sending of troops into Cambodia, they seemed omnipresent and the campus was in turmoil: some professors dismissed classes to protest Kent State; antiwar protest rallies were a part of the culture of the University Center (with large numbers of fatigue-clad veterans taking part); and student protest leader Peter Kami was standing before the administration building challenging new UT President Edward Boling to come outside and duke it out.

After requests from a local clergy committee in May 1970, the administration invited evangelist Billy Graham to conduct a crusade in the football stadium. In turn, President Richard Nixon was invited to speak at the crusade. Antiwar students and faculty were outraged. They argued that the university was being used for political purposes, that Nixon was attempting to prove that (despite national student unrest) he could still speak on a college campus, and that it was a studied insult to the University of Tennessee to think it was so backwater conservative that Nixon could speak there without major protests. About 75,000 people, including several hundred protesters and a huge contingent of police and other law enforcement officers, were in the stadium when Nixon attended the crusade on May 28. Some protesters were boisterous and shouted obscenities, but others quickly quieted them. Twenty-two persons, including Peter Kami and two professors, were arrested and charged with disturbing a religious service. There seemed to be little relationship between those arrested and their behavior at the crusade; it was clear that they had been chosen for arrest earlier. One faculty antiwar leader was so distressed at not being arrested that he took a taxi to the police station and turned himself in only to discover to his chagrin that there was not a warrant for him. "Free the Knoxville 22" became a slogan at rallies and on buttons and posters. Eighty faculty quickly came to the support of those arrested and national publicity followed, including an article by Garry Wills in *Esquire* the following August.[34]

Suspicion and distrust between trustees, alumni, and administrators on one side and students and faculty on the other lasted for years. In June, after the General Alumni Association had passed a similar resolution, the Board of Trustees resolved that the administration could "expel" students and faculty for "confrontation" and "disruption," including cancellation of classes. In August 1970, Chancellor Weaver met with the Monroe County chapter of the Alumni Association. He assured them that the professors didn't want "to destroy the American university. I can't say that about students." An alumnus responded that "there are two or three professors up there I'd frankly like to shoot." Another asked if "all the troublemakers have beards and wear sandals"? "Most of them," Weaver responded. Years later the faculty senate was still investigating the possible activities of the campus police in infiltrating protest organizations, maintaining files on political activities, and tapping faculty phones.[35]

Faculty conservatives in the College of Education were dismayed by hippie-appearing undergraduates, dressed in tie-dyed T-shirts, bell-bottom jeans, long hair, and with antiestablishment expressions on their faces. Even more obnoxious, in their eyes, was that some young professors supported the students' disgraceful appearance and behavior—and didn't look a hell of a lot better themselves. Professors scoffed that the students wanted to control the university so they wouldn't have to learn anything difficult. It was another reflection of the "do your own thing" philosophy of the counterculture. "Its like putting the animals in charge of the zoo," one senior professor liked to grumble.

One reflection of the period that found its way into mainstream education and into the curriculum of the college was "humanistic" and "sensitivity" education. Reflecting the sensitivity training popular at the time, some classes and seminars resembled T-groups where students and faculty struggled with value conflicts and engaged in "activities directed at cultivating sensitivity." The college Statement of Mission for the 1970s declared that its major goal was "to help produce professional personnel who have a sensitivity to broad spectrum of humane and democratic values. These values may include appreciation of cultural differences, sensitivity to poverty, sensitivity to cruelty, sensitivity to love."[36]

The social upheavals of the 1960s, the views of Deans Merrill and McComas, and the influx of a young and more cosmopolitan faculty brought a growing sense of responsibility for, or at least more talk about, preparing teachers for diverse populations. In part, the college responded to public education's bureaucratic expansion to teach everyone: to train educators for the young, the old, the disabled, the rural Appalachian, the urban, and racial minorities.

Almost every planning document of the 1960s and 1970s emphasized needs for early childhood and adult education. Kindergartens were rare in Tennessee as the period started; only one school system reported such classes in 1963. The state began to provide financial support for kindergartens in 1965, and their numbers grew rapidly. Other faculty worried that Tennessee was next to the bottom nationally in school dropouts and that there was a desperate need for adult educators. In 1970, 65 percent of rural Tennessee adults, over 600,000 people, had gone to school for fewer than eight years. The college hired an adult education specialist in 1970 and an early childhood specialist in 1971.[37]

Special education had long been a strong college program, and, despite the loss of Mag the Magnificent, it continued to grow, particularly in deaf education. In 1966, the Southern Regional Media Center for the Deaf was established in the college. It developed a comprehensive program for research, production, and distribution of multimedia material in deaf education: "During the school year, SRMCD staff traversed the region in station wagons, transporting equipment and materials of inservice media workshops." And the Summer Media Institute brought teachers of the deaf to UT "for six weeks of rigorous training." In the 1970s, the college led the nation in the number of deaf education graduates. In 1975, the federally funded Southeast Regional Interpreter Training Consortium was established at UT for eight southeastern states, and since 1983 the college has provided technical assistance to postsecondary schools serving the deaf and hard of hearing in fourteen southern states and the Virgin Islands.[38]

The college continued to highlight its community-based centers as a way of providing specialized student-teaching programs for diverse populations. As discussed in chapter 6, the college faculty had a vigorous outreach to rural Appalachia in the 1920s and 1930s but had not continued to give much attention to this cultural environment in which it was located, although it often reproved itself for not doing so and promised to do better in the future. Without much support from their department or college, three Curriculum and Instruction professors organized opportunities for education students to work in rural Morgan County schools one day a week for a quarter. Over 350 students participated in the project during the early 1970s. And the student-teaching director made deliberate efforts to provide teachers with experiences in the type of small, rural schools still common in isolated Appalachian communities: "The Clinch-Powell (Appalachia) Center will find 19 UT student teachers in one- and two-room rural schools."[39]

On the other hand, and despite much excellent work by MAARDAC with public schools, the college continued to ignore African Americans and other minorities in its own teacher-education program. The college relied on student teaching to give opportunities for teaching diverse populations. But none of the ten "carefully cultivated" schools that were used as student-teacher centers were primarily African American, and the director of student teaching until the late 1970s argued against sending student teachers to predominantly black schools, because "they didn't want to be assigned there." He regretfully admitted later that we "didn't respond until we had to." They "had to" because African-American community leaders, "upset with lack of placement," confronted the college administration and the director of student teaching; he was told that he was "what was wrong with the university." In a 1995 interview, the former director said that the African-American community had been right in their perceptions, and he had been wrong not only in not placing student teachers in African-American schools but also in believing that they didn't want to be assigned there. When the college finally provided opportunities, many volunteered to student teach in inner-city schools.[40]

Self-studies did not report on minority enrollments in the college until 1980. When statistics were gathered, they confirmed the obvious: the student body was not cosmopolitan. Of the 2,533 students enrolled, 180 were listed as minorities: 158 "black," 6 "oriental," 7 "American Indian," and 9 "Spanish American." And the college still offered little in multicultural education. The 1981 NCATE accreditation report tried to duck the issue by indicating that the social foundations program area is "the most natural program in which to seek experiences related to multicultural education." In addition to the formal curriculum, "faculty members in this area have engaged in diverse activities which reflect their interest in multicultural educational experiences."[41]

The Pilot Program

Surveys indicated that education students were generally "highly satisfied" with their programs. They complained, as education students often do, that their professors should use the teaching strategies that they advocate and that there was too much "theory" and not enough "practical" content in the teacher education curriculum—although it was not clear if they were really criticizing theory or simply ideas and methods that didn't seem to work very well for them in practice. But education deans are drawn to champion experimental teacher education programs, and despite general faculty and student satisfaction with the existing program, Dean Merrill, in 1966, appointed a committee to plan a program that was "sound but somewhat different from the present program." He was particularly interested in early involvement of students, even as freshmen, in the development of the theory of "contemporary phenomenology or self theory." The pilot program, as it was soon named, included a self-concept component that was to lead students to "understanding of their own selves in depth with focus on themselves as persons who are becoming teachers." Merrill wrote that the pilot program, "will deliberately exploit the idiosyncrasies and individual talents of each student."[42]

Eleven self-instructional, "self-pacing, self-direction" modules provided most of the instruction for the pilot program. Over fifty professors from education and from the College of Liberal Arts helped develop the components that were based on behavioral objectives, "process-product research," and competency-based instruction—notions that were becoming popular (and controversial) nationally. Four of the modules were "selected for national dissemination" by the American Association of Colleges of Teacher Education (AACTE). The number of students in the pilot program was quite small. In the 1969–70 academic year, 120 places were authorized, but only 58 students actually enrolled in Fall 1970.[43]

President Holt gave it his typical hyperbolic praise: "Your teacher Pilot Program is truly a courageous and significant step forward for our College of Education. Your brochure is so convincing that I am sure AACTE will feel compelled to give us the Distinguished Achievement Award." But the small program was surprisingly controversial among the faculty, leading to a number of heated exchanges in faculty meetings and hallways. In a shocking if amusing incident, an older professor, a former boxer, in a hallway encounter raised his fists and growled threats at the young, surprised director of the pilot program.[44]

In addition to generational conflict, there was a widespread perception that the dean's office imposed the program on the faculty—that it was a "top down reform." A former director of the program said that it was "Merrill's baby" and McComas was less interested and supportive. In addition, attempts to find grants to fund it were unsuccessful, "a blessing in disguise," pretended its supporters; it won't disappear when funding runs out. But the 1970 "Progress Report" was about the last that was officially heard about it. As with many other new programs in universities, there was no obituary; it just ceased to exist.[45]

Competency-Based Teacher Education

The college faculty debated the national educational issues and innovations of the 1970s. Career education, the "back to the basics" campaign, and computer-based instruction among others, were each examined in turn to see how they might affect teacher education. Proposals to change college programs to Competency-Based Teacher Education (CBTE) created the most intense debates. Far ahead of the national movement, the college had experimented with competency-based programs in the 1950s, and the Pilot Program had been centered on CBTE; but proposals to make all courses and programs competency-based caused a vigorous reaction from opponents of the idea.[46]

By 1975, half of the states were experimenting with competency-based certification. It was the current panacea for criticisms of teacher education and a major subject of debate in meetings and publications of AACTE. CBTE, also know as PBTE (performance-based teacher education) among other designations, required "specification of learner objectives in behavioral terms" and "specification of the means for determining whether performance meets the indicated criterion levels." CBTE required breaking down teacher activities into discrete behaviors and certifying teachers when they could demonstrate each behavior or competency. CBTE reached its ultimate absurdity at Florida State University where the faculty developed 1,465 competencies for teachers. Those opposed to CBTE argued that it ignored fundamental issues about values and purposes of education in a democratic society by stressing narrow instructional skills.[47]

Support for performance objectives in the college was initially strong. In a 1969 survey, the faculty agreed overwhelmingly (sixty-two to twelve) that all courses should have performance objectives. Within a few years, the issue was much more controversial. In 1975, the college sponsored a two-day conference on CBTE. Issues raised at the conference led to the college sending six faculty members to visit CBTE programs at the University of Georgia and Florida State University as part of the process of "systematically investigating the pros and cons of CBTE" to decide if it should be incorporated in Tennessee's teacher education program. Difference of opinion on the quality and successes of the visited programs depended primarily on whether the observers were for or against CBTE before they went. As the controversy continued, a school psychology professor who supported CBTE and I, in opposition, edited an eighty-page monograph published by the Bureau of Educational Research and Service: *Competency-Based Teacher Education: For and Against*. We continued the debate on Tennessee public radio.[48]

McComas, as perhaps befits deans when faculty controversies are hot, took a middle ground. He correctly saw the controversy, in part, as a struggle between humanists and behaviorists. He acknowledged the value of behaviorism: "My own personal view is that we have an obligation to measure whatever we can measure in an effective way recognizing that there is much more about teaching and learning to be known." But he also encouraged support for the social foundations' humanist position. CBTE, he wrote, did "not recognize the contribution which the foundations of education can and should make." He looked to lessons from Watergate and other recent national scandals that went beyond behaviorist thinking: "It may be time for us to reexamine our philosophical values, decide what is important for individuals and society, and explore what schools may and may not be capable of doing in helping school and society identify and clarify values."[49]

When the debate was over, things were left much as when they started. Where behaviorism was strong anyway, CBTE was embraced. The Department of Educational Psychology and Guidance submitted a proposal for competency-based counselor certification in 1975. And the state soon required competency-based certification for special education teachers, school counselors, and psychologists. Less behaviorist-oriented programs were able to resist and wait out the initial excitement accompanying the "reform."[50]

Dean William Coffield

McComas was bright, articulate, personable, and respected by the campus administration; and, according to some faculty, he started seeking a university presidency from the time he arrived in Tennessee. In 1976, he left UT to become president of Mississippi State University. He was replaced by Associate Dean William Coffield, former vice president for academic affairs at Youngstown State University, who had come to UT as head of the Department of Continuing and Higher Education. Coffield was a native of Alabama with a master's degree from George Peabody College and a Ph.D. from the University of Iowa in educational administration.[51]

McComas was dean during years of growth and optimism, whereas Coffield experienced a time of troubles. Teacher surpluses began to develop nationally as the baby boomers finished school, and reductions in public school enrollments became a preoccupation of the college. In contrast to the buoyant McComas, Coffield was a worrier. His Fall 1977 address to the faculty began with Dickens's classic sentence: "It was the best of times; it was the worst of times." He didn't indicate what was best about the times, and even the good he found seemed tinged with the bad: "Undue attention is being given to an alleged oversupply of teachers." Problems seemed to have increased by the time of his 1978 address: "The 'back to the basics' movement is still alive. Advocates of proficiency testing behave as if this is a newly discovered panacea. The 'proposition 13' mentality threatens all public supported institutions." A year later, he was still giving the faculty little cause for cheer: "The energy situation, inflation, and the possibility of an economic recession contributes to a general attitude which, to say the least, is filled with 'doom and gloom.'" As enrollments dropped in the college, he often sat in his office with a sad expression going over the statistics, fixated on falling student credit hours, and sharing the bad news with any professor who glanced into his open office. In the early 1980s, Coffield had little to say in *intercom*, a symbol of his withdrawal.[52]

Coffield was plagued with problems that were not of his making. The conservative attacks on public schools that accompanied the election of President Ronald Reagan which would find their manifesto in

A Nation at Risk (1983), as well as the antieducation school attitudes of Governor Lamar Alexander, added to the sense of "doom
and gloom" that affected the college. In the early 1980s, it was difficult to find anyone on the faculty or in the campus administration who
didn't agree on a couple of things: Coffield was a decent, honest,
thoroughly nice man—and the college was in deep trouble. Faculty
and administrators alike perceived him as a caretaker rather than an
active, idea-generating dean.[53]

Chancellor Jack Reese and the academic affairs office of the university were troubled; one college administrator said later that Reese
was "terribly disappointed" in the college. There were particularly difficult relations between the large, omnibus Department of Curriculum
and Instruction that trained most of the teachers and Ralph Norman,
assistant vice-chancellor of academic affairs, who was responsible for
undergraduate programs. Norman later recalled the bad feelings that
resulted from a 1983 academic program review of the department: "It
has to go down as the most disastrous program review in the history"
of the university. Norman recalled that the department head challenged
his support for the department in a preliminary meeting, setting the
tone for the whole review. Because the department was so large and
complex, six outside reviewers were brought to campus. They could
not agree on what they found and were unable to write the customary
joint review; each outside reviewer wrote his own separate report.
Norman said that the department was "like mainland China before
Kissinger; you knew it was big and important and things were happening in there, but nobody knew really what was going on because it
was kind of closed off."[54]

College Goals

In the spring of 1982, Chancellor Jack Reese asked for a fully developed and precise statement of the goals and priorities of the college.
A number of professors interpreted his request as a warning that the
college was on trial, adding to the siege mentality of many faculty. The
common quip, repeated in numerous hallway conversations, was "just
because you're paranoid doesn't mean that they're not out to get you."

Colleges of education engage in chronic self-examination. Goals
studies and self-studies, both self-imposed and directed by the university administration, were major activities in the history of the UT College of Education. Faculty grumbled to each other in offices and hall-

ways that self-studies left them little time to do their real work. A senior social foundations professor, braver than most, completed a survey of how he spent his time with: "10% filling out stupid question-naires such as this." A survey study of college goals had been completed in 1979, and there was widespread faculty grumbling about another, more extensive study. The results of the 1979 study, however, were obvious and gave little specific information or specific direction for planning. As an example, the highest ranked goal under Professional Education was "understand the specialized subject matter and acquire the necessary professional skills." Nearly every statement in the survey was judged statistically important and specific priorities failed to emerge.[55]

I chaired the new eight-professor goals committee. The committee used a qualitative approach with arguments for goals and priorities coming from faculty statements, position papers, hearings, and other forums. In its report the committee constructed a cultural context for the college of the future, replete with the futurist language of the time: "profound changes," "post-industrial society, a learning society, and an information-transmitting society."

The seven goals developed emphasized "enhancing quality":

Goal I, To continue the development of teacher education programs that will provide a standard of excellence by which other programs in the state and region will be measured.
Goal II, To become one of the leading colleges of education in research, scholarly writing, and creative productions.
Goal III, To provide continuing professional services to school systems, colleges, the State Department of Education, and other agencies.
Goal IV, To prepare professional educators for a variety of settings, public and private.
Goal V, To provide leadership in producing and disseminating educational innovation.
Goal VI, To promote the value of quality education to the people of Tennessee.
Goal VII, To provide leadership in the development of educational policies in Tennessee.

Lofty if general language explicated each goal statement. Under Goal I, as an example, teacher education programs were to be "academically rigorous" and "intellectually exciting." "This faculty is resolute that its graduates will be recognized and in demand as superior educators." And, even when the committee proposed specific reforms, they did not include plans for implementation. The faculty adopted the goals statement in December 1982 with the understanding that "task forces" for each goal would develop implementation plans.[56]

Ralph Norman responded for academic affairs to the goals document. His preliminary comments indicated a lack of enthusiasm: "We commend the College faculty for its work in achieving a first statement of its goals. This is a good first step. The following comments speak to the manner and conditions under which we hope you will want to refine and elaborate upon these goals." He indicated how crucial the work of the college was in a period of educational initiative by Governor Lamar Alexander, who had introduced his Better Schools legislation in January 1983. At a time of criticism of public school teachers, Norman argued that Goal I on teacher education was paramount and that the others should have lower priority.[57]

In an unprecedented move, Norman then announced that the campus academic affairs office and the college goals committee would "convene a joint seminar" to discuss the goals of the college, "to study together such documents as the new Carnegie Report on the relation of universities to the schools, Harry Judge's report on graduate education," and other documents. Administrators from other colleges were invited to the seminar. Even the paranoia of some faculty colleagues now seemed justified to others. Norman, whom many professors saw as anti-educationist, would not dare be so presumptive with other colleges. In their view it was clear that the administration was out to get the college.[58]

The members of the college goals committee and representatives with academic affairs met weekly during the Winter and Spring quarters of 1983. Norman and I co-chaired amiable discussions, and I became convinced that Norman was supportive of teacher education in general and the college in particular. In June 1983, the goals committee published an addendum to the college goals statement that reflected seminar discussions, a new statewide university task force on teacher education, as well as the increasingly shrill national debate on schools and teacher education. The committee contended that the teacher education program must be an exemplar for the state and region and a "center of excellence" in the university, that a university-wide Council for Teacher Education be established, and that admissions to teacher education be limited to smaller numbers of cohorts moving through programs together. The committee argued that higher admissions standards were crucial and recommended at least a 3.0 GPA in a student's teaching field. The addendum emphasized teacher education, but the committee also reiterated a strong expectation for demonstrated excellence in faculty research for promotion or salary increases.[59]

During the time that academic affairs was holding seminars with the goals committee, the college was also conducting a dean's search. Norman said academic affairs used the seminar to help determine the type of dean that was needed, to try to understand what the college was about, and "who were the main people thinking in the college of education [and] what were they thinking." Academic affairs took an unusually close, personal, and aggressive role in the search. Chancellor Reese said that Norman "took it as an almost religious mission." After Richard Wisniewski, dean at the University of Oklahoma, was nominated for the position, Norman and Hardy Liston, another assistant vice chancellor, went to national education meetings to hear Wisniewski present. The administration's involvement in the search process added to a sense that the college was in crisis. Years later a professor reflected that he didn't think that many faculty realized the college leadership crisis of the time: "The College was on the edge of either being omitted or subsumed within other structures. I don't think faculty realize how significant the hire was from the perspective of the chancellor and others in higher administration."[60]

The search committee and academic affairs shared strong sentiments for going outside the university to find a nationally known teacher educator. They quickly became enthusiastic about Wisniewski. He had been an innovative dean at Oklahoma for ten years, was a well-known leader in the American Association of Colleges of Teacher Education and other professional organizations, and had written widely on teacher-education reform. The major problem was that Wisniewski refused to become a formal candidate for the position. "He didn't have the slightest interest in UT when we contacted him," Norman recalled. As a noncandidate, he agreed to come to Tennessee to make presentations to the faculty on his visions of teacher education. "His platform was music to our ears," Norman said. He impressed "the hell out of a lot of people," particularly Reese. And, when the search committee selected him, Reese authorized an immediate offer. "I never saw him do that before," Norman recalled; "we rushed him." After some hesitation, Wisniewski, still not a candidate, decided to accept the offer. He liked the central administration's emphasis on quality, and he decided that UT was "more interesting and complex than Oklahoma." Second-generation Polish from Detroit, he represented a strong break from the college's southern past.[61]

After announcing his retirement from the deanship in 1996, Wisniewski reflected on the import of his appointment. He indicated that he didn't think that the college was in danger of disappearing in 1983, but it had been put on notice to "improve or be considered backwater." He thought that the campus administration perceived the education faculty as resistant to change, that they were "comfortable outwaiting" the administration's challenges to reform. But he said that he was never told that he had a mandate for change and was certainly "never commanded to carry out Jack's 10 points."[62]

Chancellor Jack Reese's "10 points" were in a 1983 memorandum, cosigned by the Vice Chancellor for Academic Affairs, and sent to the college just before the Fall faculty meeting: "It is unusual for us to send a letter such as this to a college at the beginning of a school year. These are unusual times, however." Reese emphasized the national castigation of public schools as part of the context for his memorandum. (*A Nation at Risk* had been published in April.) While the administrators wrote that they intended "to be helpful, to encourage, to exhort, to recognize and applaud the quality of the work which has been done," they proposed their own list of ten priorities for the college, beginning with increasing admissions standards and recruiting outstanding students—"the fact the College has for some time enrolled students with the lowest ACT scores in the University has been advertised widely." The chancellor proposed an intern program to replace or supplement the "limited" student-teaching program, and he endorsed a Board of Visitors and the often-mentioned university-wide Council of Teacher Preparation.[63]

After reviewing Chancellor Reese's memorandum (twelve years later), Norman observed that it was an unusual memo. He said that "very few of this length and specificity" were sent out during the twenty years he was in campus administration. Norman remembered that Reese often turned over to his assistant, Don Eastman, and others the final working of memos, "but in this instance this is very much Jack Reese . . . by and large it is his prose and his points." It was particularly unusual because Reese must have known that many faculty would feel threatened by the memo and he "did not like to ruffle people unnecessarily, to 'spook them out' as he used to say. He really did not like that at all." But Norman denied that there was an anti-education bias in the administration and indicated that Reese cared "very much" about teacher education and saw it as a "very important part of our overall mission." Norman said that the administration was reacting, in part, to Governor Alexander, "who had discovered that there was public education" and that it was good politics. The governor's office was giving the university "permission to ask more radical questions" about teacher education.[64]

After reading his memo and other documents from the period for a 1996 interview, Reese also denied that the college was in as much trouble as some faculty thought. It was not a case of shape up or else; it was "not that dire." He reiterated that he was concerned with the quality of students going into education, especially as talented women, who would have gone into teacher training in previous generations, went elsewhere. And he acknowledged that there was a "quiet criticism" of education within the university based largely on the quality of students admitted and "anecdotal" accounts of education classes. On the other hand, he said the college had done some things "really well," including preparing students to function in diverse cultures. He emphasized, as he had done in the original memorandum, that the administration's attention to education was in the context of a national "onslaught against public education in general [and] criticisms of schools and colleges of education" in particular. He agreed with Norman that Governor Alexander's "Better Schools" program was part of the context. Reese lamented Alexander's anti-teacher-education attitude and the absence of professional educators' influence in the educational reforms: "no significant input from the professional community at all—sad and rather disturbing." The issue was exacerbated when the former governor became president of the university. Reese recalled his difficulty in getting Alexander to understand the importance of professional schools in land-grant universities: "I could not get Lamar to see that."[65]

The faculty devoted its Fall 1983 meeting to worrying about the import of the chancellor's memorandum, discussing the college goals report, and appointing implementation committees for each goal. (Wisniewski attended the Fall faculty meeting even though he did not officially become dean until October.) The entire faculty was divided into seven task forces to develop implementation plans for the goals. They were to work throughout the Fall and give final reports in January 1984. The work of the task forces was quite uneven; some worked vigorously to develop "implementation strategies"; others, unwilling to rock their or someone else's boat, frankly admitted that "we must do enough to cover our asses."[66]

Richard Wisniewski and Education Reforms

The new dean quickly took charge of the goals process.

I have asked the chairs of the task forces to submit their recommendation by the end of the quarter. I have also asked each group to expand their deliberations. . . . Any issue related to the Chancellor's letter to the College, the UT Task Force on Teacher Education and other public documents provide the context for our deliberations. As a major part of these deliberations, a faculty-wide retreat is planned for January 13–14 [1984] at Fall Creek Falls State Park.[67]

Much excitement, good will, and a sense of new beginnings characterized the all-faculty retreat at the state park on the Cumberland Plateau. The lodge and cabins built over the lake were filled with faculty meeting in small groups during the day and drinking bourbon (among other things) and playing penny-ante poker far into the night. Before the retreat was over, the faculty voted on fifty-one proposals and approved forty-five wholly or in part (other proposals "tabled" at the retreat were also eventually adopted by the faculty). Many of the proposals were significant. They included higher admission standards and admission boards for each teacher education program. Each program also agreed to establish enrollment limits. The faculty accepted proposals for closer collaboration with school systems, including the appointment of faculty associates among teachers and administrators in professional development schools. And they approved the establishment of a college Board of Visitors. One professor later confessed that he thought that although a majority of professors voted for the proposals they "did not believe that they would actually come to fruition." "Fall Creek Falls" became a part of the jargon of the college as the faculty implemented and, at the same time, continued to debate the changes that they had approved. Fall Creek Falls demonstrated Wisniewski's forceful leadership style, including his eagerness to move ahead with those willing to go even if it meant leaving others behind.[68]

Using the accords reached at Fall Creek Falls, proposals in the governor's Better Schools Program, and the AACTE's *Educating a Profession: Profile of a Beginning Teacher* (which became the bible for the changes), an Ad Hoc Committee on Teacher Education redesigned the teacher education curriculum. In Spring 1984, the Curriculum Review Committee approved the new preservice programs. The reorganization included a controversial new layer of administration, the Institute for Teacher Education. Although based on a Fall Creek Falls proposal to establish an "oversight office for teacher education," the institute was very much Wisniewski's idea. He perceived the institute as a "holding company" to coordinate and articulate teacher education throughout the college as well as to "systematically address the implementation of reform goals set by the faculty." Wisniewski appointed three professors, including the director of student teaching, as tri-directors of the institute. The faculty quickly began to refer to them as the trinity or, more commonly, the troika. Some department heads and faculty saw the institute as the dean's way of wresting control of teacher education from departments to the dean's office.[69]

Wisniewski and reform-minded teacher educators in the college were dissatisfied with the short period of student teaching in the university's ten-week quarter system, and, in 1984, the faculty voted to expand student teaching to a fifteen-week semester. Only the law school was on a semester calendar, and the college's decision created what the director of student teaching called a logistical nightmare. Expanded student teaching was just a prelude to an extended teacher education program. In 1985, Wisniewski proposed a five-year teacher-preparation program; with the approval of the Faculty Council, yet another curriculum redesign was undertaken. The next year the dean proposed that student teaching be replaced with a two-semester internship. "The internship is consistent with a higher level of preparation," he argued. "Student teaching, in contrast, is embedded deeply in the traditions and expectations of four-year preparation programs."[70]

Internships were phased into the program beginning in 1988–89. Those opposed to the change argued that the college would lose students to four-year teacher-education programs and that it would devastate the master's degree program because students would be within twelve hours of completing their master's at the end of the intern year. Time has proven the opposing professors wrong on the first accusation but correct on the second. Even though the change generated raucous debate among the faculty, the five-year, post-baccalaureate program eventually received high praise from outside the college: "a move that is increasingly being praised by principals and superintendents of Tennessee." "Best thing the college did," Reese echoed. In 1986, the Holmes group, a consortium of colleges and schools of education in research universities that were undertaking similar changes, invited the college to join the organization. Wisniewski later boasted that the UT college "was among the first in the nation to implement the Holmes Group agenda for the reform of teacher education."[71]

A major legacy of Wisniewski (and the source of much animosity directed at him) was his requirement for research and publications. Some in the college had been promoted to professor without any publications or presentations at national scholarly conventions, and they planned to continue until retirement without being burdened by research efforts. These professors often felt that: "He put them on the spot. No one lost their job but he let it be known that those who did not do scholarship were second-class citizens and this created resentment." He used merit pay to reward the productive and punish the others. He shamed the "unproductive" in faculty meetings by talking about unnamed professors who had zeros, as he formed a circle with his forefinger and thumb and held it up for all to see, on their vitae under publications. In his 1988 annual address, he proposed that each professor's office hours

> include a block of time each week devoted to scholarly activity. This was not a frivolous suggestion. I believe all of us need, as part of the normal work week, a period of time for reflection, writing and reading. I also believe that stating we have such a time as part of our office hours would be an important signal to our students and to one another. I urge all members of the faculty to make a public commitment to this activity, as symbolic as it may seem, as part of their posted office hours.

Rather than doing scholarship, dissident professors often spent the time sitting in their offices, complaining that the rules had been changed since they were hired and damning the dean.[72]

More popular with almost everyone than Wisniewski's emphasis on scholarship was his support of international activities. Professors presenting at international conferences or researching in other countries could usually count on the dean's help in finding funds. Beginning with a trip to Great Britain in 1986, he found travel support for groups of faculty to Europe, Asia, and Australia to develop "relationships" with teacher educators and to foster faculty exchanges with colleges abroad. The 1989 NCATE report summarized recent visits "by scholars from different parts of the world. The Dean of Education at North East Wales Institute of Higher Education visited for ten days in April. . . . Large contingents of teachers from Australia and Japan visited the unit in 1988 and 1989. The Australians visited in January 1989 and approximately 60 Japanese teachers visited during the summers of 1988 and 1989." The exchanging program with the North East Wales Institute of Higher Education has operated since 1983 with several students each semester studying in their sister institution. And, since 1995, interns have been able to teach their first semester abroad.[73]

Although international activity fostered a more cosmopolitan atmosphere, the college community remained monocultural. The 1989 composition of the faculty was 106 whites, seven African Americans, one American Indian, and one Asian. Twenty-seven of the 115 faculty were women. The college continued to lose positions in the early 1990s; by 1993 there were only five nontenured faculty. Wisniewski held position lines open during the creation of New College (discussed below), which emphasized attention to multicultural perspectives, but announced searches for eight positions during the 1993–94 academic year. The seven faculty hired subsequently for New College included two African-American women, three white women, one African man, and one Asian man, bringing the faculty to ninety-one tenure-track positions in 1995.[74]

In 1989, the racial composition of teacher-education students was even more white than the faculty: 298 whites, two blacks, one Hispanic, two Asians, and one American Indian. In 1990, the college, through the advising center, started a concerted effort to recruit and retain African-American students. It hired an African-American recruiter to meet with high school principals and guidance counselors across the state to recruit students and set up student FTA chapters in predominantly black high schools. The college also received a grant from the Tennessee Higher Education Commission and the university to develop a program to aid minority teacher assistants in completing a teacher-education program and securing certification. In 1995–96, 37 percent of preservice scholarship money went to African Americans. But the college, despite these vigorous efforts, continued to make little progress in attracting minority students to its teacher-education program.[75]

The 1989 NCATE Report summed up sweeping, fundamental changes in the college. In a statement that was unexpectedly frank for such a document, the report admitted that: "While faculty have collaborated in decision-making at all junctures of change, this is not to say that widespread agreement or satisfaction has been achieved. Indeed, change and controversy in the College of Education go hand-in-hand. At various times, individuals or groups of faculty feel that their belief systems are not represented or their particular contributions to the program are undervalued." The report continued with the observation that "It may take several years for programs to 'settle' into different forms." In fact, programs would have no opportunity to "settle," and the changes, or, at least, the controversies of the 1980s would be dwarfed by Wisniewski's proposals for a New College of Education in the 1990s.[76]

A New College of Education

In the Fall 1990 faculty meeting, Wisniewski broached the idea of strategic planning for the college: "Today, I introduce the idea for faculty consideration. I do not offer visions of the future; I merely outline a process that can lead to new visions." Even as he introduced the idea, he anticipated faculty response and tried to comfort the disturbed. He told the faculty that "turf issues" would inevitably arise, and that every program and service provided by the college would have to be examined; but he assured them that all professors would plan the changes and that "successful strategic planning ensures that everyone wins." He indicated that foundation support would be necessary but did not name a particular funding source. After a year of courting foundations, he announced in August 1991 that the Philip Morris Companies would provide $500,000 to create a "new" college of education. A considerable amount of grumbling about tainted tobacco money came from faculty, particularly from those who were opposed to restructuring; the Philip Morris representative kept emphasizing that the company was also Kraft Foods.[77]

After recommendations by the College Faculty Council, Wisniewski appointed a seven-professor planning committee; he and Ralph Norman served as ex officio members. Dissident faculty members immediately charged that the dean had stacked the committee with his supporters; and, while insisting that the planning group was representative of the faculty, Wisniewski recognized "to this day" that the appointments were suspect to opponents of restructuring. A National Advisory Board on the creation of the new college was also established. Among its more distinguished members were Anne T. Dowing, Director of Corporate Contributions at Philip Morris Companies; Charles Smith, Tennessee Commissioner of Education; Sharon Robinson, National Center for Innovation, NEA; Arthur Wise, President of the National Council of Accreditation of Teacher Education; Linda Darling-Hammond of Teachers College, Columbia; John Goodlad, Center for Educational Renewal, University of Washington; and Theodore Sizer, Chair of the Coalition of Essential Schools. A classroom was converted to a New College Planning Office, groups of professors traveled to examine "exemplary programs" throughout the country, and the college quickly began to spend Philip Morris money.[78]

Study groups, chaired by members of the planning committee, were formed on the mission, the societal context for the college, innovative forms of organization, and innovative delivery systems. The planning committee urged all members of the college community to join a study group, and eighty-one persons (a number of them doctoral students) eventually volunteered to work in a group. In a qualitative study of the planning process, Linda Ginn found the work of the study groups "the most positive of the process. . . . Faculty and students enjoyed the opportunity to generate dialogue with newly found colleagues. They enjoyed the intellectual stimulation." Wisniewski assured the faculty that they, rather than the administration, "would be the agents of change." But old animosities toward the dean, often stemming from his hiring process and his emphasis on scholarship, affected attitudes toward restructuring, and a number of faculty refused invitations to participate in study groups. There was much talk of the dean's hidden agendas. Some professors warned that the dean had not revealed his *real* purpose for reorganizing (often thought to be to enhance teacher education at the expense of other programs), and these and other faculty insisted that the planning process was a charade: the dean had a preconceived plan that he would impose on the faculty. On the other hand, the dean received letters from professors expressing discouragement with the "fear and paranoia" of other faculty. A consultant to the college on planning new college, Barbara Brittingham, quipped that "Half the faculty are afraid the Dean has a plan in his bottom drawer, the other half are afraid he doesn't." As a member of the planning committee, I saw plans for the new college evolve from widespread debate, compromise, and reconsideration, a process in which Wisniewski did not often take positions; if he had a plan, he kept it to himself. On the planning committee, he was most active in writing a draft of the noncontroversial section on "linkages with the practicing professions."[79]

On March 6 and 7, 1992, members of the four study groups and a number of other faculty and graduate students retreated to the Glenstone Lodge, close by in the Smoky Mountains resort town of Gatlinburg. The objectives of the retreat were to increase faculty participation in planning the New College and to "share information among study groups, gain clarity regarding questions and issues, and move toward consensus and identify commonalties within and among study groups." Omnipresent flow charts documented the discussions; one from the societal context study group captured the themes and buzz words of the retreat: "Interdisciplinary, Diversity, Democratic, Collaborative, Social Justice."[80]

From the beginning of the planning process, a major issue was the construction of a mission statement that included "non-teacher ed things." There were suggestions for multiple mission statements and for schools of health, of education, of human services in the college. At the retreat, however, consensus developed that a single mission statement should include an acknowledgment of the "multiple missions that encompass education, health and human service." Perhaps the most surprising consensus that developed was acceptance of a societal context study group proposal that the college commit itself to social justice. Consensus that developed at the retreat led to five formal commitments that formed the foundation of the New College: excellence in scholarship, a leadership role in education, a commitment to social justice, innovative instructional excellence, and collaborative partnerships among faculty, students, and practitioners.[81]

After the Gatlinburg retreat, Wisniewski expressed hope that the faculty had a sense of ownership over the change process and that they understood that there was room for everyone in the new college. Encouraged by the retreat, the planning group worked throughout the summer of 1992 writing the forty-nine-page document that was to be the blueprint for New College: *Planning a New Future: The College of Education*. The document was based on accords reached at Gatlinburg, "position papers" prepared by professors, and the reports of the study groups. Preparation of the final reports of the study groups was a precursor to the debates that were to follow. A group member expressed "real irritation toward the faculty who were not involved and attempted to place roadblocks at the last minute. They would show up at the last minute and argue over every sentence and paragraph." The planning document was sent to the faculty for debate and consideration in September 1992.[82]

There was, of course, the usual professorial nit-picking: doesn't "covenants" have a religious connotation? Let's change it to "principles of association." But much of the debate was angry and often loud. The angriest and most suspicious professors were usually those who had refused to attend planning meetings or retreats. The dean and the planning committee were often accused of using undemocratic tactics; "stacked the deck" was a common expression. And there were mean-spirited personal attacks. Ginn wrote of the "pain" caused by "nastiness" and the "petty acts" of colleagues toward each other. In retrospect, there may not have been enough attention to dealing with anxieties created by the proposed fundamental changes. In February 1993, after the vigorous and bitter debates, 74 percent of the faculty voted to accept the planning document.[83]

After much "rumor mongering," the departments of Health, Leisure, and Safety and Technological and Adult Education left the College of Education and joined the College of Human Ecology. (The Adult Education faculty and a few individual professors from the leaving departments opted to stay in Education.) Those leaving had long-term conflicts with the dean, opposed restructuring, and believed that their programs were unappreciated in the college; many of their professors had been unhappy for years and the creation of New College gave them an opportunity to look for a more congenial place.[84]

In what proved to be the most fundamental change, the planning document called for the elimination of departments in favor of more temporary structures that were to cross disciplines and enhance faculty collaboration. There were seven departments in the old college, and protecting departmental turf had been a chief reason for the failure of earlier attempts to establish and implement significant, common goals. Wisniewski complained that the departments operated "as if they were colleges unto themselves." Reorganization eliminated Curriculum and Instruction, Special Education, and other traditional college of education departments. The units that replaced departments "were to be smaller, more flexible, and less formal."[85]

From the beginning of restructuring, the dean and the planning committee encouraged professors to explore the construction of new units. With traditional homes threatened, some department heads and professors accused departmental faculty of disloyalty for joining groups to discuss formations of new units. The college planning document responded with the declaration that "there should be no impediments to free and open discussions. No person needs to be granted permission to talk with anyone." In practice, rather than being based on common scholarly interests or program responsibilities, units were sometimes formed by friends or "like-minded people who enjoyed working together." An Implementation Committee required new units to develop rationales for their existence and to demonstrate that their units complied with the New College guidelines, including statements about how they would support the five commitments. Eleven units were formed in 1993–94, and more variety in teacher education resulted. For example, six elementary teacher-education programs were housed in different units that reflect quite different approaches or philosophies: holistic, inclusive early childhood, and urban/multicultural among others.[86]

Democratic governance was suppose to characterize New College. Hierarchical administration was to be replaced with "flattened" structures, and decision making was to be by consensus rather than majority rule. An inclusive College Coalition that included students, faculty, support staff, "grants and contracts personnel," and other members of the college community was created to govern New College. Department heads were replaced with unit leaders who were to be considered faculty rather than administration and who were temporary representatives of their colleagues. Wisniewski assessed the changed leadership styles of the leaders in 1995 and concluded that "they have done their best to behave as 'first among equals' in keeping with the philosophy of New College." Despite efforts by most members of the college community, in the short history of New College, the new participatory democracy is working imperfectly; old hierarchical ways continuously reemerge.[87]

Campus administrators strongly supported the Wisniewski-era reforms; but the new unit organization was an anomaly in the university structure, and they had reservations. Former Chancellor Reese called structural reorganization "the one question mark," and Norman opined that the college "splintered too much—into too many units." Wisniewski responded that the other reforms had been "widely applauded" throughout the university, but that restructuring was still "too new and different to elicit the same level of enthusiasm." The campus and university administration strongly endorsed the New College proposals before the Board of Trustees, which approved them on July 1, 1994.[88]

With some success, Wisniewski attempted to move the college from a regional to a national institution. In speeches, presentations, and articles, he publicized New College. In September 1992, during the intense debate about restructuring, he organized and hosted a national symposium of restructuring schools of education; and in 1993, the college received a $92,000 grant from the Rockefeller Foundation to establish a Network for Innovative Colleges of Education, linking institutions that were engaged in similar restructuring. When he was elected President of the American Association of Colleges for Teacher Education in 1994, he campaigned on a platform emphasizing the need to redesign schools and colleges of education.[89]

With the possible exception of Claxton, no administrator in the history of the college had as much impact on teacher education at UT as Wisniewski. Norman said that he didn't know of another dean who had so "shaped the fundamental nature" of his college. Wisniewski's ability to direct change was a result of several factors. He was decisive, articulate, and thoughtful, with vision and ideas that he placed in broad educational and societal contexts. He was also physically imposing; tall and with silver hair, he was a casting director's model of a United States senator or a distinguished dean. He singlemindedly pursued his objectives (dissenters in the college often felt as if they had been treated as knaves or fools), and he did not hesitate to work his lieutenants as hard as he drove himself. Educationists are sometimes accused of supporting change for change's sake. Wisniewski responded "Why Not? We all know how hard it is to get *anything* done. Therefore, why not go for changes in *every* way possible and at *every* turn—knowing full well that most efforts will fail." When, in the midst of one teacher education change after another, a delegation of professors went to his office to plea for closure on one reform before another began, the dean leaned toward the startled spokesman and said, "Fuck closure." Wisniewski didn't "see himself as confrontational"; he complained that some faculty thought that anytime he pushed an idea he was confrontational. And besides, he argued, those who protested didn't propose any ideas of their own. He insisted that he "never berated any member of the faculty for not agreeing with him; although it took a saint not to."[90]

While approving of his deanship and acknowledging that he "fulfilled all the hopes we had" and that he was able to create a great deal of support among the faculty ("he brought along a lot of people remarkably well"), the campus administration recognized that his leadership style as well as his proposed changes created hurt feelings. "I will be quite frank on the negative side," Norman said; "Richard was so concerned about the fundamental direction and design that he was not always sensitive to individual cases and people." There was "no great consensus on approval of his leadership" among the faculty, Reese agreed, but also observed that his dissenters were often "entrenched people" who were resistant to change itself.[91]

Recognizing Wisniewski's support by the Knoxville campus administration, dissenting faculty complained to the UT system's president, Joe Johnson; they were able to "get Joe Johnson's ears; he is a good listener." The campus administration had to "constantly protect" and "undergird" Wisniewski by restating their case to the president: "Lots of times in my experience," Norman said, "we went up to Joe Johnson's office, and we explained to him again what was happening and why it had to be backed up to the hilt, why there could not be any idea that there was a crack in this anywhere. There were such occasions again and again for years."[92]

Only a person of great imagination and vision as well as single-mindedness and forcefulness could have led the college to the fundamental changes that Wisniewski accomplished. A person with more sensitivity to emotional needs might have accomplished them with less human trauma, but it is doubtful that administrative geniuses exist who can painlessly re-create institutions as resistant to change as colleges.

Afterword

After more than twenty years of mucking around in the college records and the university archives, I have fairly much satisfied the curiosity that I had as a new assistant professor about the history of teacher education at the University of Tennessee. In constructing a history for others of UT's experience, it would have been easy to write a story of progress—from a single professor, worrying that his Teachers' Department not be mistaken for a normal school, to a comprehensive college with a student body as select as any in the university and a large, cosmopolitan faculty. But if historical lessons are honest, they are always ambiguous, and a story of perseverance and hard work leading to successful practitioners in public schools and acceptance in the university community would be as much a fairy tale as would a failure saga.

UT educationists prepared teachers for a southern society that was often ambivalent about schooling. Although through most of its history Tennessee and the rest of the South suffered from rural poverty, many southerners did not share other Americans' belief in promises of progress and modernization through education. Racial obsessions that created and maintained educational injustices and reinforced hierarchical and paternalistic attitudes had profound effects on teaching and teachers, particularly on women teachers. And UT educationists' work was circumscribed among people that Flannery O'Connor called Christ-haunted because of their preoccupation with fundamentalist religion.[1]

Yet, in most ways, UT's experience corresponds closely with the general history of teacher education. Despite their best efforts to please university administrators and their arts and science colleagues, teacher educators at UT for generations, like their counterparts elsewhere, seemed to be in "perpetual disfavor" or the subject of "contempt" and "hostility" within the university; and, as in other schools of education, "a chronic inferiority complex" was the unsurprising result.[2]

Contemporary as well as historical critics of teacher education and educationists denounce the low academic quality of programs and the anti-intellectualism of educationists and their students. Examples include two popular and influential books published in 1963: James B. Conant's *The Education of American Teachers* and James D. Koerner's *The Miseducation of American Teachers*. In 1986, Reginald G. Damerell published a mean-spirited and self-serving critique: *Education's Smoking Gun: How Teachers Colleges Have Destroyed Education in America*. And, in 1991, Rita Kramer added to the baleful genre with *Ed School Follies: The Miseducation of America's Teachers*. Although less polemic, two prestigious and influential reform reports on teachers and their preparation published in 1986—*Tomorrow's Teachers: A Report of the Holmes Group* and *A Nation Prepared: Teachers for the Twenty-First Century* (a report of the Carnegie Forum on Education)—recommended significant, far-reaching improvements in the academic preparation of teachers. Both of these documents, one from deans of education in research universities, the other from a heterogeneous but elite group of citizens and educators, concluded that school improvement depends on professionalization of teachers, which, in turn, depends on more knowledgeable and intellectual teachers.

It wasn't as if previous generations of educationists had missed hearing the message about academic standards. From the beginning of teacher education at UT, educationists tried to improve the image and status of teacher education by raising admission standards, making the curriculum more rigorous, and demanding that the faculty be more scholarly. From Teachers' Department Principal Thomas Karns's assurance that "this is not a normal course" to Dean Richard Wisniewski's claim that UT was among "the first in the nation to implement the Holmes Group agenda," educationists assured university administrators that they had achieved academic respectability. And each generation embraced new teacher education curricula that promised to produce professional teachers. Southern progressive educationists found a panacea for modernizing school and society in industrial education; a "science" of pedagogy underpinned teacher education by the First World War; later, competence-based teacher education assured competent teachers; and the Carnegie and Holmes proposals would finally provide truly professional teachers.

Since the UT College of Education was a charter member of the Holmes Group (a consortium of colleges and schools of education in research universities), since Wisniewski claimed that the UT college was among the first to implement the Holmes reforms, and since the Holmes reports have been the subject of much critical analysis, I will reflect on UT's experience with the "reforms." The three Holmes Group reports are *Tomorrow's Teachers* (1986), *Tomorrow's Schools* (1990), and *Tomorrow's Schools of Education* (1995). The first of the Holmes reports aimed at "nothing less than the transformation of teaching from an occupation into a genuine profession." Research universities with theory- and research-based educationists and with strong supporting liberal arts programs were best equipped to lead teachers to professional status. "Higher quality" persons had to be attracted to teaching; they had to have higher credentials including "a broad, coherent liberal arts foundation," and pedagogical knowledge based on rigorous, scientific research. With professionalization, teachers would finally gain the respect they deserved.[3]

Much was made of the responsibility of educationists in research universities to provide the knowledge base for professional practice. *Tomorrow's Teachers* claimed that:

> Until the last two decades, scholarship in education and the content of the hundreds of university courses in the subject had to rely heavily upon the findings in other disciplines, particularly the behavioral sciences. . . . Within the last twenty years, however, the science of education promised by Dewey, Thorndike, and others at the turn of the century, has become more tangible.

Remember, however, that seventy years earlier Professor Harry Clark had also observed that once schools of education had based their teaching on theory and ideas borrowed from psychology and philosophy but now pedagogy was becoming an "exact science." Most UT educationists were too experienced with the rhetoric of education or simply too cynical to believe that a research base leading to "best practice" existed. They were aware of the tentative, contested nature of much educational knowledge.[4]

David F. Labaree has criticized the professionalization agenda of *Tomorrow Teacher's* for its reliance on a "science" of education that "pushes technical questions into the foreground and political questions into the background as either unscientific or unproblematic." Reinforcing teaching as a scientific, technical enterprise and placing teacher education students in full-year internships in public schools

will likely reduce critical consideration of the profoundly political nature of knowledge and of educational ends. The UT experience con-
firms Labaree's misgiving. During the 1980s and 1990s, the college
reduced courses focused on the political and social aspects of education for most teacher education students from nine quarter hours to
part of a single two semester-hour course.[5]

Most faculty supported, some quite reluctantly, proposals from
Wisniewski and the college goals committee that were congruent with
those in *Tomorrow's Teachers*, including a full-year internship in public
schools and replacing the undergraduate education majors with a requirement for degrees in Arts and Sciences. Students now apply to
elementary and secondary education programs only after they have a
bachelor's degree in academic majors, and even with undergraduate
grade point averages of over 3.0, not all are accepted. Commitment
to higher scholarship requirements resulted from a general faculty belief that persons who are knowledgeable about the subjects that they
teach and who are bright enough to understand relationships between
theory and practice make better teachers. Making his point (even if in
an inelegant way) during the debate over raising admission requirements, a long-time Curriculum and Instruction professor argued that
"dumb asses can't be good teachers." Some of us were convinced that
a more critical pedagogy particularly requires scholarly, well-informed
teachers.

Critics of *Tomorrow's Teachers* condemn as elitist both the proposals for admission to teacher education and the presumption that
research universities should determine standards for public schools.
Professionalization projects in the past with their "higher" standards
had deleterious effects on women's and minorities' opportunities to
enter and practice professions. Critics suspect that a "hidden curriculum" of professionalization embedded in the Holmes proposals has
similar class and racial biases. Perhaps, in part, the authors of the
third Holmes report, *Tomorrow's Schools of Education*, were reacting to such criticisms when they emphasized strategies for recruiting
and educating minority teachers and students:

1) Develop more comprehensive measures of proficiency in teaching.
2) Mount extraordinary efforts to identify, prepare for college, and recruit students of color who would make good teachers, and then finance and sustain
   them throughout their teacher preparation.
3) Mount similar efforts to make faculties of education more representative of
   minority populations.

In addition, *Tomorrow's Schools of Education* stressed the responsibility of educationists and professional development schools to prepare teachers to work effectively with children of diverse cultural and economic backgrounds. The report admonished that both public school teachers and educationists should be recruited from diverse populations; they should "wear the face of America."[6]

UT's postbaccalaureate teacher education program is vulnerable to charges of elitism. There is inevitable tension between high academic requirements and long preparation time and the inclusion of working-class and minority students who are less likely to have high test scores and grade point averages. It is not just a matter of simple justice—access to a public profession—but also an issue of sound pedagogical practice in recruiting teaching candidates who have a sense of educational injustice and inequity based on their own experiences. Eddie Stone, a student in cultural studies in education at UT, conducted ethnographic interviews with education students for his doctoral dissertation. He found that students from privileged backgrounds were "remarkably unaware of the injustices experienced by others." They had difficulty discussing or giving examples of injustices in school and identifying a personal experience with injustice; minority and working class students were aware of the dimensions of school injustices and could easily cite examples that they had experienced or observed. A teacher education curriculum may be able to partially compensate for the privileged's lack of cultural capital. But the admission of "higher quality" candidates to teaching is not without pitfalls for educationists concerned with social justice. A recently retired UT teacher educator reflected on effects of the high admission requirements: present students are an "intellectually superior group compared to the past." But we lost "some youngsters who would make great teachers."[7]

Wisniewski had a resolute commitment, shared by most of the faculty, to increase minority enrollment in the college. UT is hundreds of miles away from a large African-American population, and the college still struggles with low numbers of black teaching candidates, but a critic is hard pressed to find a strategy to increase African-American enrollments that the college has not tried in good faith. The urban/multicultural teacher education program practices antiracist subjectivity, including vigorous affirmative action that the objectivity-minded would find unprofessional. The college, however, has not made similar commitments to justice issues involving the less-visible poor Appalachian population that surrounds it.

The call from the Holmes Group and the Carnegie Forum for higher
standards of scholarship was not just for students; education faculty
were to produce the research base that makes professionalization possible. Many professors of retirement age in the college would still be
at the assistant or associate level if they had to meet current criteria
for promotion. Most education faculty, particularly younger ones, have
ongoing research agendas and long lists of scholarly publications; and
faculty expect their colleagues to present regularly at meetings of the
American Educational Research Association and other national scholarly organizations. Unlike a generation ago, an assistant professor
candidate who does not have publications and who can not discuss
her future research agenda probably would have little chance of being
hired today.

Yet, subsequent Holmes reports criticized the more scholarly, research-oriented colleges of education that educationists created at UT.
The reports charge that educationists in research universities had
adapted to the academy culture and had become distant from public
schools. Arts and science professors were colleagues; schoolteachers
were not. *Tomorrow's Schools* emphasized collaboration with public
schools rather than scientific research. The report sanctified professional development schools (PDS), places of collaboration between
education schools and local public schools. PDS would demonstrate
exemplary practices: the ways schools ought to work. They would be
sites for educational research and professional development as well as
the location for most preservice teacher education. *Tomorrow's
Schools of Education* went further, making PDS, rather than the
university, the sites for much of the work of educationists.[8]

Tomorrow's Schools of Education advocated narrowing the mission of education professors to teacher preparation. The report complained that too many of them had separated their work from public
schools: "They are a sideshow to the performance in the center ring,
where professors carry out their work insulated from the messiness
and hurly-burly of elementary and secondary education." The report
warned that schools of education will deserve to become irrelevant
unless they turn their attention to schoolchildren's education and that
more educationists must commitment themselves to moving to PDS
as their primary work site for teaching, scholarship, and service. The
deans' proclamation that "It is time for the universities to weigh in on
the side of elementary and secondary education as they have done for
medicine, engineering, agriculture, management, and other fields"
sounds like an echo of the 1929 appeal to UT President Morgan that

the university should serve schools the way they serve agriculture, engineering, and industry.[9]

For their critics in research universities, the most disturbing implication of the education deans' 1995 report is that education schools should narrow their mission to teacher education and research on teaching and learning and that most of this work should take place in PDS. Not only have research universities, particularly state universities, served the public interest in their states by educating school administrators, counselors, curriculum specialists, and other school-related personnel; they have produced the educational researchers, policy makers, and teacher educators for other institutions—valuable work treated as a sideshow by Holmes reports. And if most educational research was centered on teaching and learning in PDS, theory construction and educational research on educational issues beyond classroom teaching and learning would "devolve into industrial-style research and development."[10]

Many professors in non-teacher-education programs, about half of the faculty, feared that Dean Wisniewski's call for a New College was part of a strategy to strengthen teacher education at the expense of other programs, or even to eliminate them. (They did not necessarily associate New College planning with the Holmes Group reports; there is little evidence that either the critics of New College or most of its architects had paid much attention to the reports.) But the dean's interest obviously centered on teacher education, and, during the earlier college goals debate, Ralph Norman had signaled for campus administration that they saw teacher education as the prime mission of the college. Wisniewski assured non-teacher-education faculty early and often that there was a place for all existing programs in New College, but many professors remained unconvinced.

In part because of these suspicions, a non-teacher-education professor (in exercise physiology) was asked to chair the task force on writing the New College mission statement. *Tomorrow's Schools of Education* complains of the ambiguity surrounding the mission of schools of education, but those who constructed the mission statement saw virtue in ambiguity. They worked diligently to create an inclusive mission that did not privilege any programs in the college:

> The College of Education is a professional school that promotes critical inquiry, reflection, and social action through interdisciplinary studies. Its graduates are prepared to work in a changing and multicultural world in leadership roles in educational programs and institutions, health and social institutions, and private and corporate sectors. The College is committed to providing life-

long learning for both faculty and students by promoting courses of study that
involve students and faculty in academic peer relationships that stress shared
responsibility for learning and for the discovery of new knowledge. The faculty is committed to research, scholarship, and creative work that results in
superior teaching and service to the community and to the professions. The
College is committed to work towards equity and economic and social justice
within the University community and throughout the broader society.

This is obviously just the sort of mission that was causing despair
among the Holmes deans. Nevertheless, two departments that consisted largely of non-teacher-education faculty left the college, and other
programs continue to flirt with other colleges.[11]

In 1997, two researchers from the UT College of Communications
released a report on the culture of the College of Education: *Implementing a Vision*. After three years of experience, faculty were distressed by a lack of identity in New College; only 41 percent of the
faculty thought that the college "had a strong sense of direction." And
some were troubled by the college's unwillingness to commit itself to
particular programs and not others. Some faculty argued for a Holmes-
type commitment to teacher education rather than to continue emu-
lating colleges of arts and sciences: "We need to become more clini-
cally oriented." Another professor agreed, finding a model in the School
of Nursing and insisting that more professors become involved with
teacher interns. And professors from non-teacher-education programs
continued to feel that they "don't quite fit in."[12]

The researchers found great variation in how strongly professors
embrace the vision of New College. The most vocal group of faculty
were enthusiastic from the beginning and remain committed to the
changes. But others are still resentful about the processes for forming
New College and see its legacy in mistrust and "bitter relationships
across the whole College." One professor proposed opening discussions aimed at bringing back the departments that had left the college; at the same time other non-teacher-education programs were
negotiating with other colleges. In addition to programs, some individual professors who opposed the changes have withdrawn from the
college emotionally and, as much as possible, physically, coming to
campus only to teach their classes or when it is otherwise absolutely
necessary.[13]

Perceptions of faculty about New College may be colored by the
financial exigency of UT. Because of budget cuts in 1996, an almost
competed dean's search to replace Wisniewski had to be abandoned

and an interim dean appointed. All faculty searches were also called off. And, in 1997, the college's budget suffered one of the severest cuts in the university. There was a sense that, despite all of the work in raising standards, creating an "exemplary" teacher education program, and restructuring, New College remained just a low-status college of education and that their reforms made no difference to the university administration in the allocation of resources. Throughout their history, educationists experienced a lack of respect, regardless of how hard they worked to earn it.

Ironically, embracing research and publications at the expense of field service may have weakened the college's capability to lobby effectively for shrinking resources. A veteran teacher educator complained that the college is no longer viewed as the comprehensive teacher education institution in the state. He lamented that the college has lost "intimate contact" with Tennessee's public schools: "School people used to call first thing with a problem or issue, but we are no longer looked to for answers. If there is a problem in Carter County—they no longer call on us. Serving the state is no longer the prime mission." Increasing emphasis on faculty research and publications as the source of prestige for universities was a national phenomenon in the 1980s, and Presidents Edward Boling and Lamar Alexander championed faculty research enthusiastically as the way to make UT a "flagship" institution. And Wisniewski, intent on gaining national recognition for the college, demanded publications for faculty rewards. When asked if emphasis on faculty scholarship had been at the expense of the land-grant function of serving public schools, he answered, not unexpectedly, negatively: "Balderdash, service to the state is bedrock."[14]

Nevertheless, current budget shortfalls find the college in an inferior position compared to its support in high places and to its political savvy during the economic crisis of the 1930s. During the depression, the College of Education was able not only to weather but to expand. It was prepared as most other campus units were not to actively campaign for a share of scarce resources. Because the education faculty seldom had much support within the university, they were forced to become adept at gaining political and monetary support from outside—from public school leaders, state politicians, and foundation administrators. They put their skills and experience into effective promotion of activities and mission that led to expansion of the college. Over the last generation, intellectual inquiry and greater contributions to scholarship have made educationists more at home in the university, and they had no choice but to publish more in order to survive, but attempts to achieve the norms of the academy have been at the expense of service to public school educators and of their reciprocal support for the college.

Educationists at UT have always been concerned with their status in the university community; in *Implementing a Vision*, 90 percent of faculty agreed or strongly agreed that they were "concerned about how the College was viewed by others." Despite the disillusionment resulting from budget cuts, it is too early to know if rising research productivity and New College reforms will make a difference in the ways the college will be perceived in the long run by arts and science professors and university administrators. If history is a guide, I suspect it probably won't make much difference. The status of colleges of education is affected by biases over which educationists have little control: despite lip service to the contrary, public school children and their teachers have low status; despite much progress by feminists, gender biases are still strong and public school teachers are mainly women; despite growing sophistication and rigor of educational research, it is still considered soft and applied when compared to the hard and theoretical research of arts and sciences professors; and, despite ever-increasing standards in teacher education, past images of marginal students and Mickey Mouse education courses remain part of the university's folklore.[15]

In the history of the University of Tennessee, educationists understood that preparing teachers, administrators, and other educators and striving to improving public schools was important work. Most educationists in every generation were dedicated to doing it well. There were lazy and indifferent education professors at UT and a few blatant hustlers, but most educationists were hard working, dedicated to preparing teachers, and committed to quality public schools—although they often lacked consensus on how to train teachers and what the characteristics of quality schools were. Their liberal arts colleagues often saw their work as too practice oriented and nontheoretical, and their public school clients often saw it as too theoretical and impractical. Their "failures" were caused partly by limited resources or limited vision, but in large part they were caused by the difficulties of their tasks. Educationists simply could not satisfy critics from both worlds.

At the risk of sounding like a worried parent telling her unpopular adolescent that it doesn't really matter (you are a good kid; just work hard and be nice to others), I argue that for educationists to worry about upgrading their status is a waste of energy. We need to be about the work of trying to help create more humane, equitable, and intellectually honest public schools. Among some of my more left-leaning colleagues for whom angst is de rigueur, my optimism about educationists' ability to work with teachers to improve schools and teacher education is considered a character defect, if not a pathology. But while recognizing the obstacles in front of educationists who struggle to help prospective teachers do good work, I believe we must persevere. It is the work that is important, not the prestige that will probably never accompany it.

Notes

Chapter 1

1 James Riley Montgomery, Stanley J. Folmsbee, and Lee Seifert Greene, *To Foster Knowledge: A History of The University of Tennessee, 1794–1970* (Knoxville: The University of Tennessee Press, 1984), 30–37.

2 Stanley J. Folmsbee, *East Tennessee University 1840–1879: Predecessor of The University of Tennessee*, *The University of Tennessee Record* 62 (May 1959): 8–11; Catalogue of East Tennessee University (1844).

3 Catalogues of East Tennessee University (1845) and (1849).

4 Clinton B. Allison, "The Southern Teacher in the Twentieth Century: Race Mattered," in *Southern Education in the Twentieth Century: Exceptionalism and Its Limits*, ed. Wayne Urban (New York: Garland Press, in press).

5 Montgomery, Folmsbee, and Greene, 78–80.

6 Montgomery, Folmsbee, and Greene, 55, 93–96; Stanley J. Folmsbee, *East Tennessee University 1840–1879*, 85, 92.

7 Catalogue (1873).

8 Faculty Minutes (14 April), (21 April), (28 April), (19 May), (22 May), (30 May), and (2 June 1873). All minutes, documents, and manuscripts used in these notes may be found in Special Collections, Hoskins Library, the University of Tennessee, Knoxville.

9 Catalogue of East Tennessee University (1872–73): 27.

10 *Report of the Board of Trustees of the East Tennessee University* (1875): 6. Preparatory courses were finally eliminated in 1887.

11 Ibid., 6, 7; Catalogues (1875–1879).

12 Minutes of the Board of Trustees of East Tennessee University (21 March 1878) and (28 March 1878).

13 "Report of Special Board of Trustees Committee in Reference to Normal Schools" (1878).

14 For a general discussion of summer normal institutes see, Dick B. Clough, "Teacher Institutes in Tennessee, 1870–1900," *Tennessee Historical Quarterly* 31 (Spring, 1972). The Institute at The University of Tennessee was for whites only. Institutes for African-American teachers were held during the same years, often on the same dates, at Austin School, the black public school in Knoxville at the time. Lockett, Joynes, Karns, and other University of Tennessee professors who were prominent in the State Normal Institute also lectured at the "Colored Teachers Institute." Neither the Knoxville newspapers nor the state superintendent's *Reports* devoted much attention to the black institutes, often offering little more than an announcement of sessions and a summary conclusion such as "the colored teachers are well equipped and are making rapid strides in educational advancement," *Report of the State Superintendent of Public Instruction* (1900): 208.

15 *Knoxville Daily Chronicle*, 1 July 1883, 9 June, 2 July, 5 July, and 9 July 1881.

16 Edgar Wallace Knight, *Education in the United States* (Boston: Ginn and Company, 1929), 332; *Knoxville Daily Chronicle*, 11 July 1883 and 14 July 1882.

17 *Knoxville Tribune*, 19 July 1892 and *Knoxville Daily Chronicle*, 9 June 1882.

18 *Knoxville Daily Chronicle*, 21 and 23 July 1881.

19 *Knoxville Sunday Chronicle*, 22 July 1883; *Knoxville Tribune*, 26 July 1894; *Report of the State Superintendent of Public Instruction* (1896).

20 *Knoxville Daily Chronicle*, 7 July 1880; *Knoxville Journal*, 29 May 1896; *Knoxville Tribune*, 16 July 1894; *Report of the State Superintendent of Public Instruction* (1892): 42.

21 *Knoxville Daily Chronicle*, 9 July 1881 and 1 July 1884.

22 *Report of the State Superintendent of Public Instruction* (1880): 37.

23 *Biennial Report,* Board of Trustees of The University of Tennessee (1881–82): 13; *Knoxville Daily Chronicle*, 2 July 1881, 11 July 1883, 9 July 1883, 10 July 1883, and 19 July 1882.

24 *Knoxville Daily Chronicle*, 3 and 11 July 1883.

25 Ibid., 18 July 1884, 11 July 1883, and 15 July 1883.

26 *Knoxville Daily Chronicle*, 2 July 1881 and 5 July 1881; *Knoxville Journal*, 29 May 1892.

27 *Knoxville Tribune*, 20 July 1892; *Knoxville Journal*, 20 July 1892.

28 *Knoxville Sunday Chronicle*, 1 July 1883; *Knoxville Journal*, 20 July 1892.

29 *Knoxville Daily Chronicle*, 4 and 11 July 1883.

30 *Knoxville Journal,* 15 May 1898; *Knoxville Daily Chronicle,* 2 July 1881; *Knoxville Tribune,* 19 July 1892.

31 *Knoxville Daily Chronicle,* 19 July 1881.

32 Ibid., 22 July 1881.

33 Ibid., 20 July 1881, 11 July 1883, 1 August 1880, 20 and 21 July 1881.

34 *Knoxville Daily Chronicle,* 1 July 1883; *Biennial Report,* Board of Trustees of The University of Tennessee (1883–84): 40; Clough, 68.

35 Hunter Nicholson, "Relation of the Science College to the Common School," handwritten paper. AR 1, Box 1.

36 Ibid.

37 "Annual Report" of the Department of Natural History and Geology for 1879–1880. AR 1, Box 2; *Report of the State Superintendent of Public Instruction* (1878): 18–19. Superintendent Leon Trousdale was particularly interested in the establishment of special industrial schools.

38 A copy of the questionnaire, in Temple's handwriting, and the professors responses may be found in AR 1, Box 2.

39 Ibid.

40 Ibid.

41 See Joynes's "letter concerning the Establishment of a Normal School for the Women of Virginia" written in 1864 and printed in *U.S. Bureau of Education Report,* 1900–1901 (Washington, DC., 1902).

42 Detailed (and much the same) accounts of the deposing of Humes may be found in James Riley Montgomery, Stanley J. Folmsbee, and Lee Seifert Greene, *To Foster Knowledge,* Chapter 6, and in Stanley J. Folmsbee, *Tennessee Establishes a State University: First Years of The University of Tennessee, 1879–1887, The University of Tennessee Record* 64 (May 1961), Chapter 5.

43 Faculty Minutes (20 December 1878); *Catalogue* (1879–80): 28. See documents in AR 1, Box 2.

44 President's Report (January 30, 1879).

45 Faculty Minutes (13 January 1879); Board of Trustee Minutes (15 February 1879); *Knoxville Daily Chronicle,* 18 February 1879.

46 *Catalogue* (1879–80): 25, 29.

47 *Board of Trustees Report* (1881): 15; *Report of the State Superintendent of Public Instruction* (1879–80): 36; Faculty Minutes (21 November 1882).

48 *Knoxville Daily Chronicle,* 20 July 1881; Faculty Minutes (23 January 1882); Board of Trustees Minutes (26 January 1882).

49 Michael Hailey, "African American Cadets and the University of Tennessee, 1880–1890 (Paper presented to the Southern History of Education Society, Knoxville, Tennessee, 1997), 3–4.

50 Board of Trustee Minutes (16 August 1881), (25 August 1881), and (26 August 1881); Montgomery, Folmsbee, and Greene, 102–104.

51 *Catalogue* (1881–82): 36. This announcement continued until 1887–88.

52 Catalogues (1887–88), (1888–90): 37.

53 *Philo Star* 1 (September 1882): 10; *Chi-Delta Crescent* 3, (November 1883): 24–25.

54 Brown Ayres to "our Loyal Students," 27 December 1904; Catalogue (1874–75): 31.

55 James Riley Montgomery, *The Volunteer State Forges Its University: The University of Tennessee, 1887–1919, The University of Tennessee Record* 69 (November 1966): 67; Rhey Boyd Parsons, "Teacher Education in Tennessee," (Ph.D. diss., University of Chicago, 1935), 44.

56 *Biennial Report* (1878): 7.

57 "Report of Board of Visitors," *Biennial Report* (1881): 62.

Chapter 2

1 *Report of the State Superintendent of Public Instruction* (1893): 202.

2 Ibid., (1891): 44.

3 "Announcement of the Teachers' Department," 1891; *Morristown Gazette*, 2 January 1890.

4 James Riley Montgomery, *The Volunteer State Forges Its University: The University of Tennessee, 1887–1919, The University of Tennessee Record* 69 (November 1966): 31–33.

5 UT *Register* (1891): 11–13; *Knoxville Tribune*, 18 June 1891.

6 "Announcement of the Teachers' Department," 1891; UT *Register* (1893–94): 49.

7 *Knoxville Journal*, 8 December 1893; "Editorial," *Tennessee University Student*, (February 1892): 16–17.

8 "Announcement of the Teachers' Department"; UT *Register* (1894–95): 52.

9 *Board of Trustees Report* (1891): 27; UT *Register* (1890–91): 41; See also "Announcement of The Teacher's Department," and *Board of Trustees Report* (1891): 26–27.

10   *Knoxville Tribune*, 9 June 1892.

11   *Tennessee University Student* (December 1890): 53 (October 1891): 14 and (April 1889): 110.

12   *Board of Trustees Report* (1891–92): 7.

13   *Report of the State Superintendent of Public Instruction* (1893): 202–203; *Tennessee University Magazine* (November 1894): 42; UT *Biennial Report* (1891): 80.

14   *Board of Trustees Report* (1894): 32, 33, 55; Faculty Minutes (September 20), (December 10), and (February 24, 1894); *Tennessee University Magazine* (February 1895): 171.

15   *Report of the State Superintendent of Public Instruction* (1890–91): 43; *Knoxville Tribune*, 12 May 1892.

16   *Knoxville Journal*, 17 May 1894.

17   Faculty Minutes (3 October 1892); *Board of Trustees Report* (1894): 32–33; "Teachers' Department," *Report of the State Superintendent of Public Instruction* (1893): 202–203.

18   Smith served as state superintendent from 1887 to 1891 and from 1893 to 1895.

19   Editorial in *Nashville Banner*, reprinted in *Knoxville Journal*, 25 February 1893; *Knoxville Journal*, 3 March 1893.

20   *Knoxville Journal*, 12 March 1893.

21   Ibid., 19 February 1893.

22   *Knoxville Journal*, 29 February 1893; *Knoxville Tribune*, 20 February 1893; *Knoxville Journal* , 21 February 1893.

23   *Knoxville Tribune*, 23 February 1893; *Knoxville Journal*, 22 February 1893.

24   *Knoxville Journal*, 12 March 1893.

25   Nugent Fitzgerald, "History of the College of Education, The University of Tennessee," AR 4, Box 24, mimeographed, undated: 7, 8.

26   *Knoxville Journal*, 2 and 7 February 1895.

27   *Knoxville Journal*, 9 June 1893; Much of this sketch of Karns is taken with permission from Clinton B. Allison, "Early Professors of Education: Three Case Studies," in *The Professors of Teaching: An Inquiry*, eds. Richard Wisniewski and Edward R. Ducharme (Albany: State University of New York Press, 1989).

28   Charles Dabney, *Letterbook*, 29 July 1896.

29   Madge Parham-McCoy, "Two East Tennessee Educators," unpublished term paper, undated [1929?].

30   Faculty Minutes (1 November 1897) and (3 October 1898); *Knoxville Tribune*, 24 January 1894; *Tennessee University Magazine*, (December 1894): 87.

31   *Knoxville Sentinel*, 10 June 1897; *Tennessee University Student* (March 1889): 84.

32   Parkham-McCoy, 16; UT *Register* (1899–1900): 33; Karns to Dabney, 29 May 1893.

33   *Tennessee University Magazine* (October 1895): 36; Karns to Dabney, 29 May 1893.

34   *Knoxville Tribune*, 8 December 1896. In 1892, the National Education Association established the Committee of Ten on Secondary School Studies, which was chaired by Harvard President Charles Eliot; it recommended the same curriculum for students who were going or not going to college.

35   *Tennessee University Magazine* (November 1894): 42–43; Karns, "Report of the Teachers' Department," UT *Biennial Report* (1893–94): 82, 83.

36   Karns, "Report of the Teachers' Department," in UT *Biennial Report* (1893–94): 82, 83.

37   *Tennessee University Magazine* (March 1896): 247.

38   *Board of Trustee Report* (1893–94): 84; *Report of the State Superintendent of Public Instruction* (1892): 245.

39   See, for example, *Tennessee University Student* (October 1893): 174–175.

40   Karns to Ira Meese, 12 March 1896; Karns to Ralph L. Smith, 9 April 1891.

41   For the history of coeducation at The University of Tennessee and other southern universities, see Elizabeth Lee Ihle, "The Development of Coeducation in Major Southern State Universities" (Ed.D. diss., University of Tennessee, 1976). Nugent Fitzgerald; *Board of Trustee Minutes* (8 January 1891); *Knoxville Journal*, 4 February 1891; Faculty Minutes (10 December 1894).

42   Montgomery, 37–38; *Tennessee University Student* (December 1890): 55 and (February 1892): 17.

43   Montgomery, 36; *Knoxville Tribune*, 6 June 1893; *Tennessee School Report* (1892): 206.

44   Faculty Minutes (26 January 1894).

45   *Knoxville Tribune*, 14 September 1894, and James Hoskins, "Admission of Women," in "History of the University of Tennessee," unpublished manuscript, AR 76; quoted in Montgomery, 37.

46   *Board of Trustees Report* (1893–94); The name "Teachers' Department" does not appear in the 1896–97 UT *Record*.

47   Karns to Miss Dorthy White, 1 November 1893.

48   Karns to Dabney, 29 May 1893.

49   Karns to Dabney, 18 February 1893.

50   UT *Register* (1893–94): 18.

51   Karns to J. N. Odom, 10 January 1896; Dabney to Mr. W. J. Miller, 6 December 1898; UT *Register* (1897–98).

52   Faculty Minutes (3 February 1896); Karns to Dabney, 18 February 1898.

53   Martha Fain, secretary, to Prof. William Dinwiddle, 4 July 1899; Dabney to Mr. J. T. Gose, 12 July 1899. The following letters are in Dabney's *Letterbook* 32: to Dr. William E. Dodd, 22 January, 31 January, and 17 March 1900; Professor Richard J. Street, 20 March 1900; Professor P. P. Claxton, 3 April 1900; and in *Letterbook* 40, to Prof. Edward E. Sheib.

54   UT *Register* (1900–1901) and (1903–04).

Chapter 3

1   This sketch of Claxton is extracted by permission from Clinton B. Allison, "Early Professors of Education: Three Case Studies," in *The Professors of Teaching: An Inquiry* , eds. Richard Wisniewski and Edward R. Ducharme (Albany: State University of New York Press, 1989).

2   Charles Lee Lewis, *Philander Priestley Claxton: Crusader For Public Education* (Knoxville: The University of Tennessee Press, 1948.), 31–36.

3   Ibid., 52.

4   Claxton to Dabney, 23 May 1905.

5   Lucile Cole to Claxton, 18 January 1911; Claxton to Cole, 21 January 1911.

6   Claxton to W. C. Bagley, 18 October 1910.

7   Lewis, 98–109.

8   Claxton to C. O. Ruch, 7 April 1908.

9   Board of Trustees Minutes (22 July 1902): 74; UT press release, 1902, AR 2, Box 2; James Riley Montgomery, *The Volunteer State Forges Its University*, UT *Record*, 69 (November 1966): 52; James E. Russell to Dabney, 11 November 1902; Dabney to George Foster Peabody, 22 August 1903.

10   Announcement: "Department of Education," 1902, AR 5, Box 1; *Knoxville Journal and Tribune*, 3 January 1903 and 22 November 1902. A list of the teachers' journals may be found in AR 3, Box 7; samples of the advertisements may be found in AR 2, Box 3.

11   Claxton, "Public High Schools-II," undated [1909]), MS 278, Box 14. For information on the education of southern teachers, see Clinton B. Allison,

"The Southern Teacher in the Twentieth Century: Race Mattered," in *Southern Education in the Twentieth Century: Exceptionalism and Its Limits*, ed. Wayne Urban (New York: Garland Press, in press).

12   Edward L. Thorndike to Dabney, 7 October 1902; Carroll Dunham to Dr. Shaw, 30 September 1902.

13   Dabney to Claxton, 7 January 1903; Dabney to Miss Lilian W. Johnson, 16 October 1902. Several professors in other university departments (including two of the few women on the faculty: Florence Skeffington, graduate of Minnesota State Normal College and the University of Chicago in methods of teaching English, and Mary Comfort, graduate of the Philadelphia Academy of Art in drawing) offered special courses for the education students.

14   UT *Record* 7 (March 1904): 53.

15   J. P. Gray to Dabney, 1 March 1902; Dabney to Gray, 3 March 1902; Board of Trustees Minutes (10 December 1903): 258; Board of Trustees Minutes (February 1903): 61, 64, 115.

16   Board of Trustees Minutes, 5 (3 February 1903): 116.

17   *Knoxville Journal and Tribune*, 24 October 1904; Dabney to Walter Hines Page, 22 August 1903; Dabney, "Confidential Report," 1903, MS 310, Box 18.

18   Dabney to Wallace Buttrick, 18 August 1903.

19   Wallace Buttrick to Dabney, 26 June 1903; Dabney to Wallace Buttrick, 18 August 1903.

20   Dabney to George Foster Peabody, 22 August 1903.

21   Board of Trustees Minutes, 5 (26 September 1903): 254; UT *Record* 7 (March 1904): 54; *The Biennial Report of the State Superintendent of Public Instruction* also reported that the Department had a "model and practice" school. *Biennial Report of the Superintendent of Public Instruction* (1902–1903): 333. In 1915 the name of Rose Avenue School was changed to Staub School. For a time, the department was responsible for Farragut School, a Knox County "model rural school." See Clinton B. Allison, "Farragut School: A Case Study in Southern Progressivism," *Curriculum as Psychoanalysis: Essays on the Significance of Place*, eds. Joe L. Kincheloe and William Pinar (Albany: State University of New York Press, 1991).

22   Dabney to Peabody, 20 June 1903; Dabney to Wallace Buttrick, 18 August 1903.

23   Claxton to Dabney, 20 September 1904. See letters from Claxton to Dabney, 23 May and 12 June 1905 in MS 278, Box 14 and additional correspondence in AR 5, Box 1.

24   Brown Ayres to Buttrick, 22 September 1904; Buttrick to Ayres, 14 September 1904 and 28 September 1904; Ayres to Robert S. Ogden, 24 October 1904; Buttrick to Ayres, 11 January 1905.

25 Claxton to Mari R. Hofer, 16 January 1905.

26 "School of Education," UT *Record* 14 (July 1911); *Knoxville News-Sentinel*, 7 June 1915; UT *Register* 23 (1919–1920); *Orange and White*, 4 November 1916, 24 November 1911, and 15 December 1911.

27 Letter to "My dear President Thompson" of Ohio State, 16 May 1912.

28 E. E. Rall to Ayres, 2 October 1911; Ayres to Rall, 5 October 1911.

29 *Knoxville Sentinel*, 3 June 1911; *Knoxville Journal*, 4 June 1911.

30 E. E. Rall, "The County High School Curriculum," *University of Tennessee Magazine* (January 1913): 116–122.

31 Rall to Ayres, 31 May 1916.

32 Ayres to Rall, 27 July 1916.

33 UT *Record* 3 (1903): 208–209. Some grandiose plans of the department were never initiated, such as the announcement that a School of Kindergarten to train early childhood teachers would open on January 6, 1903, with no effort spared "in making the instruction and management as nearly ideal and perfect as possible," Claxton, "announcement," AR 3, Box 7.

34 "School of Education," undated [1906], MS 278, Box 5; UT *Register* 8 (April, 1905): 57.

35 UT *Register* 8 (April, 1905): 57.

36 Dabney to Claxton, 7 January 1903; *Knoxville Journal and Tribune*, 29 September 1915; Harry Clark, "Work of University Schools of Education," [undated] AR 4, Box 27; *Knoxville Sentinel*, 23 November 1916; "The University of Tennessee: Its Service, Resources and Needs," pamphlet, AR 2, Box 3.

37 Harry Clark, "Work of University Schools of Education," AR 4, Box 27.

38 Claxton to Ayres, 25 November 1908; "School of Education," undated [1906], MS 278, Box 5.

39 "Announcement," Department of Education, 1902, AR 5, Box 1; Board of Trustees Minutes (29 October 1902): 106; Claxton to Ayres, 25 November 1908.

40 Rall to Ayres, 18 October 1911; *Orange and White*, 24 November 1911.

41 Claxton to Ayres, 25 November 1908; UT *Record* 7 (March 1904): 55.

42 *Orange and White*, 11 December 1913.

43 *Orange and White*, 26 March 1914, 29 April 1914, 1 April 1914, 11 February 1915, and 22 April 1915; *Knoxville Sentinel*, 11 January 1916 and 11 November 1920.

44 "Editorial," *Tennessee University Magazine* (November 1903): 71.

45   Claxton to Frederick A. Bolton, 7 December 1906, The survey from Bolton is in MS 278, Box 5, File B.

46   Clark to "Dear Friend," 10 March 1913; UT *Record* 28 (1915): 7.

47   *Orange and White*, 23 September 1914.

48   Mrs. F. H. Cothren to Claxton, 25 March 1910; P. P. Claxton, "Tennessee Hall," UT Scrapbook, February 1903, AR 79.

49   Claxton to Miss M. W. Haliburton, 24 March 1903.

50   Claxton to Ayres, 25 November 1908.

51   Harry Clark, "Get Thee to Mop and Broom for Profit," *Knoxville Sentinel*, 8 March 1914.

52   Ayres to W. T. Robinson, 10 February 1918.

53   See, for example, "Knox County Colored Teachers' Association," *Knoxville Journal and Tribune*, 28 January 1914; Dabney to Hon. W. T. Harris, 15 February 1902; Dabney to J. H. Goddard, 22 April 1901, *Letterbook* 43.

54   Rhey Boyd Parsons, "Teacher Education in Tennessee," (Ph.D. diss., University of Chicago, 1935), 125; Ayres to State Superintendent J. W. Brister, 6 December 1911; The attitude of many in the university community remained antagonistic toward African Americans for a long time to come. As late as 1921, a well-attended, spirited debate conducted by the Chi Delta Literary Society was on the question: "Resolved that the negro [sic] is a greater menace to the United States than the immigrants from any foreign country." To the credit of the students on the racial, if not the immigrant, issue the judges decided unanimously in favor of the negative side, *Orange and White*, 7 April 1921.

55   Clinton B. Allison, "The Southern Teacher in the Twentieth Century: Race Mattered."

56   Telephone interview with Franklin Parker, 25 April 1997. For information on the life and philanthropic work of Peabody, see Franklin Parker, *George Peabody: A Biography* (Nashville: Vanderbilt University Press, 1995). For an example of accusations of favoritism, see Ayres to Superintendent S. W. Sherrill, 29 November 1916, AR 4, Box 26.

57   Board of Trustees Minutes (27 May 1912); Ayres to Judge E. T. Sanford, 12 April 1912.

58   Charles G. Maphis to Ayres, 4 December 1912; Ayres to Maphis, 7 December 1912.

59   Jurgen Herbst, "Teacher Preparation in the Nineteenth Century: Institutions and Purposes," in *American Teachers: Histories of a Profession at Work*, ed. Donald Warren (New York: Macmillan Publishing Co., 1989), 218.

60   Rhey Boyd Parsons, 118–119, 125.

61   Claxton, "Answers to Questions of Dr. A. A. Murphree," 20 October 1906.

62   Claxton to Frederick A. Bolton, 7 December 1906. The survey is in MS 278, Box 5, File B.

63   Claxton to Moses E. Wood, 27 February 1911; Ayres to E. E. Rall, 5 October 1911.

64   Ayres letters were postmarked 22 April 1912.

65   Seymour A. Mynders to Ayres, 25 April 1912; Sidney G. Gilbreath to Ayres, 25 April 1912.

66   Ayres to Gilbreath, 29 April 1912.

67   Gilbreath to Ayres, 3 May 1912; Ayres to Gilbreath, 6 May 1912.

68   H. W. Terry, "The Summer School of the South: An Educational Revolution," 1902, unpublished paper, MS 278, Box 17B.

69   Jessie Lee Willcox, "Where Two Thousand Teachers Were Trained this Year," Circular, 1905, MS 278; Tennessee University Magazine (October 1902): 33; "Report of Summer School of South," 1902, AR 2, Box 3; "Confidential Report," MS 310, Box 20.

70   Letters from Dabney to William H. Baldwin, 4 November 1902.

71   James R. Montgomery, "The Summer School of the South," Tennessee Historical Quarterly 22 (December 1963): 375; H. W. Louis to P. P. Claxton, 11 May 1903.

72   Board of Trustee Minutes (7 January 1902).

73   Board of Trustee Minutes (22 July 1902); "The Relations of the University to the Summer School," MS 278, Box 20.

74   James Riley Montgomery, The Volunteer State Forges Its University: The University of Tennessee, 1887–1919, UT Record 69 (November 1966): 148–49; Terry, "The Summer School of the South: An Educational Revolution."

75   "Do you Remember," Knoxville Sentinel, 13 June 1924; "White Caps," memorandum, MS 278, Box 20; "Knoxville is the Home of the Great Summer School of the South," Knoxville Journal and Tribune, 11 May 1905.

76   UT Record (1904): 77; Dabney to J. D. Eggleston, 18 February 1943.

77   Dabney to Prof. Junius Jordon, 27 November 1901, Letterbook 43; Brown Ayres to the Board of Trustees, 29 May 1911; Knoxville Journal and Tribune, 12 April 1908; "Lectures and Recitals at the Coming Session of the Summer School of the South," announcement, AR 2, Box 3; UT Record 7 (1904): 10.

78　*Knoxville Sentinel*, 10 July 1902; "Lectures and Recitals at the Coming Session of the Summer School of the South," announcement, AR 2, Box 3; David Williams, "Teacher Training and Educational Evangelism: The Summer School of the South," *Proceedings of the Twenty-ninth Annual Meeting of the Southwestern Philosophy of Education Society* 29 (1978): 207; Montgomery; UT *Record* 7 (1904): 10.

79　Terry, "The Summer School of the South: An Educational Revolution."

80　*Biennial Report of the Superintendent of Public Instruction* (1903–04): 241; *Winston-Salem Twin-City Sentinel*, 13 July 1903; *Knoxville Journal and Tribune*, 21 July 1903; *Tupelo Journal* [Mississippi], 17 July 1903; Jessie Lee Willcox, "Where Two Thousand Teachers Were Trained This Year," 1905, MS 278, Box 20.

81　Memorandum from Dabney to Summer School of the South faculty, MS 278, Box 20.

82　*Yearbook*, Summer School of the South, 1908, MS 278, Box 17D.

83　Terry, "The Summer School of the South: An Educational Revolution."

84　*Summer School News*, 7 July 1914.

85　*Dublin Telephone* [Texas], 10 July 1914.

86　Willis A. Sutton, "The Summer School of the South—As I Remember It," MS 278, Box 17D; Lisa Pollard, "Just Peddling Out Their Wares: The Formal Lectures of the Summer School of the South, 1902–1918," *Tennessee Education* 25 (Fall 1995): 1; and Williams, "Teacher Training and Educational Evangelism," 207.

87　"Report on second session of the Summer School of the South," MS 278, Box 17.

88　*The Orange and White*, 5 April 1912; Claxton to Mrs. David G. Ray.

89　Terry; *Knoxville Sentinel*, 2 May 1910; *Summer School News*, 7 July 1914.

90　UT *Record*, "Summer School of the South," (1903), (1910), (1913), and (1915).

91　Pollard; *Knoxville Sentinel*, 8 July 1902; [Claxton], "A Visit to the Summer School Kindergarten [1903], MS 278, Box 17B.

92　*Knoxville Sentinel*, 23 April 1907 and 10 July 1902.

93　*Knoxville Journal and Tribune*, 11 June 1912; *Knoxville Sentinel*, 10 June 1912.

94　William B. Eigelsbach, "The Rise and Fall of a Summer School," *The Library Development Review/1987–88*, The University of Tennessee; Claxton, "Summer School of the South: In Retrospect," *Teacher Education Journal* 3 (December 1941); *Knoxville Journal and Tribune*, 11 June 1902. The fee was gradually increased to $10.00.

95   W. MacDonald, "The Status of the Summer School," *The Nation* 89 (September 1909): 202-203, quoted in Pollard; Clinton B. Allison, "Training Dixie's Teachers: The Summer School of the South," Symposium, Photography as a Historical Tool: A Southern Perspective, American Educational Research Association, 1989; "The Rest Room" [1903] MS 278, Box 20. A feminist interpretation of the Summer School of the South may be found in Lisa Pollard, "Just Peddling Out Their Wares: The Formal Lectures of the Summer School of the South, 1902–1918," *Tennessee Education* 25 (Fall 1995).

96   *Knoxville Journal and Tribune*, 24 July 1902.

97   T. S. Stribling, "The Summer School of the South," *Florence Herald* [Alabama], 17 July 1903, AR 68, Box IIIB.

98   Pollard, 9; *Knoxville Journal and Tribune*, 9 April 1913. On gender differentiated curriculums, see John L. Rury, *Education and Women's Work* (Albany: State University of New York Press, 1991) and Jane Bernard Powers, *The "Girl Question" in Education: Vocational Education for Young Women in the Progressive Era* (Bristol, PA: The Falmer Press, 1992).

99   *Knoxville Sentinel*, 18 July 1903.

100   *Knoxville Journal and Tribune*, 23 July 1918; Montgomery, "The Volunteer State," 158–159.

101   Dabney to Walter Hines Page, 22 August 1903.

102   Terry; Edgar Gardner Murphy to Claxton, 11 March 1903; Dabney to Page, 22 August 1903.

103   Montgomery, *The Volunteer State*, 158–159; Ayres to the Board of Trustees, 29 May 1911.

104   Board of Trustees Minutes (4 August 1908); Ayres to Claxton, 26 June 1909 and 25 August 1908.

105   Montgomery, *The Volunteer State*, 162–163.

Chapter 4

1   Clinton B. Allison, "The Conference for Education in the South: An Exercise in *Noblesse Oblige*, *Journal of Thought* 16 (Summer 1981). Accounts of the southern educational campaigns may be found in: Charles William Dabney, *Universal Education in the South*, Volume II (Chapel Hill, University of North Carolina Press, 1936); Louis R. Harlan, *Separate and Unequal: Public School Campaigns and Racism in the Southern Seaboard States, 1901–1915* (Chapel Hill: University of North Carolina Press, 1958); Henry Allen Bullock, *A History of Negro Education in the South from 1619 to the Present* (Cambridge: Harvard University Press, 1967); and James D. Anderson, *The Education of Blacks in the South, 1860–1935* (Chapel Hill: The University of North Carolina Press, 1988).

2   Edwin A. Alderman, "The Child and the State," *Proceedings of the Fifth Conference for Education in the South* (1902): 75.

3   Address by P. P. Claxton," *Proceedings of the Seventeenth Conference for Education in the South* (1914): 3–4.

4   *Memphis Commercial Appeal*, 10 April 1903.

5   "Campaign Opened for More and Better School in the Southern States," *Knoxville Journal and Tribune*, 15 January 1902.

6   Dabney to Wallace Buttrick, 14 April 1903; Dabney to Claxton, 14 April 1905.

7   *General Education Board: Review and Final Report* (1902–1964): 5–7; *The General Education Board: An Account of its Activities, 1902–1914* (New York, 1915): 84.

8   Ayres to Wallace Buttrick, 23 October 1905; Claxton to Buttrick, 6 May 1905; Ayres to Claxton, 25 August 1908; Ayres to Buttrick, 5 May 1905; Buttrick to Ayres, 15 May 1905; Ayres to Buttrick, 25 April 1906.

9   Ayres to Claxton, 25 August 1908.

10   Claxton to Mari Hofer, 17 November 1906; Walter Hines Page to Claxton, 11 April 1908.

11   Seymour A. Mynders to Dabney, 11 May 1903.

12   S. A. Mynders, "Tennessee," *Proceedings of the Ninth Conference for Education in the South* (1906): 68.

13   *Knoxville Journal*, 1 December 1935; *Memphis Commercial Appeal*, 7 September 1905 and 8 October 1906; *Knoxville Sentinel*, 23 November 1907.

14   P. P. Claxton, *Proceedings of the Eleventh Conference for Education in the South* (1908): 79.

15   Claxton to Superintendent H. G. Farmer, 12 August 1905; manuscript, "Education Campaign in Tennessee," MS 278, Box 14; Wallace Buttrick to Claxton, 5 August 1905. Claxton was generally a cosmopolitan rather than a sectional chauvinist. When a Tulane University professor requested his support for a series of southern public school textbooks, Claxton responded that he thought southerners should stop thinking of themselves "as a peculiar people set apart from the rest of the nation and the world, and I know no reason why there should be publishing houses, books and authors for the South more than there should be for the West or the North or for any other section": Walter Miller to Claxton, 10 November 1909; Claxton to Miller 16 November 1909.

16   Claxton to E. A. Alderman, 28 November 1907. See correspondence with D. S. Chandler, Knoxville passenger and ticket agent, Louisville and Nashville Railroad and with C. A. Benscotter, Assistant General Passenger Agent, Southern Railroad, Company, MS 278, Box 3.

17   Manuscript, "Education Campaign in Tennessee," MS 278, Box 14; *Tennessee High School Report*, September, 1917; *Nashville Tennessean,* 16 March and 12 October 1908; *Knoxville Journal and Tribune*, 12 January 1907; *Knoxville Journal,* 1 December 1935; and "Programme," East Tennessee Farmers' Convention and Institute (27 May 1908): 18–19.

18   Claxton to Ayres, 18 April 1906.

19   Claxton to S. A. Mynders, 3 August 1905; Claxton's letter to J. L. Barnes of Coal Creek is typical of letters sent to county superintendents, 5 August 1905, MS 278, B3; *Bristol Courier*, 15 October 1906.

20   Circular letter from Claxton, January 1908.

21   *Nashville Banner*, 3 October 1906.

22   Circular letter from Harry Clark, "High Schools," undated, AR 4, Box 26; *Knoxville Sentinel*, 4 May 1907 and 17 August 1912; Claxton to McIver, 10 January 1906. For discussions of the "administrative" progressives see David B. Tyack, *The One Best System: A History of American Urban Education* (Cambridge: Harvard University Press, 1974) and Jeffery E. Mirel, "Progressive School Reform in Comparative Perspective," in *Southern Cities, Southern Schools: Public Education in the Urban South*, eds. David N. Plank and Rick Ginsberg (New York: Greenwood Press, 1990).

23   Henry Allen Bullock, *A History of Negro Education in the South from 1619 to the Present* (Cambridge: Harvard University Press, 1967); James D. Anderson, *The Education of Blacks in the South, 1860–1935* (Chapel Hill: The University of North Carolina Press, 1988). For the class bias argument, see Clinton B. Allison, "The Conference for Education in the South: An Exercise in *Noblesse Oblige*," *Journal of Thought* 16 (Summer 1981); Claxton quoted in the *Nashville American*, 2 February 1908.

24   Draft of Claxton's campaign speech, MS 278, Box 3.

25   Seymour A. Mynders to Claxton, 6 November, 1905; *Knoxville Sentinel*, 17 August, 1912.

26   *Knoxville Journal*, 1 December 1935.

27   Claxton to Robert C. Ogden, 6 January 1905.

28   Dabney to Claxton, 30 January 1906. For an account of Farragut School, see Clinton B. Allison, "Farragut School: A Case Study in Southern Progressivism," in *Curriculum as Psychoanalysis: Essays on the Significance of Place*, eds. Joe L. Kincheloe and William F. Pinar (Albany: State University of New York Press, 1991).

29   Dabney to Claxton, 30 January 1906.

30   Ayres to Claxton 25 August 1908; see also Ayres address: "School Boys and an Intellectual Life," *Proceedings of the Ninth Conference for Education in the South* (1906).

31　Wallace Buttrick to Ayres, 27 June 1905.

32　Ayres to Clark, 17 November 1911; Morgan to Abraham Flexner, 25 September 1920.

33　Buttrick to Ayres, 11 November 1916; Ayres to Buttrick, 6 July 1917.

34　Harry H. Clark to Ayres, 13 November 1911 and 22 November 1911; Ayres to Buttrick, 26 January 1912; *Orange and White*, 6 January 1921 and 13 January 1921; Clark vitae, AR 4, Box 27.

35　Ayres to Clark, 6 November 1911, 12 July 1912, and 22 August 1912; Clark to Morgan, 14 June 1919.

36　Clark to Ayres, 14 January 1914.

37　Clark to Ayres, 1 November 1914.

38　Jane Bernard Powers, *The "Girl Question" in Education: Vocational Education for Young Women in the Progressive Era* (Bristol, PA: The Falmer Press, 1992); John L. Rury, *Education and Women's Work* (Albany: State University of New York Press, 1991); Clark to Ayres, 14 January 1914.

39　*Knoxville Sentinel*, 21 February 1913; James L. Leloudis, *Schooling the New South: Pedagogy, Self, and Society in North Carolina, 1880–1920* (Chapel Hill: The University of North Carolina Press, 1996), 169.

40　Clark to Ayres, 1 October 1914.

41　"Plans of Harry Clark—Tennessee 1916," AR 4, Box 13.

42　Clark to E. C. Sage, 28 June 1916.

43　Clark to E. C. Sage, 28 June 1916; Harry Clark, "High School Report—Tennessee: An Estimate of My Year's Work," 7 January 1917, AR 4, Box 27.

44　*Knoxville Journal and Tribune*, 18 February 1920.

45　"Plans of Harry Clark—Tennessee, 1916," AR 4, Box 13; *Orange and White*, 9 December 1915; Clark to Dear Superintendent and Friend, 22 August 1914; Clark to Morgan, 14 June 1919; Harry Clark, "High School Report—Tennessee: An Estimate of My Year's Work," 7 January 1917, AR 4, Box 27.

46　Clark to Morgan, 1 January 1920; Clark to Ayres, 14 January 1914 and 5 September 1916.

47　Clark to Ayres, 1 November 1914; Clark to Ayres, 31 October 1917.

48　Clark to Ayres, 14 January 1914; Clark, "Tennessee High School Report," February 1918, AR 4, Box 27.

49　Circular letter from Harry Clark to "High School teachers," AR 4, B26; *Nashville Tennessean*, 17 September 1905; *Knoxville Sentinel* 14 March 1913; *Knoxville Journal and Tribune*, 24 March 1913; *Bristol Courier*, 24 October 1916.

50 Buttrick to Ayres, 2 October 1914; Ayres to Buttrick, 10 October 1914.

51 Clark to Ayres, 31 October 1917; Clark to Ayres, 14 January 1914; Clark to Ayres, 1 October 1914.

52 Clark to Ayres, 14 January 1914; "Plans of Clark, Report to the General Education Board, 1916," AR 4, Box 13.

53 Charles William Dabney, *Universal Education in the South*, 5–11; *New York Herald*, 10 January 1903.

54 J. L. M. Curry, "Education in the Southern States," *Proceedings of the Second Capon Springs Conference* (1899): 28; Edwin A. Alderman, "The Child and the State," *Proceedings of the Fifth Conference for Education in the South* (1902): 61.

55 Clippings may be found in MS 278, Box 15. *The State* (Columbia, SC), 27 April 1903, MS 278, Box 15; "Southern Men Behind This New Movement," *Knoxville Journal and Tribune*, 21 November 1901;"The Southern Education Board," *The Daily Progress* (Charlottesville, VA), 15 April 1902, MS 278, Box 15; Robert Ogden of the Wanamaker department stores of New York and Philadelphia was the president of the Conference for Education in the South during most of its existence.

56 *Chattanooga Times*, 13 October 1906; Louis R. Harlan, "The Southern Education Board and the Race Issue in Public Education," *The Journal of Southern History* 23 (May 1957): 194; "Within the Year," pamphlet, Southern Education Board, MS 278, Box 17 B.

57 *Memphis Commercial Appeal*, 10 April 1903.

58 Amelia Hofer to Claxton, 5 January 1905; Claxton to Hofer, 17 January 1905.

59 Mynders to Claxton, 1 August 1905; Claxton to Mynders, 2 August 1905; P. P. Claxton, *Proceedings of the Eleventh Conference for Education in the South* (1908): 80; Claxton to G. Stanley Hall, 9 December 1904.

60 Claxton to J. C. Wright, 9 December 1904; *Knoxville Journal*, 23 December 1904.

61 "Plans of Clark for 1916: Report to Sage," AR 4, Box 13.

62 "High School Report, Clark to Sage," 7 January 1917, AR 4, Box 27.

63 "Plans of Clark: Report to Sage," January 1916, AR 4, Box 13; "High School Report for February 1916"; Clark to Ayres, 31 October 1917; "Tennessee High School Report," December 1918, AR 4, Box 27.

64 "Tennessee High School Report," December 1918, AR 4, Box 27; Clark, "September Report to Brown Ayres," 1 October 1914, AR 4, Box 27; "Tennessee High School Report," September 1917, AR 4, Box 27.

65 "Tennessee High School Report," April 1917, AR 4, Box 27; "Tennessee High School Report," December 1918, AR 4, Box 27.

66 *Orange and White*, 29 May 1919; Montgomery, *To Foster Knowledge*, 170–172.

67 Clark's "Monthly Report," December 1917; Clark to Morgan, 14 June 1919; Clark to Morgan, 24 December 1920.

68 Clark to Morgan, 20 June 1919; Morgan to Clark 23, June 1919.

69 Clark to Ayres, 16 December 1918.

70 Clark to Morgan, 4 June 1919.

71 "Secondary Education in the Southern States: A Memorandum for Consideration of the Conference of University Presidents and State Superintendents," Congress Hotel, Chicago, 14 and 15 November 1919; Abraham Flexner to Morgan, 15 December 1919.

72 "*Resolutions*, adopted by State Superintendents of Education and Presidents of State Universities of the Southern State," 19 December 1924, AR 4, Box 13; George H. Denny to H. A. Morgan, 6 October 1919; Morgan to Denny 10 October 1919.

73 Myrtle E. Harris to Morgan, 9 December 1924; Morgan to Buttrick, 28 September 1923; Morgan to Buttrick 6 October 1924; Morgan to Frank P. Bachman, 15 January 1926. The three men who held the post after Clark's resignation in 1921 were much less able than Claxton and Clark. The first of these, Jesse W. Sprowls, was a disaster. He was fired in 1923, precipitating the "Great Professor War" at the university, a story told in some detail in chapter 5. Sprowls was replaced by Forest E. Long who left for Washington University in Saint Louis almost immediately after his appointment. E. R. Gabler was the final appointment to the position.

Chapter 5

1 *Orange and White*, 7 October 1916; James Riley Montgomery, Stanley J. Folmsbee, and Lee Seifert Green, *To Foster Knowledge: A History of The University of Tennessee, 1794–1970* (Knoxville: The University of Tennessee Press, 1984), 194–205.

2 "Report on the University of Tennessee," *Bulletin of the American Association of University Professors*, 10 (April 1924); Hoskins to Paul J. Kruesi, 18 October 1946.

3 Editorial, *Knoxville News*, 15 April 1923; "Report on the University of Tennessee," AAUP *Bulletin*, 25.

4 Cloide Everett Brehm, quoted in James Riley Montgomery, *Threshold of a New Day: The University of Tennessee, 1919–1946*, UT *Record* 74 (November 1971): 20.

5   Philip Hamer diary, 11, MS 526; "Report on the University of Tennessee," AAUP *Bulletin*: 25.

6   Copies of *The Independent Truth* may be found in Special Collections, UT Hoskins Library; *Knoxville Journal and Tribune*, 17 April 1923; "Report on the University of Tennessee," AAUP *Bulletin*, 31; Hamer diary.

7   University papers on the hearings may be found in University Archives 3, Box 8.

8   *Knoxville Journal and Tribune*, 8 January 1922 and 16 April 1923; *Knoxville Sentinel*, 17 May 1923 and 24 May 1923; *Knoxville Journal and Tribune*, 19 April 1923. Educationists, including Dean Thackston, took prominent roles in Sunday school activities of mainline churches. For twenty-five years, educational psychology Professor Joseph Avent conducted the Standard Training School for the Knoxville District of the Methodist Church. A discussion of the pervasive Protestant influence at UT was prepared by the Office of the University Historian, "To Promote No Creed: Religion at UT," Historical Vignette, *Context*, 13 (2 February 1996): 6–9.

9   Unsigned letter to Morgan, 16 May 1924.

10   A. R. Wilson to Morgan, 21 July 1923.

11   "Report on the University of Tennessee," AAUP *Bulletin*, 64. The AAUP again censored the university after the dismissal of education Associate Professor A. D. Mueller in 1936.

12   Jno. A. Thackston to President H. A. Morgan, 11 January 1921.

13   Ibid.

14   Minutes of Board of Trustees Executive Committee, 23 February 1926.

15   *Tennessee Alumnus*, 10 (April 1926): 4; UT "News Letter" (27 March 1926). For historical essays on the science of education, see Erwin Johanningmeier, ed., "Science of Education and the Education Professoriate," *Occasional Papers Series—Set #10*, Society of Professors of Education, 1978.

16   *Knoxville Journal and Tribune*, 15 August 1916; *Knoxville News-Sentinel*, 18 August 1949.

17   *Orange and White*, 19 January 1932.

18   *Orange and White*, 19 January 1932; *Knoxville Sentinel*, 8 April 1919, 28 April 1920, and 29 March 1917; *Memphis Press-Scimitar*, 24 September 1946; *Knoxville Sentinel*, 5 February 1933.

19   UT *Record* 29 (May 1926); UT "News Letter" 5 (27 March 1926).

20   Jno. A. Thackston to Dean James D. Hoskins, 25 March 1926; Minutes of the Board of Trustees (1 June 1926).

21   *Knoxville Sentinel*, 22 July 1923.

22 Thackston to Morgan, 19 March 1927; Jos. E. Avent, "The Place of the State University College of Education in a State Program of Education," undated [1927], AR 4, Box 24.

23 Harry C. Humphreys, "Objectives of the College of Education, undated [1927]. In 1918 the NEA's Commission on Reorganization of Secondary Education promulgated the Seven Cardinal Principles of Secondary Education: health, command of fundamental processes, worthy home membership, vocational efficiency, civic participation, worthwhile use of leisure time, and ethical character. Professor R. B. Parsons and B. O. Duggan also developed wide-ranging objective statements.

24 Thackston to Morgan, 19 March 1927; R. B. Parsons, "Objectives of the College of Education, University of Tennessee," undated [1927].

25 *Orange and White*, 4 March 1926; "Some Objectives to be Attained by Graduates of Universities," mimeographed, undated, AR 4, file 459-A; The UT "Newsletter" (27 March 1926).

26 *Nashville Tennessean*, 1 August 1943; Duggan to Morgan, 31 July 1928.

27 Duggan to Morgan, 22 January 1929.

28 Duggan to Morgan, 22 January 1929; Duggan to Morgan, 31 July 1928.

29 Chenault to Morgan, 25 June 1929.

30 Chenault to Morgan, 25 June 1929; Robt. N. Chenault to Morgan, 19 January 1929; Morgan to Chenault, 26 June 1929.

31 Duggan to Hoskins, 8 April 1932; For documents on reorganization, see AR 4, Box 24.

32 Duggan to Morgan, 21 March 1932.

33 Harcourt A Morgan to Dr. Leonard V. Koos, 30 July 1931; Morgan to Doctor William J. French, 15 May 1930; Morgan to Dr. Chas. E. Little, 7 February 1931. For a time, the liberal arts faculty did take an active role in educating high school teachers. Working with educationists and high school teachers, professors in biological sciences, chemistry and physics, social sciences, English, Latin, and modern foreign languages prepared syllabi in their fields for secondary school courses. See "Project A. 1. a. Relation of Secondary Schools to Higher Institutions and to the College of Education," AR 4, Box 24.

34 See, for example, letters to William E. Drake, 6 October 1933, E. M. Highsmith, 30 March 1936, and Fred C. Smith to Sidney B. Hall, 30 April 1938 in AR 4, Box 24; Board of Trustee Minutes (31 July 1937).

35 See Jurgen Herbst, *And Sadly Teach: Teacher Education and Professionalization in American Culture* (Madison: The University of Wisconsin Press, 1989) and Robert A. Levin, *Educating Elementary School Teachers: The Struggle for Coherent Visions, 1909–1978* (Lanham, MD:

University Press of America, 1994). Such a division between training elementary and secondary teachers was common.

36   B. O. Duggan, "The Teacher-Training Situation in Tennessee, 1931–32," mimeographed, AR 4, Box 24.

37   Duggan to Thackston, 22 April 1929; Duggan, "The Inter-Dependence of Public Education on Its Various Levels," mimeographed, 1924, AR 5, Box 4; "Project II—Elementary Education," undated [1929], 3.

38   Duggan, "The Inter-Dependence."

39   Duggan, "The Inter-Dependence"; Duggan to Morgan, 22 January 1930.

40   "A Few Reasons Why Colleges Should Give Professional Training for Elementary School Teachers," undated [1922], AR 4, Box 38; Knoxville Sentinel, 22 March 1922.

41   Harcourt Morgan to Mr. H. North Callahan, 3 December 1932; "The Place of the University in the Training of Elementary Teachers," undated [1935], AR 5, Box 4.

42   Duggan, "The Inter-Dependence"; Morgan to Hoskins, 21 June 1928.

43   Paul J. Kruesi to Dr. Alexander Guerry, 13 December 1931.

44   "University of Tennessee: Information for Normal School Students," flyer, 28 May 1914. For correspondence on the transfer issue for normal school students, see Archives 4, Boxes 29 and 30; Sidney G. Gilbreath to Dean J. D. Hoskins, 18 November 1920; Harcourt A. Morgan to President Sidney G. Gilbreath, 21 December 1920; Gilbreath to Morgan, 21 December 1920. Even this limited credit was not allowed for all majors, premedicine was an example. See Harcourt A. Morgan to P. L. Harned, 4 January 1924.

45   Hubert F. Fisher to Morgan, 26 October 1923; Morgan to Fisher, 29 October 1923; Knoxville Journal, 1 March 1933. See also Hoskins to Paul J. Kruesi, 17 April 1934; Hoskins to Kruesi, 25 July 1934 ; Kruesi to Hoskins, 26 July 1934.

46   Kruesi to Hoskins, 26 July 1934; Hoskins to Kruesi 25 July 1934.

47   Kruesi to Hoskins, 26 July 1934; Kruesi to Hoskins, 1 August 1934; Minutes of Meeting, Committee on the Study of Curricula (11 June 1938).

48   Mabel W. Hardin, "Teacher-Training in High School," master's thesis, University of Tennessee, May 1923, 29; "Teacher Training in County High Schools," The Tennessee Educational Bulletin 1 (July 1922): 2. An irony is that the university's professor of secondary education, Harry Clark, had been a chief lobbyist for the development of teacher-training courses in high schools in 1916. He had lamented that Tennessee was "lagging badly behind our sister southern states" in such programs. "Plans of Harry Clark-Tennessee 1916," AR 4 Box 13.

49   *Biennial Report of the Superintendent of Public Instruction* (1919–1920): 249–252; Duggan to Thackston, 15 January 1931; Duggan to Hoskins, 21 March 1932; Hoskins to Claxton, 26 February 1935.

50   Hardin, 1, 65.

51   Montgomery, Folmsbee, and Greene, 181; *Knoxville Journal*, 7 September 1930; *Maryville Times*, 6 November 1930. In 1935, UT professors William E. Cole and Frank B. Ward published a study of the poorest families of Knox County, Tennessee: 39 percent owed money for food bought on credit, 49 percent were surviving by eating less, 56 percent had been forced from their homes, 68 percent had dropped insurance plans, and 15 percent were keeping their children out of school for financial reasons. Study quoted in *Knoxville Journal*, 18 August 1935.

52   UT press release, 27 November 1930; *Knoxville Journal,* 7 September 1930; *Orange and White*, 7 October 1932 and 14 October 1932.

53   David Tyack, Robert Lowe, and Elizabeth Hansot, *Public Schools in Hard Times* (Cambridge: Harvard University Press, 1984); *Knoxville Journal*, 3 February 1933, 3 March 1933, 8 March 1933, 21 April 1933; *Knoxville Sentinel*, 7 February 1933; *Orange and White*, 8 February 1935; "Report of Dean Jno. A. Thackston to President J. D. Hoskins," 25 October 1934.

54   *Orange and White*, 14 October 1932 and 17 January 1933; *Knoxville Journal*, 9 October 1932; I. E. Gillenwater to Officials of the University of Tennessee; Petition of Elementary Teachers Association Grainger County, 24 December 1932; Loudon County Superintendent to Officials of the University of Tennessee, 17 December 1932, AR 5, Box 4; Elementary Teachers Association, Grainger County, Tennessee, to Officials of the University of Tennessee, 24 December 1932, AR 4, Box 25.

55   *Knoxville Sentinel*, 21 October 1934; mimeographed proposal from College of Education, 27 January 1932; *Orange and White*, 4 October, 7 October 1933, and 6 October 1933; "Education College at U.T. Offers New Expanded Program," UT press release, 6 May 1938; "Activities of the College of Education Carried Out in 1938–39 and Proposed for 1939–40," July 13, 1939, AR 4 Box 27.

56   *Orange and White*, 12 October 1938.

57   Clinton B. Allison, "Early Professors of Education," in *The Professors of Teaching: An Inquiry*, eds Richard Wisniewski and Edward R. Ducharme (Albany: State University of New York Press, 1989), 44.

58   Tyack et al., 110; *Knoxville Sentinel*, 2 April 1931.

59   *Orange and White,* 16 April 1937.

60   *Orange and White*, 8 February 1935.

61 *Orange and White*, 5 May 1939. The Spring of 1939 was a particularly difficult time for the College of Education. Because of impoundment of funds by the state budget director, the Spring Term for teachers was eliminated; 400 teachers had been expected to enroll.

62 Hoskins to United States Bureau of Education, 15 June 1934; W. B. Overton to Hoskins, 25 June 1934; Ernestine L. Friedmann to Hoskins, 27 June 1934; *Knoxville Sentinel*, 12 August 1934; "Activities of the College of Education Carried Out in 1938–39 and Proposed for 1939–40."

63 In 1934, amidst rumors that the General Education Board was soon to liquidate its assets, the college looked again to their old benefactor. In September 1935, the college prepared an elaborate seventeen-page proposal for the GEB. It asked for the then huge sum of $500,000 to build a demonstration school and an annual grant of $40,000 to $50,000 for up to twenty years. Leo M. Favrot, General Field Agent of the GEB, warned Hoskins that he was unlikely to get the funds, that it was not board policy to support construction of that type, and that it was too much money. On November 22, the GEB made it official: "I regret to inform you that the Committee did not find it practicable to act favorably on your request." Morgan to Abraham Flexner, 17 March 1920; "Details and Description of Experimental-Demonstration Projects, University of Tennessee," September 1935; Hoskins to Leo M. Favrot, 7 October 1935; Favrot to Hoskins, 22 October 1935; W. W. Brierley to Hoskins, 22 November 1935.

64 Mimeographed proposal from College of Education, undated [1937], AR 4, Box 13; *Orange and White*, 30 October 1940.

65 Montgomery, Folmsbee, and Greene, 183; *Biennial Report of the College of Education for the years 1932–33 and 1933–34*; Thackston to Hoskins, 25 October 1934.

66 Thackston to Frank Smith, 19 March 1938.

67 Margaret Ragsdale, "Teacher's Ills Blamed on Bad Boys," Clipping, 39 October 1949, UT Scrapbook, AR 79; *Orange and White*, 26 October 1931; *Knoxville Journal*, 14 April 1936.

Chapter 6

1 *Knoxville Sentinel*, 12 October 1925; H. A. Morgan, "The State University in Its Public Relations," Commencement Statement, June 1930, AR 2, Box 3.

2 "Immediate Projects to be Undertaken by the College of Education," 13 November 1929, AR 4, Box 13.

3 *Orange and White*, 8 November 1932.

4   *Knoxville Journal and Tribune*, 6 March 1922; *Knoxville Sentinel*, 7 March 1922; *Orange and White*, 17 May 1922.

5   Thackston to Dean D. S. Burleson, 26 March 1930; *Knoxville Journal*, 30 October 1926; *Knoxville Sentinel*, 29 October 1927; *Orange and White*, 28 October 1926; *Knoxville Sentinel*, 30 October 1931. For a mean-spirited editorial on teachers' misbehavior at an ETEA meeting, see "Teachers Only Sub-Human; Not So Austere at ETEA," *Orange and White*, 1 November 1939.

6   *Orange and White*, 4 April 1929 and 18 April 1933; Morgan to Dean D. S. Burleson.

7   James Riley Montgomery, Stanley J. Folmsbee, and Lee Seifert Greene, *To Foster Knowledge: A History of The University of Tennessee, 1794–1970* (Knoxville: The University of Tennessee Press, 1984), 172.

8   Frank L. Teuton to Harcourt Morgan, 12 July 1920; E. A. Sutherland to Morgan, 16 September 1927; Morgan to Dwight Sanderson, 15 January 1924; Sanderson to Morgan, 8 January 1924; "Progress Report of the Committee on Rural Social Organizations and Agencies Essential to a Permanent and Efficient Agriculture," Chicago, 16 November 1923, AR 4, Box 46. For information on the country life movement see William L. Bowers, *The Country Life Movement in America, 1900–1920* (Port Washington, NY: Kennikat Press, 1974) ; James H. Madison, "John D. Rockefeller's General Education Board and the Rural School Problem in the Midwest, 1900–1930," *History of Education Quarterly* 24 (Summer, 1984).

9   Address of Morgan before the Southeastern Division, National Electric Light Association, Memphis, 14 April 1927, AR 4, Box 34.

10 Bowers, 82; Hugh MacRae to John McDowell, 10 April 1924; R. B. Pratt, Jr. to Morgan, 12 March 1926 and 5 August 1927; Morgan to J. D. Canaday, 11 July 1927; Canaday to Morgan, 9 July 1927; John W. Shackford to Morgan, 18 January 1927; unpublished paper by Shackford, AR 4, Box 33.

11 Morgan to Howard W. Odum, 8 March 1923.

12 Morgan to B. O. Duggan, 3 October 1921.

13 Morgan to P. P. Claxton, 4 February 1924.

14 N. E. Fitzgerald to Morgan, 2 January 1924; "The Need of a Special Course For the Training of Rural Teachers," memorandum, AR 4, Box 16; Duggan to Morgan, 22 October 1925; *Knoxville Sentinel*, 24 February 1926.

15 Duggan to Morgan, 21 November 1924; Morgan to W. J. Field, 6 April 1926; Morgan to F. L. Browning, 3 November 1924; Morgan to William McNeely, 5 March 1926.

16 Morgan to Miss Sue M. Powers, 13 November 1922; Morgan to Claxton, 4 February 1924; McNeely to Morgan, 3 March 1926. The university had been

willed $50,000 to be used as a loan fund for agricultural students. Morgan decided that rural education students also qualified. Morgan to State Superintendent Harned, 3 January 1924.

17 UT *Registers* (1921–22), (1926–27), and (1928–29); Duggan, memorandum, MS 330, BI-D; Duggan to Thackston, 11 February 1929; Duggan to Thackston, 14 February 1929.

18 "Education and Economic Survey of Union County," September and December 1922; Duggan, unpublished report, 16 May 1933, AR 4, Box 14.

19 "Rural Education Project," AR 4, Box 47.

20 Duggan, "Educational and Economic Survey of Union County."

21 Duggan, "Educational and Economic Survey of Union County; Duggan to Morgan, 23 October 1922. In addition to questionnaires and interviews, Duggan and his students documented conditions by "making pictures freely" of schools, houses, barns, water-mills, and even livestock. County surveys in the form of master's theses were profusely illustrated with photographs.

22 Duggan, "Educational and Economic Survey of Union County"; *Knoxville Sentinel*, 26 August 1930; H. L. Callahan to Morgan, 11 February 1925; R. Beecher Witt to Morgan, 11 February 1925; J. D. Johnson to Morgan, 7 January 1927; Morgan to Johnson, 10 January 1927.

23 Hixson to Duggan, 22 May 1926; Duggan to Hixson, 26 May 1926.

24 "Rural Education Project," mimeographed questionnaire, AR 4, Box 24.

25 Ibid.

26 Duggan, "Educational and Economic Survey of Union County."

27 Thackston to Morgan, 7 December 1923.

28 Duggan to Morgan, 26 March 1926.

29 *Knoxville News-Sentinel*, 26 August 1930.

30 Everett M. Smith to Morgan, 21 December 1928; J. D. McFarlin to Morgan, 8 December 1928; Chas. S. Kitts to Morgan, 17 December 1928. These and other testimonials may be found in AR 4, Box 47.

31 Rhey Boyd Parsons to Thackston, 21 May 1928; "Sub-Project Statement— C," Department of Rural Education, 1932–33, AR 4, Box 24.

32 Duggan, memorandum, 16 May 1933, AR 4, Box 10.

33 Duggan to W. W. Carpenter, 24 July 1931; Bowers, 4–15.

34 Bowers, 43–44.

35 "The Development of a Science Program for Elementary Schools," Project Statement, 1931, AR 4, Box 10; F. C. Lowery to Howard, undated; Morgan

to Powers, 2 February 1931; "Curriculum Guide," Rural Education Project, AR 4, Box 16. Duggan was particularly pleased with a 1931 revised edition of the guide. Enlarged, printed (rather than mimeographed), and then called a manual, it included information from the sciences "to the race" and then to the farm and the home and to life itself. He wanted the state superintendent to understand how well it correlated with nearly all of the other subjects in the elementary school: it "vitalized these subjects in a most pleasing way." Duggan to P. M. Harned, 18 June 1931; Duggan to Thackston, 23 January 1931.

36 Duggan to Harned, 18 June 1931; *Orange and White*, 26 October 1931; Duggan to Thackston, 23 January 1931; "Sub-Project Statement—B," Department of Rural Education, 1932–33, AR 4, Box 24; "The Development of a Science Program for Elementary Schools," Project Statement, 29 September 1932, AR 4, Box 24; UT press release, 12 November 1937.

37 Duggan to Powers, 15 October 1931.

38 Duggan, "Report of the Rural Education Department," 16 May 1933, AR 4, Box 10; A. W. Hobt, "Socialization of Rural Communities," memorandum, 13 November 1930, AR 4, Box 33; Duggan to Mrs. Hugh Bryan, 20 March 1930.

39 Bryan to Duggan, 3 March 1930; Duggan to Bryan, 20 March 1930; *Knoxville Journal*, 16 June 1931; *Knoxville Sentinel*, 15 June 1932.

40 Duggan to Bryan, 20 March 1930; Hines to Duggan, 19 April 1932.

41 Hines to Duggan, 19 April 1932; *Orange and White,* 29 November 1932.

42 "Department of Rural Education—1932–1933, Sub-Project Statement—BS," MS 330, Box 1-A; Lecture Report, AR 4, Box 24.

43 Mary S. Hoffschwelle, "Organizing Rural Communities for Change: The Commonwealth Fund Child Health Demonstration in Rutherford County, 1923–1927," *Tennessee Historical Quarterly* 53 (Fall 1994): 157–162.

44 William J. French to Morgan, 6 February 1930; Morgan to French, 8 February 1930; E. L. Bishop to Morgan, 4 March 1930; Morgan to French, 15 May 1930; Morgan to French, 31 May 1930.

45 *Knoxville Sentinel*, 21 October 1934.

46 E. L. Bishop to Morgan, 2 July 1930; Board of Trustee Executive Committee Minutes, 28 August 1930; W. F. Walker to Morgan, 10 June 1930; Scamman to Morgan, 13 September 1932; "Health Education Project, The University of Tennessee," undated [1933], AR 4, Box 11.

47 Paul W. Allen, "General Statement Concerning Health Education Project," 15 April 1934, AR 4, Box 11; Cara L. Harris, "Tentative Outline for Health Education Courses and School Health Project," 17 June 1931, AR 4, Box 11; Cole to Allen, 15 October 1934; "New Course in Public Health at the University of Tennessee," UT press release, 13 October 1935; "Health Edu-

cation—A New Program," *Health Briefs* (Tennessee Department of Public Health), 15 December 1935, AR 4, Box 11.

48 Robert H. White to Hoskins, 16 February 1941.

49 William L. Bowers, *The Country Life Movement in America, 1900–1920.*

50 E. H. Edwards to Morgan, 7 December 1926.

Chapter 7

1 *Orange and White*, 11 October 1940 and 18 October 1940.

2 *Orange and White*, 16 October 1940 and 24 September 1940; *Knoxville Sentinel*, 11 August 1942.

3 UT press release, 23 January 1942; "Historical Vignette," *Context* (29 November 1990).

4 *Knoxville Journal*, 29 May 1942

5 *Knoxville Journal*, 4 September 1942.

6 *Knoxville Sentinel*, 21 July 1942

7 A. W. Hobt to Dean F. C. Smith, 29 January 1943; Hobt to President J. D. Hoskins, 6 May 1943; "Notice to Staff, Army Air Corps P. T. Program," 5 May 1943.

8 Robert Lindsay Mason to Hoskins, 10 June 1940; Hoskins to Mason, 19 June 1940.

9 *Orange and White*, 2 October 1942, 14 February 1947, and 29 March 1946.

10 *Knoxville Sentinel*, 2 November 1940; UT press releases, 6 June 1941 and 10 April 1942.

11 UT press releases, 10 April 1942 and 10 January 1942; *Orange and White*, 22 May 1942; *Knoxville Journal*, 26 March 1944.

12 N. E. Fitzgerald to Lt. Henry Gibson; UT press release, 25 June 1943. Fitzgerald corresponded regularly with former students of the college who were serving in the armed forces. Copies of his letters may be found in his papers, MS 302, Special Collections, Hoskins Library.

13 "The Function of College of Education—Point of View," mimeographed, undated [1941].

14 Ibid.

15 Ibid.

16 Ibid.

17   Flyer, "Wartime Courses for Teachers!" University of Tennessee, AR 5, Box 12; Thackston to Duggan, 3 June 1942; UT press release, 26 June 1942.

18   *Knoxville Journal and Tribune*, 1 November 1917 and 24 April 1920; "Activities in Teacher Education now Being Carried on at the University of Tennessee," typed report, undated [1939], AR 5, Box 11. Physical Education Professor John Bender's 1922 *The Progressive Teacher* article, "Play in Education," was typical progressive fare. *Knoxville Sentinel*, 7 May 1922.

19   *Knoxville Sentinel*, 14 February 1938 and 25 June 1943; *Orange and White*, 10 December 1941; UT press release, 24 May 1940.

20   *Knoxville Sentinel*, 24 April 1940; UT press release, 3 May 1940.

21   UT press release, 2 July 1943.

22   *Knoxville Sentinel*, 10 November 1946; *Orange and White*, 22 October 1948.

23   Sue Downs, "The Case of Progressive Education Versus Twelve Student Teachers," *Tennessee Alumnus* 29 (Spring 1949).

24   Ibid.

25   Ibid.

26   Commencement Address, "Education for Democracy," 1942, AR 5, Box 34. Hoskins appreciated the antiprogressive stance of *School and Society*. In 1947, he sent a copy to university trustee Paul Kruesi, commenting that it was "an excellent publication which I have been taking for some time." Hoskins to Paul J. Kruesi, 10 July 1947.

27   Commencement Address at East Tennessee State College, 1943; *Knoxville Journal*, 22 April 1944; UT press release, 28 May 1943; *Orange and White*, 14 May 1943.

28   Commencement Address, East Tennessee State College.

29   Bob Jones to President James D. Hoskins, 26 August 1943; Hoskins to A. D. Holt, 1 August 1942.

30   Mrs. James Clark to Hon. D. M. [sic] Hoskins, 16 January 1943 [sic, 1944]; Hoskins to Mrs. James Clark, 18 January 1944.

31   Florence V. Essery to Hoskins, 1 March 1944; Hoskins to Essery, 9 March 1944.

32   Hoskins to Clark, 3 September 1941.

33   Thackston to Hoskins, 20 April 1943.

34   Board of Trustees Minutes (29 April 1943): 12–13; Hoskins to Charles William Dabney, 21 May 1943. The university press release following the meeting emphasized that the College of Education would have greater control over teacher education. UT press release, 30 April 1943.

35 Hoskins to Thackston, 11 May 1943; Thackston to Hoskins, 9 July 1943; Hoskins to Thackston, 10 July 1943.

36 *Knoxville Sentinel*, 19 September 1943.

37 *Orange and White*, 19 May 1944.

38 *Knoxville Journal*, 24 February 1945.

39 James Riley Montgomery, Stanley J. Folmsbee, and Lee Seifert Greene, *To Foster Knowledge: A History of The University of Tennessee, 1794–1970* (Knoxville: The University of Tennessee Press, 1984), 204–217.

40 H. Vandiver to Brehm, 18 December 1946; Brehm to Vandiver, 26 December 1946; Montgomery, Folmsbee, and Greene, 216.

41 *Orange and White*, 16 October 1946; UT press release, 11 February 1947; *Knoxville Journal*, 3 June 1946. I taught a class in one of these "temporary" buildings in the early 1970s.

42 Ralph E. Dunford to Chancellor Clark Kerr, 30 June 1956; Ralph W. Frost to Brehm, 31 July 1952; "Police Fire to Halt Trophy Raid," London *New Chronicle*, 20 May 1952, typed transcript, AR 6 Box 16; John B. Elliott to Brehm, 20 May 1952; Brehm to Elliott, 27 May 1952; "Reader Knocks Panty Raids; Calls them 'Symbolic Rape,'" *Orange and White*, 12 May 1955.

43 Williams to Hoskins, 31 January 1936; H. C. Byrd to Hoskins, 4 February 1936; Byrd to Hoskins, February 1939. In *Missouri* ex rel. *Gaines v. Canada, Registrar of the University, et al.*, the United States Supreme Court found that the state must provide education for all of its citizens within the state. Tennessee passed legislation in 1937 providing out-of-state grants for graduate and professional training after William B. Redmond filed suit to be admitted to the School of Pharmacy.

44 *Knoxville Sentinel*, 27 September 1939 and 28 November 1939.

45 Hoskins to Congressman George H. Bender, 3 February 1948; Hoskins to Duggan, 23 July 1941.

46 Vic to My dear Friend, undated, AR 5, Box 9.

47 Duggan to Hoskins, 13 February 1941; Hoskins to Duggan, 15 February 1941; Duggan to President W. J. Hale, 12 December 1942; Holt to Brehm, 13 October 1950.

48 *Orange and White*, 29 September 1950; *Knoxville News-Sentinel*, 4 December 1950; *Knoxville Journal*, 10 January 1952; Board of Trustee Minutes (April 9, 1952): 274.

49 *Orange and White*, 29 September 1950 and 27 May 1954; see columns for 22 October 1947 and 5 March 1948.

50 *Knoxville News-Sentinel*, 18 March 1948; *Orange and White*, 29 March 1956.

51 UT press release, 15 June 1953.

52 *Orange and White*, 6 January 1955; "Desegregation at UT: The Undergraduate Experience," *Volunteer Moments, 1794–1994*, University Historian's Office, 1994.

53 Burgin Dossett to Brehm, 10 December 1946; UT press release, 8 October 1948.

54 UT press release, 9 December 1946.

55 UT press release, 11 March 1947.

56 "College of Education Enrollments, 1936–1948," typed report, AR 6, Box 26; *Orange and White*, 1 October 1947. In 1953, Governor-Elect Frank Clement selected Quill E. Cope, professor of Administration and Supervision, as Tennessee Commissioner of Education.

57 *Orange and White*, 5 December 1951; Montgomery Johnston, "Dr. Edward S. Christenbury (1902–1984): A Tribute, " *The Claxton Educator* 2 (Spring 1985); *Tennessee Alumnus* 33 (Winter 1953): 12, 21; *Tennessee Alumnus* 32 (Spring 1952): 14; *Tennessee Alumnus* 35 (Fall 1955): 12. By the early 1950s, an integral part of the student teaching experience was "action research," with the ambitious aim of having student teachers learn the "techniques of on-the-spot" research to solve local problems immediately. UT press release, 25 October 1954.

58 *Orange and White*, 29 October 1947; Florence V. Essery, "Our Exceptional Life Together," mimeographed, 1965.

59 *Orange and White*, April 16, 1948; Essery, 28, 49, 54–55; *Knoxville Journal*, May 10, 1945.

60 *Orange and White*, 29 October 1947 and 14 January 1948; *Knoxville News-Sentinel*, 14 November 1946; *Knoxville Sentinel*, 8 October 1947; Essery, 31; telephone interview with Lawrence Haaby, 29 February 1988.

61 *Knoxville News-Sentinel*, 11 November 1915; Essery, 72–73.

62 Essery, 60, 69; *Knoxville Sentinel*, 5 July 1950; L. G. Dethick to N. E. Fitzgerald, 27 June 1947.

63 Brehm to Burgin Dossett, 19 September 1947; Fitzgerald to Brehm, 12 January 1953.

64 Essery, 88; Eugene E. Doll, "In Memoriam: L. X. Magnifico," mimeographed, undated.

65 *Knoxville Journal*, 24 June 1957.

66 UT press release, 1 December 1951; *Tennessee Alumnus* 36 (Summer 1956): 10; Board of Trustees Minutes (30 March 1946): 152; Thackston to Hoskins, 11 December 1945.

67 Board of Trustees Minutes (15 February 1940): 120; *Knoxville Journal*, 20 July 1949 and 24 August 1951; *Knoxville News-Sentinel*, 4 July 1952.

68 Fitzgerald to Brehm, 18 November 1947.

69 Fitzgerald to Fred C. Smith, 26 February 1951.

70 "Program of Teacher Education in the University of Tennessee," 1955–1956, mimeographed.

71 "Smith Urges Fundamentals in Education," *Knoxville Journal*, 21 July 1950.

72 Notes made by Brehm, 22 April 1952, typescript, AR 6, Box 26.

73 Ibid.

74 Ibid.

75 Ibid.

76 "Progress Report of Teacher Education Curriculum Development at The University of Tennessee," mimeographed [sent to Brehm, 26 August 1953].

77 Ibid.

78 "Program of Teacher Education at the University of Tennessee," 1955–1956, General Education, I-54, I-55.

79 UT Catalogs, 1952 and 1962; telephone interviews with Montgomery Johnston and Lawrence Haaby, 29 February 1988.

80 Fitzgerald to Brehm, 5 May 1949.

81 "Minutes of Staff Meeting," May 6, 1952; See also Reports of Sub-committees on Reorganization, December 1951, AR 6, Box 26; Fred Smith to Brehm, undated memorandum [1953], AR 6, Box 26.

82 Haaby telephone interview; undated memorandum [1952], AR 6, Box 26; Brehm to Vice President E. A. Waters, 13 January 1954.

83 Fitzgerald, "Reorganization of C & I Department," 18 May 1954, AR 6, Box 26.

84 I. L. Kandel, "Teacher Preparation and the State of Education." *School and Society* 74 (6 October 1951): 219; Lester M. Emans, "Where Are We Going in Teacher Education?" *The Journal of Teacher Education* 3 (September 1952): 163–165; Mother Elizabeth Boyter, "A Study of Five-Year Programs," *The Journal of Teacher Education* 5 (September 1954): 194; P. W. Hutson, "A Proposed Program for the Fifth Year Plan Teacher Education," *School and Society* 82 (7 August 1954); Harold Rugg, "The Teacher of Teachers: A Preface to Appraisal," *The Journal of Teacher Education* 2 (March 1951): 4; Theodore C. Blegen, "Toward A Common Front," *School and Society* 76 (13 September 1952): 163. Both *School and Society* and *The Journal of Teacher Education* devoted considerable space to discussions of five-year

plans. Readers were assured that a "five-year requirement will become standard practice throughout the United States." The University of Tennessee began a five-year program in 1988.

85 See, for example, Raymond S. Moore, "The Distinctive Opportunity of the Small Liberal-Arts College in Teacher Education—A Challenge," *The Journal of Teacher Education* 1 (September 1950); Jack Allen, "Toward A Synthesis of the Academic and Professional in Teacher Education," *The Journal of Teacher Education* 2 (September 1951); "Principles Underlying an Effective Program of Teacher Education," *The Journal of Teacher Education* 4 (September 1953); Burton W. Jones, "Closing the Gap," *The Journal of Teacher Education* 4 (September 1953): 206; Brehm notes; Quill E. Cope to Brehm, 12 November 1953.

86 Fitzgerald to Vice President E. A. Waters, 27 September 1956; Fitzgerald to Brehm, 30 May 1957; "Dean N. E. Fitzgerald's Personal Comments Contributing to the Development of a History of the U. T. College of Education," undated [1972].

87 "Revised Suggestions on Organizational Procedures For the Selection and Certification for Teaching," mimeographed, 2 February 1957, AR 6, Box 24; Fitzgerald to Brehm, 9 February 1957; Brehm to Cope, 16 February 1957; "Conference About the State Testing Service in The University of Tennessee," mimeographed, 9 March 1957.

88 *Teacher Education at the University of Tennessee: A Report to the National Council for Accreditation of Teacher Education* (April 1962): 11, 15; Johnston and Haaby telephone interviews; telephone interview with Bain Stewart, 9 March 1988; conversation with William Coffield, 1 March 1988; James D. Koerner, *The Miseducation of American Teachers* (Boston: Houghton Mifflin Company, 1963), 268.

89 Board of Trustees Minutes, 20 July 1920; *Orange and White*, 24 January 1947; *Knoxville News-Sentinel*, 5 September 1935; Thackston to Hoskins, 19 April 1939; *Orange and White*, 30 April 1947; *Knoxville News-Sentinel*, 18 March 1957.

90 "Editorial" and Dave Walker, "Education Building Completed; Called 'Milestone' By Dean," *Orange and White*, 22 March 1956 and 29 October 1953.

91 Mrs. Claxton's correspondence is in MS 310, Box 17; Hoskins to Mrs. P. P. Claxton, 7 September 1949 and 19 December 1949; see, for example, the *Knoxville Journal*, 17 May 1954 and the *Maryville Times*, 13 March 1955.

92 *Knoxville News-Sentinel*, 18 March 1957; N. E. Fitzgerald, "P. P. Claxton Education Building, " *The University of Tennessee News Letter* (August 1957); "Dedication, Philander P. Claxton Education Building," 15 November 1957; *Orange and White*, 22 March 1957.

Chapter 8

1 "Obituary," Dr. Edward C. Merrill, Jr., Gallaudet College, January 1995; Howard F. Aldmon and E. C. Merrill, "Open Letter to the Faculty," 14 September 1963.

2 Office of the University Historian, "Historical Vignette: Andrew D. Holt, UT's Sixteenth President (1959–1970)," *Context* 14 (October 1966): 4–5. For a biography of Holt, see Susan H. McCue, "Life History of Andrew David Holt," (Ph.D. dissertation, University of Tennessee, Knoxville, 1995).

3 Holt to Merrill, 12 December 1968; Holt to Merrill, 25 October 1966; See letters of 4 November 1969, 30 January 1970, 2 May 1970, and 23 June 1970 as examples, AR 7, Box 17.

4 James Riley Montgomery, Stanley J. Folmsbee, and Lee Seifert Green, *To Foster Knowledge: A History of The University of Tennessee, 1794–1970* (Knoxville: The University of Tennessee Press, 1984), 203–04, 318; *Teacher Education at the University of Tennessee: A Report to the National Council for Accreditation of Teacher Education* (April 1962): 21; *intercom* (13 August 1971; UT *Record* (1981–1982): 249; "Clayton Arnold, Education Benefactor Dies," *The Claxton Educator* 4 (Fall 1987): 1–2. A story about Arnold's gift appeared in the 13 June 1971, *National Inquirer*.

5 *Southern Association Report, College of Education, The University of Tennessee* (June 1970): 48, 51; *Teacher Education at the University of Tennessee*, 62; *Southern Education Report*, 48; *intercom* (4 June 1971) and (April 1977). The June 1970 *Southern Education Report* included enrollments in various certification programs: 1,090 in elementary education, 306 in special education, 504 in social studies, but only 28 in foreign language teacher preparation.

6 *Southern Association Report*, 199; *intercom* (7 July 10 1970) and (26 May 1972); *Accreditation Report for the National Council for the Accreditation of Teacher Education, College of Education, The University of Tennessee* (Winter 1981): 149–152; *intercom* (19 November 1973); Cyrus Mayshark, "A Survey of Selected University of Tennessee, Knoxville College of Education Graduate Degree Recipients," Publication No. 4, Bureau of Educational Research and Service (February 1971): 6. Ninety-seven of the Ed.Ds were in Curriculum and Instruction, 89 in Educational Administration and Supervision, and 71 in Educational Psychology and Guidance. The college offered 427 courses in 1970, and the Claxton Education Building was bursting at its seams. In 1968 the college began planning a major addition to Claxton that didn't open until 1984. In 1970, the 175,000 square-foot Health, Physical Education, and Recreation Building was occupied. *Southern Association Report*, 43, 109, 105.

7   *Accreditation Report to the National Council for Accreditation of Teacher Education* (Spring 1971): ii; *intercom* (10 September 1971): 2; "A Statement of the Mission for the 1970's of the College of Education, U.T., Knoxville," 3; *intercom* (10 November 1972) and (14 October 1974).

8   UT Record 52 (May 1949): 232; *Southern Association Report* (June 1970): 79, 88.

9   *intercom* (18 September 1974) and (September 1975); *Accreditation Report for the National Council for the Accreditation of Teacher Education* (Winter 1981): 61–67, 177; *Southern Association Report* (June 1970): 65. According to accreditation reports for 1971 and 1981, about 74 percent of tenure-track faculty held a doctorate in 1970 and 83 percent in 1980.

10 "A Statement of the Mission for the 1970's of the College of Education, U.T., Knoxville," 2; *Southern Association Report* (June 1970): 64; "Questionnaire on Goals Relative to Program, Students, and Faculty," *A Self Study Conducted by the College of Education, The University of Tennessee, Knoxville, Tennessee* (1969–1970); *Accreditation Report for the National Council for the Accreditation of Teacher Education* (Winter 1981): 61–67; *General Catalog* (1979–1980): 113.

11 The October 28, 1969 address was reprinted in *A Self Study Conducted by the College of Education* (1969–1970); "The Program Mission of the College of Education For the Decade Ahead," *A Self Study Conducted by the College of Education* (1969–1970): 136, 139.

12 Aaron Montgomery Johnston, "Aptitude, Achievement and Other Characteristics of University of Tennessee Education Seniors," *A Research Project Sponsored by The University of Tennessee* (February 1962): 14–17; vocational education student teachers were not included in the study.

13 Ibid., 42–44.

14 Ibid., 61–66.

15 *Teacher Education at the University of Tennessee. A Report to the National Council for Accreditation of Teacher Education* (April 1962): 24–27. A considerable amount of grade inflation has taken place. In Fall quarter 1960, the university grade point average for undergraduates was 2.13.

16 The visiting committee was particularly concerned with limited requirements for general education in vocational fields and music education. W. Earl Armstrong to President A. D. Holt, 7 September 1962; E. C. Merrill to Dr. W. Earl Armstrong, 20 September 1962.

17 *Teacher Education at The University of Tennessee, A Supplementary Report to The National Council for Accreditation of Teacher Education* (January 1963): 1–2; A. D. Holt to Dean E. C. Merrill, 3 March 1964.

18   *A Supplementary Report to The National Council for Accreditation of Teacher Education* (January 1963): 11–13; W, Earl Armstrong to President A. D. Holt, 27 May 1963; Holt to Merrill, 31 May 1963.

19   *Southern Association Report* (June 1970): 93–94; A. Montgomery Johnston, "Education Faculty as Critic, Truth-Seeker, and Model, " *A Self Study Conducted by the College of Education* (1969–1970): 23; *Accreditation Report to the National Council for Accreditation of Teacher Education, College of Education, The University of Tennessee* (Spring 1971): 75; "Questionnaire on Goals Relative to Program, Students, and Faculty."

20   *intercom* (7 May 1971); *Southern Association Report* (June 1970): 188.

21   *intercom* (12 March 1971) and (24 September 1973).

22   *Accreditation Report for the National Council for the Accreditation of Teacher Education, College of Education, The University of Tennessee* (Winter 1981): 87–88, 97–100. The state also required education students to take the National Teachers Examination for certification.

23   *Southern Association Report* (June 1970): 70; *Accreditation Report to the National Council for Accreditation of Teacher Education* (Spring 1971): 6, 69; "Questionnaire on Goals Relative to Program, Students, and Faculty."

24   *A Report to the National Council for Accreditation of Teacher Education* (April 1962): 38.

25   Howard F. Aldmon and E. C. Merrill, "Open Letter to the Faculty," 14 September 1963; James D. McComas, "The UT College of Education—An Immovable Object or An Irresistible Force?" in *A Self Study Conducted by the College of Education* (1969–1970): 14–15; "A Statement of the Mission for the 1970's of the College of Education, U.T., Knoxville," 2; "Questionnaire on Goals Relative to Program, Students, and Faculty."

26   *Southern Association Report* (June 1970): 113–116.

27   *Southern Association Report* (June 1970): 116–117; *intercom* (14 October 1974); Frances Fowler and Fred Venditti, "A History of the Department of Educational Leadership, undated; *Knoxville Journal*, 1 April 1978; *UT Daily Beacon*, 3 April 1978.

28   *Southern Association Report* (June 1970): 125; Joe Johnson to Holt, 9 August 1965; Frank G. Clement to Holt, 2 September 1965.

29   *Southern Association Report* (June 1970): 127; *intercom* (December 1982); for other MAARDAC accounts in *intercom*, see issues for October 1975, February 1980, July 1981, January 1983.

30   *intercom* (15 December 1970) and (19 November 1973).

31   *intercom* (May 1970) and (June 1970); "Questionnaire on Goals Relative to Program, Students, and Faculty." The 1970 *Southern Association Report* reported 36 funded projects in the college but concluded that only a few could be "classified as research," 166. The debate about the place of research in the college was serious and sometimes bitter, but there was also humor. The lead story in the February 12, 1971, *intercom* was that three educational psychology professors had started *Decline*, a non-journal: "It will invite and accept but not publish the works of both renowned and new, unknown authors, thus giving ambitious young professors on their way up as well as established persons in their respective fields a chance not to be published. . . . Articles are accepted and not published for subscribers only!"

32   *Southern Association Report* (June 1970): 156–160. The college complained that even though it produced more than 20 percent of the doctoral degrees in the university, it received only 3.2 percent of university research funds, a much smaller percentage than the colleges of liberal arts and engineering; "Report of the Committee on Research in the College of Education," *A Self Study Conducted by the College of Education* (1969–1970): 50; *intercom* (12 April 1971). The M.S. was authorized in 1938, the Ed.D. in 1950, and the Ph.D. in 1980.

33   "Which Direction Graduate Education?" *Proceedings, Conference on Graduate Studies in Education* (April 30– May 1, 1971): 21–25.

34   Protest Newsletters, undated, mimeographed; Faculty Statement of June 3, 1970, dittoed; *UT Daily Beacon*, 14 August 1970.

35   *UT Daily Beacon*, 19 June 1970 and 18 August 1970; "From the President's Office, Intercampus Newsletter," The University of Tennessee, 1 (June 26, 1970); Arthur Jones to Members of the "Committee on procedural guideline for Safety and Security," 23 May 1975.

36   "A Statement of the Mission for the 1970's of the College of Education, U.T., Knoxville," 1–4.

37   *A Self Study Conducted by the College of Education* (1969–1970): 16; *Southern Association Report* (June 1970): 173; *Accreditation Report to the National Council for Accreditation of Teacher Education* (Spring 1971): 3.

38   *intercom* (29 April 1974) and (December 1979); *Southern Association Report*, 123; Information supplied by Bill Woodrick, 18 March 1997. Special education professors were particularly adept at securing federal grant funds.

39   Karl J. Jost, "The Morgan County Project," undated. The university paid for the transportation of student teachers to schools at the beginning of the term and back to Knoxville at the end. *Teacher Education at the University of Tennessee* (April 1962): 89–90; *Southern Association Report* (June 1970): 37–41; "A Statement of the Mission for the 1970's of the College of Education, 4; *A Self Study Conducted by the College of Education* (1969–1970); *intercom* (10 September 1971).

40   Cyrus Mayshark, "A Survey of Selected University of Tennessee, Knoxville
     College of Education Graduate Degree Recipients," 23; *Teacher Education
     at the University of Tennessee* (April 1962): 89; *Accreditation Report to
     the National Council for Accreditation of Teacher Education* (Spring 1971):
     42–44; interview with William L. Butefish, 12 November 1995. Butefish gave
     credit to Professor Everett Myer, who then worked in the Mid-Atlantic/Appa-
     lachian Race Desegregated Assistance Center, for making the case to place
     student teachers in predominantly black schools.

41   *Accreditation Report for the National Council for the Accreditation of
     Teacher Education, College of Education, The University of Tennessee*
     (Winter 1981): 29, 94.

42   Cyrus Mayshark, "A Survey of Selected University of Tennessee, Knoxville
     College of Education Graduate Degree Recipients," 14–15, 20; "The Pro-
     gram Mission of the College of Education For the Decade Ahead," *A Self
     Study Conducted by the College of Education* (1969–70): 144; *intercom* (5
     November); "A Proposal for a Pilot Program in Teacher Education, University
     of Tennessee," undated, dittoed; "UT's Pilot Teacher Education Program, A
     Self Study (1969–1970): 43; E. C. Merrill, "Experimental Program in Teacher
     Education, Assumptions," 30 January 1967.

43   "A Proposal for a Pilot Program in Teacher Education"; "A Progress Report of
     the Pilot Program in Teacher Education at The University of Tennessee, Pre-
     sented to the Faculty of The College of Education," 13 October 1970; Com-
     mittee on Experimentation and Innovation, "A Model for the Preservice Prepa-
     ration of Teachers," 8 August 1967. The Committee on Experimentation
     discussed three major components: micro teaching, simulation, and analysis
     of teaching. Micro teaching consisted of videotaped "abbreviated lessons" to
     three to five students. Simulation—"alternative solutions to critical teaching
     problems presented in a simulated school environment. The first simulation
     component recreated the "classroom of Pat Taylor, a new fifth-grade teacher."
     Each education student assumed the role Taylor. Analysis of teaching focused
     on "the effects of verbal and nonverbal influence" on students, using the
     Flanders' System of Interaction Analysis. The designers of the program said
     that the program was based "heavily" on the educational research of the pe-
     riod, including the hierarchical learning model in Robert M. Gagne's *The
     Conditions of Learning*.

44   Holt to Merrill, 25 November 1968; "U-T's Pilot Program in Teacher Educa-
     tion: A Rationale."

45   "A Progress Report of the Pilot Program," 13 October 1970; Butefish inter-
     view; Russell L. French, former director of the pilot program, telephone con-
     versation, 13 February 1997.

46   *intercom* (May 1975) and (June 1977); *Accreditation Report for the Na-
     tional Council for the Accreditation of Teacher Education* (Winter 1981):
     35. The college's computer experience paralleled national technological ad-
     vancements and trends. In 1962, data processing machines and a computer
     were available in the College of Business Administration building for educa-

tion faculty and graduate student use. A new era began in 1981 when five terminals (3 Digital VT100's and 2 DECriter IV's) were installed in the college's Media Center. In 1987, BERS announced that it had a LaserWriter printer and a Macintosh work station: "We are still learning, but we'll try to offer you some service in this area." By 1996, all faculty (except the few who refused them) had a computer in their office and were on e-mail. And the students had a "state-of-the-art" College Computing Instructional Laboratory. *Teacher Education at the University of Tennessee* (April 1962): 105; *intercom* (November 1981) and (October 1987).

47 John Pitman, "Competency-Based Certification: What Are the Key Issues," New England Program in Teacher Education, Working Paper #6 (June 1973); Robert W. Houston and Robert B. Howsam, eds., *Competency-Based Teacher Education: Progress, Problems, and Prospects* (Palo Alto, CA.: Science Research Associates, 1972). For some of the contemporary literature on CBTE, see American Association of Colleges of Teacher Education and ERIC Clearing House on Teacher Education, *Performance-Based Teacher Education: An Annotated Bibliography* (Washington D.C.: American Association of Colleges of Teacher Education, August, 1972, No. 7); Stanley Elam, "Performance-Based Teacher Education: What Is the State of the Art? (Washington, D.C.: American Association of Colleges of Teacher Education December, 1971); Harry S. Broudy, "A Critique of PBTE" (Washington, D.C.: American Association of Colleges of Teacher Education, May 1972); James W. Popham, "Teaching Skill Under Scrutiny," *Phi Delta Kappan* 52 (June 1971); Ward Sybouts, "Performance-Based Teacher Education: Does It Make a Difference?" *Phi Delta Kappan* 54 (January 1973).

48 "Questionnaire on Goals Relative to Program, Students, and Faculty"; Clinton B. Allison, "Why I Am Against CBTE," in *Competency-Based Teacher Education: For and Against*, College of Education Monograph Series, No. 7, eds. Donald J. Dickinson and Clinton B. Allison, Bureau of Educational Research and Service, College of Education, The University of Tennessee (1975): 5–7; Lewis Hodge, ed., "CBTE at The University of Georgia and Florida State University—An Interview with the UT Visiting Team," in Dickinson and Allison.

49 James D. McComas, "Preface," Dickinson and Allison, v.

50 *intercom* (12 May 1975).

51 McComas later served as president of the University of Toledo and Virginia Tech University; interview with Ralph Norman, 11 December 1996; *The Claxton Educator* 10 (Fall 1993): 3.

52 *intercom* (22 May 1973), (September 1977), (September 1978), and (September 1979).

53 National Commission on Excellence in Education, *A Nation at Risk* (Washington, D.C.: U.S. Government Printing Office, 1983); interviews with Norman, William L. Butefish, 12 November 1995, and Jack Reese, 2 December 1996. For an interpretation of the conservative attack on public education, see Ira

Shor, *Culture Wars: School and Society in the Conservative Restoration, 1969–1984* (New York, Rouledge & Kegan Paul, 1986). *Tennessee Education*, a publication of the College of Education, published "Five Deep Ruts," Alexander's article that was critical of colleges of education, 15 (Fall 1985): 5–10.

54   Butefish interview; Norman interview.

55   "College of Education Goals Study, Primary Report," The University of Tennessee (April 1979): 15.

56   "Goals of the College of Education, The University of Tennessee, Knoxville," adopted by the faculty, December 1982. A continuing issue was the place of non-teacher education programs such a counseling psychology, exercise science, or recreation in a comprehensive college of education. The chair borrowed the language of cultural revisionist educational historian Lawrence Cremin to defend a place for these programs in a broad conception of education as systematic and sustained efforts "to transmit or evoke knowledge, attitudes, values, skills, and sensibilities."

57   "Academic Affairs Comments on the December 1982 Statement of Goals for the College of Education, UTK," January 1983.

58   "Academic Affairs Comments on the December 1982 Statement of Goals for the College of Education, UTK," January 1983; Harry Judge, *American Graduate Schools of Education: A View from Abroad* (New York: Ford Foundation, 1982).

59   Memorandum: "Addenda to the College Goals Statement," College of Education Goals Committee to College of Education Faculty and Office of Academic Affairs, 2 June 1983.

60   Norman interview; Reese interview; "Faculty Meeting Considers Proposed Changes in Education," *intercom* (September 1983); Linda W. Ginn, "Crossing Boundaries, Creating Community, Reorganizing a College of Education," Paper presented at the 1996 Annual Meeting of the American Educational Research Association, New York City (April 8–12, 1996): 4.

61   "New Dean Named for College," *intercom* (August 1983); Norman interview; Reese interview. Wisniewski's Ed.D. from Wayne State University was in educational sociology. Among the national positions that he has held are AACTE Board of Directors, AACTE president (in 1995), NCATE Board of Examiners, president of the Association of Colleges and Schools of Education in State Universities and Land-Grant Colleges, the executive board of the Holmes Group, and member of the National Commission on Teaching and America's Future. *The Claxton Educator* 13 (Spring 1996): 4.

62   Interview with Richard Wisniewski, 3 June 1996.

63   Walter Herndon and Jack Reese, "Memorandum to the Faculty, College of Education," 15 September 1983. Although the 1962 accreditation report included a description of "an important University-wide advisory and coordi-

nating committee," a 1969 faculty questionnaire found that nearly all faculty thought there should be such a committee, but only nine of the eighty-one faculty surveyed thought that one already existed. *Teacher Education at the University of Tennessee* (April 1962): 11; "Questionnaire on Goals Relative to Program, Students, and Faculty."

64   Norman interview.

65   Reese interview. In 1988, shortly after becoming president of UT, Alexander met with a delegation of faculty members from the college at Blackberry Farm, in part to reduce misunderstanding. Alexander was particularly interested in reviving the name Summer School of the South for publicity purposes. He indicated that he might be able to get some outside funding, but little came from it. *The Claxton Educator* 5 (Fall 1988): 1–2.

66   "Faculty Meeting Considers Proposed Changes in Education," *intercom* (September 1983). Task force chairs were often unhappy with faculty participation. The final report for Goal IV listed the thirteen "active members" of the twenty-nine member task force. And task force five reported that they had met five times: "Approximately one-half of the assigned faculty participated in the first meeting; numbers dwindled thereafter!" "A Report: Task Force on Producing and Disseminating Educational Innovation, Goal V."

67   Wisniewski to Faculty, College of Education, 24 October 1983.

68   Minutes, College of Education faculty meetings, 30 May 1984 and 18 February 1986; Ginn, 4.

69   "Curricular Redesign and Characteristics of Graduates" (March 1984) in NCATE Institutional Report, College of Education, University of Tennessee (November 1989): 25–26, 155; Butefish interview.

70   During the late 1970s, James Johnson of Northern Illinois University conducted a nationwide "criteria-based" study to identify outstanding student-teaching programs; UT was placed in the 96th percentile in Johnson's study: note from William Butefish, 8 May 1997. In 1988, the university moved to a semester system. Support for a five-year program culminating in a masters program was an old issue. In a 1969 questionnaire, the faculty had supported such a proposal—46 to 39, "Questionnaire on Goals Relative to Program, Students, and Faculty"; Butefish interview; NCATE (1989): 27; Minutes, faculty meeting, 18 February 1986.

71   Minutes, faculty meeting, 18 February 1986; C. Glennon Rowell, "Beyond the Crossroads," *The Claxton Educator* 13 (Fall 1996): 3; Reese interview; Richard Wisniewski, "The Transformation of a College," *Teacher Education Quarterly* 23 (Winter 1996): 10. Full year internships were first implemented at UT in the small alternative Lyndhurst program in 1984.

72   Ginn, 5; "Dean's Annual State of the College Statement," *intercom* (May 1988). It may have been a result of the new emphasis on research in the college that doctoral students' dissertations received national honors from the

mid-1980s to the mid-1990s: Tracy Cross, John Habel, and Rosa Kennedy from the American Educational Research Association; Robert Bruce Cooter from the College Reading Association; Barbara Cary from the International Reading Association; and Gregory A. Dale from the Sport Psychology Academy. Faculty publications increased as well. Of 99 professors reporting their publications for 1988, 41 listed at least one article in a refereed journal and 14 published one or more books with national publishers. Wisniewski also supported a qualitative research thrust in the college. In 1987, two professors were hired primarily to teach qualitative research courses, to assist other faculty to develop qualitative research skills, and to sponsor "support groups" for students and faculty engaging in research. By the early 1990s, qualitative doctoral dissertations were as commonly accepted as more traditional quantitative dissertations in most departments and, in fact, had become chic.

73   NCATE (1989): 311; *intercom* (September 1989).

74   NCATE (1989): 10; "We're Questioning Everything," *Continuing Accreditation Report*, prepared for the National Council for Accreditation of Teacher Education, The University of Tennessee, Knoxville (November 1995): IR 5–6. About half of the faculty in 1989 had their terminal degrees from southern institutions, 16 from UT, NCATE (1989): 301, 317.

75   NCATE (1989): 247; *intercom* (February 1990).

76   NCATE (1989): 40, 176. The college was re-accredited under new, stiffer NCATE standards in 1989 when one third of the institutions visited lost accreditation. The college passed all standards despite the major changes it had undergone.

77   "Strategic Planning and the Future of the College of Education," *intercom* (October 1990); Richard Wisniewski, "The Transformation of a College," 11; *intercom* (August 1991).

78   Richard Wisniewski, "The Transformation of a College," 11–12; "News" from The New College Planning Office, 3 February 1992; *intercom* (June 1992). Among the schools visited were the Bowman Gray School of Medicine at Wake Forest University and Evergreen State College in Washington.

79   "Planning a New Future," The College of Education, The University of Tennessee, Knoxville (September 1992); Ginn, 9–10; Joan Paul, "Riding New Waves," draft of book chapter, (February 1997): 3, 5, 9. For the treatment of faculty attitudes about New College, I am much indebted to Linda W. Ginn's qualitative study in which she included data from 40 interviews collected in the summer of 1994. Linda W. Ginn, "Crossing Boundaries, Creating Community, Reorganizing a College of Education," Paper presented at the 1996 Annual Meeting of the American Educational Research Association, New York City, April 8–12, 1996. Lynn Cagle repeated the quip to me in a memo, 8 May 1997.

80   Anand Malik, Portfolio, New College of Education Retreat, 12 March 1992; "News" from The New College Planning Office, 24 February 1992.

81   Malik; "News" from The New College Planning Office, 24 February 1992; *Planning a New Future,* The College of Education, The University of Tennessee, Knoxville, September 1992.

82   *Planning a New Future;* "News," 16 March 1992; Richard Wisniewski, "The Transformation of a College," 11; Ginn, 22. Ginn listed eight different "modes of entry into the restructuring process" by professors, from "those who where captured by the idea from the beginning and worked throughout the change process to facilitate the effort" to some who "were opposed to the notion of restructuring from the beginning and actively worked against those who were supporting the efforts"; most were somewhere in between, including those who became "involved because they did not want something imposed on them" that they hadn't help develop. Ginn, 17.

83   Paul, 5–6; Richard Wisniewski, "The Transformation of a College," 11, 13, 14; Ginn, 1, 21.

84   Richard Wisniewski, "The Transformation of a College," 14, 15; Ginn, 14, 23; Norman interview.

85   Malik; Ginn, 12–13; "Units" was a descriptive, working term for the new subdivisions and was to be replaced by a better designation later, but no suggestion for a better name was accepted.

86   Paul, 14, 15; *Planning a New Future,* revised (July 1993): 47; Ginn, 16; C. Glennon Rowell, "Beyond the Crossroads," *The Claxton Educator* 13 (Fall 1996): 3. Everyone in the process underestimated the significance to professors of desirable offices (location, size, windows), and one of the unanticipated consequences of reorganization was bruised egos over the assignment of offices for new units. (The University's decision to take much of the Claxton Education Building for a computer center exacerbated the problem.) One program faculty went so far as to leave their new unit, in part because they were unhappy with their assigned offices.

87   *Planning a New Future,* revised (July 1993): 36–39; Paul, 21–22; "Dean's Remarks," Faculty Meeting, August 31, 1995; *intercom* (September 1995): 3.

88   Reese interview; Norman interview; Richard Wisniewski, "The Transformation of a College," 10.

89   "Rockefeller Foundation Awards Grant to College to Establish Network," *The Claxton Educator* 10 (Fall 1993): 1; *intercom* (March 1994); "Dean's Remarks," Faculty Meeting, August 31, 1995; *intercom* (September 1995): 2. The other members of the Innovative Network were the University of New Mexico, George Washington University (Washington, D.C.), Miami University (Oxford, Ohio), and California State University at San Marcos. In 1995, *U.S. New and World Report* ranked the college among the top 50 graduate schools of education.

90   Norman interview; Reese interview; Richard Wisniewski, "Reforming Schools of Education—Or Martin Luther Had It Easy," paper for Centripetals [undated];

Wisniewski interview. A symbol of faculty bitterness was the request by a senior professor from a department leaving the college to address the trustees. He refused to accept his assigned place on the agenda, insisting on speaking last after the supporters of the proposals, and condemned the changes, the process, and the change leaders.

91   Norman interview; Reese interview.

92   Norman interview.

Afterword

1   For an essay on the uniqueness of the southern educational experience, see John Best, "Education in the Forming of the American South," *History of Education Quarterly* 36 (Spring 1996).

2   Donald Warren, "Learning from Experience: History and Teacher Education," *Educational Researcher* 14 (December 1985): 10; Mark B. Ginsberg, "Teacher Education and Class and Gender Relations: A Critical Analysis of Historical Studies of Teacher Education," *Educational Foundations* 2 (Spring 1987): 15.

3   *Tomorrow's Teachers* (East Lansing, MI: Holmes Group, 1986): ix; *Tomorrow's Schools of Education: A Report of the Holmes Group* (East Lansing, MI: Holmes Group, 1995): ii–iii; David F. Labaree, "A Disabling Vision: Rhetoric and Reality in *Tomorrow's Schools of Education*," *Teachers College Record* 97 (Winter 1995): 167.

4   *Tomorrow's Teachers*, 52.

5   David F. Labaree, "Power, Knowledge, and the Rationalization of Teaching: A Genealogy of the Movement to Professionalize Teaching," *Harvard Educational Review* 62 (Summer 1992): 148. For critiques of the Holmes reports, I am indebted to the thorough, scholarly work of David F. Labaree.

6   Andrew Gitlin, "Gender and Professionalization: An Institutional Analysis of Teacher Education and Unionism at the Turn of the Twentieth Century," *Teachers College Record* 97 (Summer 1996): 615, 619; Ginsberg, 26; *Tomorrow's Schools of Education*, iv–vii, 48.

7   Eddie Stone, "Students' Perceptions of Educational Justice" (Ph.D. diss., The University of Tennessee, 1996): 133–139, 153–154; Interview with William L. Butefish, 12 November 1995.

8   *Tomorrow's' Schools: Principles for the Design of Professional Development Schools* (East Lansing, MI: Holmes Group, 1990); *Tomorrow's Schools of Education*, 63, 74.

9   *Tomorrow's Schools of Education*, 10, 17–18, 64.

10   Labaree, "Disabling Vision," 167–168, 190. Labaree criticized the Holmes Group for its about-face in switching from the research-oriented university to

the public school classroom as the place where educationists could best serve the professionalization project. He complained that *Tomorrow's Schools of Education* caricatured education schools with the charge that they ignore teacher education. All but a tiny number of elite graduate schools of education recognize educating teachers as their bedrock activity—as does the UT College of Education, a typical Holmes institution. David F. Labaree, "The Trouble with Ed Schools," *Educational Foundations* 10 (Summer 1976): 42.

11 *Tomorrow's Schools of Education*, 17; *Planning a New Future: The College of Education, The University of Tennessee*, Knoxville (July 1993): 6.

12 Ronald E. Taylor and Eric Haley, *Implementing a Vision: A Study of the Culture of the College of Education: A Component of the Overall Evaluation of the New College*, College of Communications, University of Tennessee (April 1997):13, 36, 39.

13 Ibid., 7, 10, 18, 19, 24, 42, 48.

14 Interview with Richard Wisniewski, 3 June 1996.

15 *Implementing a Vision*, 63.

Index

History of Schools and Schooling

THIS SERIES EXPLORES THE HISTORY OF SCHOOLS AND SCHOOLING in the United States and other countries. Books in this series examine the historical development of schools and educational processes, with special emphasis on issues of educational policy, curriculum and pedagogy, as well as issues relating to race, class, gender, and ethnicity. Special emphasis will be placed on the lessons to be learned from the past for contemporary educational reform and policy. Although the series will publish books related to education in the broadest societal and cultural context, it especially seeks books on the history of specific schools and on the lives of educational leaders and school founders.

For additional information about this series or for the submission of manuscripts, please contact the general editors:

Alan R. Sadovnik
118 Harvey Hall
School of Education
Adelphi University
Garden City, NY 11530

Susan F. Semel
Dept. of Curriculum and Teaching
243 Gallon Wing
Hofstra University
Hempstead, NY 11550